THE COMPASSIONATE ACHIEVER

THE
COMPASSIONATE
ACHIEVER

How Helping Others Fuels Success

CHRISTOPHER L. KUKK, PH.D.

HarperOne
An Imprint of HarperCollinsPublishers

HarperCollins books may be purchased for educational, business, or sales promotional use. For information, please email the Special Markets Department at SPsales@harpercollins.com.

FIRST EDITION

Designed by Ad Librum

Ambigram art, pages 80 and 81 © Mark Palmer, www.wowtattoos.com

Library of Congress Cataloging-in-Publication Data

Names: Kukk, Christopher L., author.

Title: The compassionate achiever : how helping others fuels success / Christopher L. Kukk.

Description: First edition. | New York, NY : HarperOne, 2017. | Includes bibliographical references and index.

Identifiers: LCCN 2016051065 (print) | LCCN 2017009145 (ebook) | ISBN 9780062457899 (hardcover) | ISBN 9780062563040 (audio) | ISBN 9780062457912 (ebook)

Subjects: LCSH: Compassion. | Success.

Classification: LCC BJ1475 .K85 2017 (print) | LCC BJ1475 (ebook) | DDC 177/.7–dc23

LC record available at https://lccn.loc.gov/2016051065

18 19 20 21 LSC(H) 10 9 8 7 6 5 4 3

To Elly, Cade, Quinn, and Cole . . .
You are my equation for love: $E=QC^2$

Contents

Introduction: Compassionate People Finish on Top—Together   1

PART ONE   SURVIVAL OF THE KINDEST

1. The Connection Between Compassion and Success   9

2. LUCA: The Four-Step Program for Cultivating Compassion   23

PART TWO   THE FOUR STEPS FOR CULTIVATING COMPASSION

3. Listen to Learn   29

Skill 1: Less Is More: Focusing Your Attention   34

Skill 2: Open the Closed and Close the Opened:
Asking Great Questions   41

Skill 3: Mind the Gaps: Appreciating Silence   52

4. Understand to Know   65

Skill 1: Flight, Fight, or Freeze: Recognizing Mindset   69

Skill 2: Three Monkeys and a Bonobo:
Developing Emotional Intelligence   82

Skill 3: Only Connect: Turning Facts into Concepts
and Relationships into Networks   95

5. Connect to Capabilities   109

Skill 1: Take No One for Granted: Tapping into the
Human Potential Hidden in Plain Sight   111

Skill 2: The Web of Connections: Expanding Your Reach   125

Skill 3: Walk This Way: Shifting Your Perspective   130

6. Act to Solve   147

Skill 1: The Courage to Try: Overcoming Fear   150

Skill 2: Testing Your Mettle: Strengthening Responsibility
          and Resilience   162

Skill 3: Just Sit There: The Power of Nondoing   174

PART THREE   THE RIPPLE EFFECT

7. Conquest of the Common Virtue   185

Conclusion: The Modern Spartacus   191

Acknowledgments   199

Notes   203

Index   229

About the Author   239

THE COMPASSIONATE ACHIEVER

Compassionate People Finish on Top—Together

Compassion is the chief law of human existence.

—FYODOR DOSTOYEVSKY

My wife, Elly, and I were on an elevated train traveling home after spending the day in Boston, when a loud blast fractured the silence of the car. I didn't need to see the pellets embedded in the window above Elly's head to recognize the source of the sound immediately: a shotgun. I guessed that someone had fired from one of the rooftops parallel to the tracks. As Elly and I dropped to crouch on the floor, the train car slammed to a stop. Now we were trapped like fish in a bowl.

Across from us, we watched in disbelief and horror as a woman holding a baby slowly rose from the floor and stood directly in front of a window. Several people yelled at her to get down, but she didn't move and didn't seem to register anyone's instruction. She was clearly in shock.

Then Elly did something I will never forget. She calmly stood up, looked the woman in the eye, and said, "Everything is going to be all right." She hugged the mom and her baby and slowly guided them all to the floor of the train car. Almost simultaneously, the train began to move again. Elly's was one of the most brave and compassionate acts that I have ever personally witnessed.

Most of us will never need to risk our lives to show our compassion for another, but whether you practice compassion in a boardroom, a classroom, or your very own living room, you have the power to save and change lives. And you have the power to dramatically improve the quality of your own life.

What is compassion? *Compassion* is a holistic understanding of a problem or the suffering of another with a commitment to act to solve the problem or alleviate the suffering. Understanding a problem or the suffering of another can happen instantaneously, as it did in Elly's case, or it can develop over time. But the most important thing to know about compassion is that it involves a commitment *to act*. This is what distinguishes compassion from empathy. Empathy is understanding what another person is experiencing, but for compassion understanding isn't enough. Compassion means actually doing something to help.

Being compassionate is not about trying to be a saint or being so kind that you become a doormat for other people. Being compassionate is not a sign of weakness. In fact, it's the exact opposite. It takes strength to remain caring and rational when the easiest thing to do is to stop caring or give in to anger. And it takes bravery to act, when it is much easier to do nothing.

Given the definition of compassion, you might think it is more emotionally and physically taxing than empathy, but that's not the case. Tania Singer, director of neuroscience at the Max Planck Institute for Human Cognitive and Brain Sciences, has found that compassion and empathy "are two different phenomena associated with different brain activity patterns." When we think compassionately, we use the same neural pathways as love, but when we think empathetically we use the brain regions associated with pain. The constant use of the brain's pain neural pathways leads to feelings of burnout; empathy is not sustainable. Because compassion is connected to feelings of love, we are nourished and the brain is primed for achievement. Research focused on a dopamine-processing gene known as DRD4, for instance, has shown that the more compassionate a classroom environment becomes, the greater the level of learning that occurs.

Compassion is commonly accepted as a quality of a "good" person, but only recently have we begun to make the connection between compassion and success. I started to make the connection when I was a counterintelligence agent for the military. During my service, I noticed that the best agents were the ones who made time to help other agents. Because they assisted fellow agents, they had a large network of colleagues who would in turn help them and "have their back" even in the most difficult situations. By helping others, these compassionate agents built trust with the members of their team, and that helped them to make better tactical decisions. Over time, compassion has become the focus of my professional and personal life, and scientific research has confirmed what I had anecdotally realized: compassion is the foundation for success.

Success is defined as the accomplishment of an aim or purpose, and being successful means different things to different people. Whether you are trying to get a promotion, reach a financial milestone, complete a degree, or help a child learn to read, compassion will help you to accomplish your goal more efficiently and effectively, and it will make the achievement more enduring, fulfilling, and rewarding. Compassion is win-win. It will help you to be successful, and it will help solve problems and create opportunities for others. The ripple effect takes over from there, spreading success throughout the community. I call people who achieve success by helping others *compassionate achievers*. It is never lonely at the top if you are a compassionate achiever.

Throughout my professional life, from my military service to my current teaching position, I've noticed that compassion has been one of the most underappreciated but consistent characteristics of successful people across a wide range of occupations. People usually mention grit, courage, strength, and intelligence when they discuss success—but not compassion. One of the reasons I wrote this book is to help people recognize the link between compassion and success and to demonstrate why compassion should be brought into our discussions of what enables individuals and groups to achieve their goals and overcome difficulties.

Part of my work over the last several years has been focused on building compassion on the local, national, and global levels in an effort to find ways to successfully address problems in areas ranging from education to policing. I've been trying to weave compassion into the activities and discussions involving every aspect of daily life anywhere I can, primarily through my work as the founding director of the Center for Compassion, Creativity and Innovation (CCCI) at Western Connecticut State University.

Launched with seed money from the Dalai Lama, the CCCI states its purpose as "to create awareness within the university as well as the regional and global communities about the importance of compassion, creativity, and innovation in daily and professional life." The CCCI works with local high schools to address homelessness, coordinates with the Charter for Compassion International, an organization founded by bestselling author Karen Armstrong to establish and sustain cultures of compassion locally and globally; and helps colleges around the world become universities of compassion. I have been asked to lead roundtables as well as help employ

compassion in organizations ranging from police and social-service departments to schools and hospitals. I've helped mayors, through the Charter for
Compassion International, find ways to become designated "cities of compassion," which place compassion at the forefront of the discussion to generate
policies and address problems in their locales. We know now that compassion
builds successful businesses, governments, schools, and civic communities.

With this book, I hope to inspire you to be a compassionate achiever and
give you the tools to be an agent of compassion in your community. We need
compassionate achievers and compassion in general now more than ever.
The National Center for Education Statistics reports that there has been a
21 percent increase in bullying since the center began tracking it in 2003.
A child is bullied every seven minutes, and 160,000 children in the United
States miss school each day for fear of bullying; 1 in 10 kids drop out of
school altogether because of bullying. Clearly, we need more compassion in
our classrooms.

Our boardrooms could do with some as well. Some companies consider
"nice" a four-letter word and are encouraging their employees to practice
"radical candor" or "front-stabbing" and to be as critical as they want. The
costs of such frankness, or what I would consider incivility, are many. In the
latest survey about the state of civility in America, for example, 70 percent of
Americans believe "that incivility in America has risen to crisis levels" and
"even more alarming is that 81 percent believe uncivil behavior is leading
to an increase in violence." Incivility causes stress, which in turn creates a
multitude of health problems such as high blood pressure, diabetes, heart
disease, depression, and other mental and physical illnesses, and the health
costs to individual Americans are not only obvious but also increasing. Stress
from work alone is estimated to cost American businesses approximately
$300 billion each year. Extra costs to businesses come from worker turnover
due to incivility in the workplace: over a third of Americans have said that
they experienced incivility at work and 26 percent of them have quit their
jobs because of it.

In addition to spreading compassion, I hope to alter the common perception of how to achieve success. For too long, we've heard that it's a "push or
be pushed" world. It's dog eat dog out there in the "real" world. Compassion
costs too much. It means having to sacrifice something to help another. It's
a zero-sum game of resources, whether of time, money, or space; your loss
is another's gain; you have to give up something to help another. Countless
times I've heard the argument that you have to choose between being kind
and being successful. The science shows that such thinking is false and

that it is easier, more fulfilling, and more sustainable to be a compassionate achiever.

Yet our children are learning that you can be either successful *or* someone who helps others, but you can't be both at the same time. "Almost 80 percent" of middle- and high-school students, according to a 2014 study by Harvard's Graduate School of Education, ranked "high achievement or happiness" over "caring for others." The report's authors highlight a "rhetoric/reality gap"—a mismatch between what parents and teachers say is important and what children and students see adults do—as "the root" cause of the student rankings. Our kids are shifting into a black hole of self-absorption, and our communities are becoming more violent and less productive, because we are not modeling compassionate behavior.

It's time for this to change. This book shows not only that we should "rank" caring for others at least as important as success, but that when we do, our success is greater and more sustainable. And our individual success makes our community stronger.

My hope is that compassion becomes your lodestar and that with the help of the ideas on the following pages, you never feel lost. No matter who you are or what the context is, compassion is always an option—the best option.

PART ONE

SURVIVAL OF THE KINDEST

1

The Connection Between Compassion and Success

When we practice loving-kindness and compassion, we are the first ones to profit.

—RUMI

"You need to be ruthless, Kukk. If you want to defeat the enemy, you need to learn to be absolutely ruthless." As a budding counterintelligence agent for the U.S. army, I remember my drill sergeant's words from boot camp like they were yesterday. The words were loud and clear, and they were absolutely wrong. We are taught that being ruthless—not just in boot camp, but from movies, television, books, and sports—is a key part of successfully defeating an opposing side. It's not only wrong generally speaking, but, according to a person who had a much higher perch than I in the intelligence world, ruthlessness creates more problems than it solves. You may know him by his fictional name "M" in the James Bond movies, but he was one of the Chiefs, known as "C," of MI6, the British Secret Intelligence Service. His real name is Sir Richard Dearlove.

When I asked Sir Richard if it was better to be a compassionate or callous and ruthless agent, he unhesitatingly said, "Compassionate." He continued by saying: "You need to work with people, get to know them, and be able to keep going back to them; being compassionate helps to cultivate sources. If you're callous or ruthless, it makes it much more difficult to get the information you need" to succeed.

He talked about an example that made headlines in the United States during the height of America's war on terror to make his point: the use of enhanced interrogation techniques, or what others describe as torture. Sir Richard said: "Enhanced interrogation techniques are not worth the costs. Their use provides a strong recruitment tool [for your enemies], and the prisoners who go through them tell you what you want to know and not what you need to know. When they were used against [members of] the Irish Republican Army, they did not work and made the problem worse in a lot of respects." When it comes to attaining success, even in the world of espionage, compassion trumps ruthlessness.

Survival of the Kindest

We've often heard that if you want to succeed in life, you need to subscribe to the idea of "survival of the fittest." Success in life, we are commonly told, has to be grabbed; it has to be taken or someone else will get it. Richard Dawkins famously argued in *The Selfish Gene* that we human beings are "lumbering robots" programmed by our genes to be "selfish," a concept that is at the heart of survival-of-the-fittest thinking. If you're compassionate, according to this line of reasoning, then you're expending resources, time, and energy toward helping others succeed at the expense of your own success; the path of compassion is the path of the loser. Individuals, the survival-of-the-fittest theory concludes, have to find and fight their way through life by their own effort and means, and those who rise to the top deserve all the rewards they get. If you falter or fall, you are simply not deserving of anything at all. You either win or lose on your own. Humankind's evolutionary success is framed by the survival-of-the-fittest argument as one in which competition between its members created a species that has conquered all others.

Yet, according to biologists from Charles Darwin to E. O. Wilson, cooperation has been more important than the idea of competition in humanity's evolutionary success. A cooperative perspective is more important than a competitive mindset to any group's success. Compassion is the reason for both the human race's survival and its ability to continue to thrive as a species.

Charles Darwin not only did *not* coin the phrase "survival of the fittest" (the phrase was invented by Herbert Spencer), but he argued against it. Charles Darwin, in *The Descent of Man,* wrote: "I perhaps attributed too much to the action of natural selection or the survival of the fittest" in *On the Origin of Species* and "it hardly seems probable that the number of men gifted with such virtues [as bravery and sympathy] . . . could be increased through natural selection, that is, by the survival of the fittest." Darwin was very clear about the weakness of the survival-of-the-fittest argument and the strength of his "sympathy hypothesis" when he wrote: "Those communities which included the greatest number of the most sympathetic members would flourish best and rear the greatest number of offspring." What Darwin called "sympathy," in the words of Paul Ekman, "today would be termed empathy, altruism, or compassion."

Darwin goes so far in his compassion argument as to tie the success of human evolution (and even "lower animals") to the evolution of compassion. He outlines in chapter 4 of *The Descent of Man* that as the human race evolved from "small tribes" into large civilizations, concern about the well-being of others extended to include not just strangers but "all sentient beings." Charles Darwin clearly argued in his writings that our evolutionary success is linked to an ever-widening circle of compassion or survival-of-the-kindest mindset rather than to narrow self-interest or survival-of-the-fittest thinking.

He even calls compassion "the almost ever-present instinct" when a fellow human being witnesses the suffering of another. In other words, Darwin believed that compassion was a natural instinct that we all share. The bumper-sticker way of teaching and labeling Darwin's ideas as exclusively focused on the "survival of the fittest" is not only misleading; it completely misses his idea that humanity's success hinges on its level of compassion or sympathy.

Since Darwin's fieldwork and writings, researchers from various fields have supported his perspective. Biologist and theorist Edward O. Wilson, who is known for his studies of ants and bees that have yielded insights into human existence, has shown that our evolution from tribal into a global society increasingly favors compassionate and cooperative over callous and competitive approaches to human interaction. Wilson calls our "selfish activity" in interpersonal relations "the Paleolithic curse" that "hampers" success at all levels where groups of humans interact. Although selfishness may have been an advantage during the Paleolithic Era, when *Homo sapiens* lived more independently of each other, Wilson contends that it is "innately dysfunctional" in our highly interconnected societies and world. Wilson demonstrates in *The Social Conquest of Earth* that evolution favors a "group selection" mechanism in which "groups that work together altruistically, regardless of how closely related their members are," will have an advantage over others who are not as compassionate and collaborative.

One of the main reasons that compassion helps people succeed is called "group selection" in science or "teamwork" in sports and business. Although Darwin discussed the importance of group selection in evolutionary success in *The Descent of Man*, David Sloan Wilson and Edward O. Wilson (no relation) have recently "double-downed" on Darwin's argument, stating that "our ability to function as team players in coordinated groups enabled our species to achieve worldwide dominance, replacing other types of hominid and a range of other species along the way." Elsewhere, the Wilsons show that, although "exploitation" of and "cheating" by people exist in groups, the low levels at which such selfish acts occur is evidence that we think and act for the greater good because we understand that we are "unable to succeed at each other's expense."

The Wilsons are not saying that selfishness, ruthlessness, and meanness play no part in evolution or reality; instead, they contend that when you look at the larger successes in life, compassion, altruism, generosity, and cooperation play greater roles. If you overlay their logic onto sports teams, local communities, and national societies, both Darwin and the Wilsons are arguing that groups made up of mainly "survival of the fittest," self-interested people will fail more than they succeed. In contrast, groups consisting of mainly "survival of the kindest," compassionate people will succeed more than they fail. Why? The members of the selfish group are looking out only for themselves, and if others in their group fall, they see it as strengthening their own survival within it: one less competitor to worry about. Over time, as Darwin noted, their membership dwindles relative to the compassionate group, where there is an "all for one and one for all" mentality. As E. O. Wilson writes in *The Meaning of Human Existence:* "Within groups selfish individuals beat altruistic individuals, but groups of altruists beat groups of selfish individuals."

Selfish people and even bullies may win a couple of rounds or sets in the game of life, but they rarely win the match or game; it is the compassionate people who win. Biologists from Michigan State University, Harvard University, and other academic institutions have reached similar conclusions from a diverse set of research projects. The key to long-lasting success— whether it is on a sports team, in town hall, or in private business—is to cultivate and surround yourself with compassionate and caring people.

James Q. Wilson, one of the world's most respected social scientists, uses a wide range of human interactions, stretching from a mother's love to the reconstruction of Russian civil society, to demonstrate in *The Moral Sense* that human beings, at their very core, are moral creatures and that "our moral sense is a central fact of humanity." He shows that humanity shares a common moral sense, which can be found in the "universal dispositions" of people and not in any "universal rules" that we may invent either philosophically or legally. He examined human "dispositions" or "sensibilities" such as sympathy and fairness across societies to demonstrate that the evolutionary process "favored" such traits over "the opposite tendencies" of "ruthless pre-dation . . . or a disinclination to share." In other words, Wilson showed that people with the "psychological orientation" toward compassion have found much more success than those with a selfish disposition since the beginning of our evolutionary process.

Anthropologist Karen Strier's work, which has been compared to the work of Jane Goodall and Dian Fossey, shows "that the roots of primate social behavior, including that of people, might be more accurately reflected in the flexibility, tolerance, cooperation and affection that predominate among most primates, and that these qualities are at least as recognizably human as aggressiveness, competition and selfishness." Strier's field studies echo Darwin's observations that human instincts are more compassionate and generous than aggressive and selfish.

From Charles Darwin's American monkey case to E. O. Wilson's insects, scientists have shown that the notion of "survival of the kindest" explains more evolutionary success than the "survival of the fittest." Darwin, after pro-viding a list of "instance[s] of sympathetic and heroic" acts by animals rang-ing from dogs to pelicans to prove his point about survival of the kindest, cites the case of the "little American monkey" that attempted to save his zoo-keeper. The monkey, according to Darwin, lived in a "large compartment" at the zoological garden with a "fierce baboon" that caused the monkey to live in constant fear for his life. However, when the little American monkey saw that the zookeeper—who had become a "warm friend"—was in danger from the baboon, "he rushed to the rescue . . . running great risk to his life."

E. O. Wilson's work on ants has shown how insects that favored coopera-tion over "selfish" existence were the ones that successfully achieved "world domination." The concept is called eusociality, which Wilson defines as "the condition of multiple generations organized into groups by means of an altruistic division of labor." Ants, for example, created cooperative and "symbiotic relationships" with other insects such as aphids (bugs that feed by sucking the sap from plants) that helped them to "rise to dominance among the invertebrates of the terrestrial world." He describes how ants risk their own lives to "protect" their "symbionts" against any potential danger or intruders. Cooperation and compassion breed success.

As for humans, Wilson provides hope for our own continued evolution-ary success as long as we nurture the "heritable group-level traits" of "coop-erativeness, empathy, and patterns of networking." He collectively calls our compassion, empathy, and cooperativeness "the final reserve of altruism that may yet save our race." From E. O. Wilson's idea of the "final reserve" to J. Q.

Wilson's emphasis on "psychological orientation," both physical and social scientists have come to the same conclusion: evolutionary success favors the compassionate.

Our psychological disposition toward compassion can also be seen in the evolution of the brain. The early reptilian brain, composed of the cerebellum and brain stem, developed into the paleo-mammalian brain with the addition of the hippocampus, amygdala, and hypothalamus; with the addition of the cerebral neocortex it became the primate/human brain. Thus we evolved from being exclusively focused on basic reactionary instincts of self-preservation and self-interest to being capable of understanding the value of compassion and cooperation. Such neuro-evolution helped our ancestors survive by enabling them to cooperate with one another when faced with animal species that were more powerful and stronger than they were. Our brain's development shaped a civilization in which individual success is determined more by how well "you play with others" than how well "you take down others." We left our self-interested reptilian and paleo-mammalian lives back in evolutionary history to establish a mainly neocortex-based compassionate civilization.

We Are Hardwired for Compassion

Given the role of compassion in our species' survival, it should be no surprise that recent research has shown that we are hardwired for compassion. We may not be born saints, but we are born with compassion. It's a natural instinct, woven into the biology of what makes us human.

"Selflessness is the default option" of the brain. Research by Leonardo Christov-Moore and others published in *Social Neuroscience* found that "our primary drive" is to act "prosocially, perhaps due to reflexive forms of empathy that blur the boundaries between individuals." In other words, it showed that our brains have to exert more effort when we pursue selfish acts than when we act selflessly, because we seem to be neurologically wired for compassion and empathy. Throughout history, many great thinkers have intuited this, including the eighteenth-century philosopher Jean-Jacques Rousseau, who argued that we are all born with "natural compassion," but now we have scientific support from recent studies in neuroscience and psychology that our brains are chemically configured for compassion.

The things that give us pleasure, such as eating our favorite foods and making love, release the peptide hormone oxytocin in the brain. Oxytocin activates the neurotransmitters dopamine (brain reward) and serotonin (anxiety reduction), contributing to happiness and optimism, two characteristics that have been shown to contribute to success by enhancing both cognitive and social intelligence. Oxytocin is also released when we act in compassionate and altruistic ways. In other words, our brain chemistry is structured so that we are stimulated to pursue compassion and altruism in the same way we desire our favorite foods and our spouse. "Oxytocin," according to Paul Zak in *The Moral Molecule*, "orchestrates the kind of generous and caring behavior that every culture, everywhere in the world, endorses as the right way to live, . . . that every culture everywhere on the planet describes as 'moral.'" If human beings are, in the words of Richard Dawkins, "programmed," we are more strongly programmed to be kind and generous than to be mean and selfish.

The idea that humanity is programmed for compassion is supported when examining the part of the brain known as the nucleus accumbens. Research on generosity has shown that dopamine is released in the nucleus accumbens when we give to charity. In fact, one research team from the University of Oregon found that giving to charity is "neurologically similar" to eating your favorite food, seeing a loved one after a long absence, or winning the lottery. The dopamine pathway in our brain plays an important role in the human search for pleasure and avoidance of pain. Because compassion activates our neuronal pleasure circuits, we are naturally wired and predisposed toward compassion.

We are also physiologically wired for compassion through a bundle of nerves that are called, all together, the vagus nerve. The vagus nerve is a cranial nerve that extends from the brain stem down through the body (*vagus* is Latin for "wandering"), connecting to numerous muscles and organs such as muscles in the face and vocal chamber, and the heart, lungs, and digestive organs. It's the nerve that gives us the "warm fuzzies" and causes us to feel relaxed and safe. Stephen Porges, a physiological psychologist, calls the vagus nerve the "nerve of compassion" for several reasons. One is "that the vagus nerve innervates the muscle groups of communicative systems involved in caretaking" such as vocalization, prosody, and listening. In other words, the vagus nerve helps you to calm your voice so you don't yell, keep a soothing rhythm and intonation to your words, and, overall, slow your talking so that you are better prepared to listen—all attributes that contribute to acting in a compassionate manner.

The second reason, the centerpiece of Porges's research, is that when the nerve is activated (Porges calls it a high vagal tone), it reduces a person's heart rate (Porges's vagal brake). The more a person's vagus nerve is activated, the slower the heart rate; a less active vagus nerve (Porges's low vagal tone) causes a high heart rate. Porges's insight into vagal tones explains why our heart races when we are angry and fearful and why it beats gently when we feel happy and safe. When we have a lower heart rate, according to Porges, we tend to follow more constructive "social engagement" behaviors, such as compassion rather than callousness. A strong vagus nerve, in other words, helps a person take a calm and soothing approach rather than a fight-or-flight reaction to life's problems and sufferings.

Another reason for calling it the nerve of compassion is that an active vagus nerve stimulates the release of the "moral molecule": oxytocin. Dacher Keltner writes, in a vein similar to Paul Zak's, "As the vagus nerve fires . . . it triggers the release of oxytocin, sending signals of warmth, trust, and devotion throughout the brain and body and, ultimately, to other people." Other researchers in psychology, such as Nancy Eisenberg, have reached conclusions similar to those of Porges and Keltner. If we strengthen the vagus nerve, we strengthen compassion in each of us and, thereby, in society. We've all heard of the saying that what happens in Vegas, stays in Vegas, but if it happens in vagus, it spreads from vagus—to all of us.

The "Everyday" Compassion–Success Connection

Compassion helps our species survive and, by promoting the release of oxytocin, makes us feel good. But how does practicing compassion improve our everyday lives? The research is overwhelming.

Achieving high-level lasting success, whether it is climbing a professional ladder, living a life you are proud of, accomplishing a personal goal, or effectively helping someone else do the same, is based upon finding meaning and purpose in your life. Studies in areas from political economics to psychology have shown that people who have a strong sense of meaning in their lives, whose lives are based on *intrinsic* values, attain high levels of success and can sustain them for much longer than people whose lives are based on *extrinsic* values, which are direct personal benefits such as money or status. These extrinsic values may foster a "goal-achieving mentality," according to the research of Kathleen Vohs, of the University of Minnesota, and may help in achieving short-term objectives (earning a raise at work, buying a new car, or making partner by age thirty), but the feeling of success is short-lived.

Because extrinsically motivated people are driven by the desire for money or status, they treat others as instruments to achieve their goals; they are "less interpersonally attuned . . . and are not prosocial." As they try to summit their objective, they tend to cut the ropes of everyone else around them. Their social insensitivity, in short, makes them less effective as employees and coworkers, because people don't like working with them. Furthermore, once an extrinsic goal is realized, people's motivation diminishes, because they achieved what they sought to accomplish. If they don't find another extrinsic motivation, they start to lose what they earned or become less effective in their job. As Mariano Grondona highlights in his work on economic development: "Only intrinsic values are inexhaustible."

How do we bring more meaning into our lives? Compassion. A research team from Florida State University, University of Minnesota, and Stanford University has shown that meaningfulness comes from being a "giver," helping others while maintaining a healthy level of self-interest. This is on-the-ground survival of the kindest. The positive effects of practicing compassion are short-term, long-term, and real. A recent study of over eleven thousand West Point cadets concluded: "Helping people focus on the meaning and impact of their work, rather than on, say, the financial returns it will bring, may be the best way to improve not only the quality of their work but also—counterintuitive though it may seem—their financial success." The researchers found that those cadets who were driven by intrinsic values outperformed their fellow cadets who were extrinsically motivated on both long- and short-term goals. They also found that cadets who had a mixture of intrinsic and extrinsic motivations were outperformed "on every measure" by their intrinsically motivated peers. Following an intrinsic path through life, such as a compassionate achiever does, provides not only meaning in your life, but also professional and financial success.

Financial success is just the tip of the iceberg. The following represents a small but broad sampling of research about the benefits of compassion:

- *Compassion fosters greater self-esteem and health.* Rachel Piferi, of Johns Hopkins University, and Kathleen Lawler, of the University of Tennessee, demonstrated that people who were compassionate toward others lowered their blood pressure and reported "greater self-esteem, less depression, and less stress."

- *Compassion strengthens resilience.* Practicing compassion is one path to building resilience, which is the ability to respond to adversity and despair. As the late Jerilyn Ross, president and CEO of the Anxiety Disorders

Association of America for thirty years, showed: "Doing things for other people, thinking about other people, is like giving your brain a break from despair. . . . It creates a sense of satisfaction that increases endorphins and therefore a sense of well-being." Meredith Maran calls it the "activism cure."

- *Compassion creates a happier workplace, boosts productivity, and improves the bottom line.* Sigal Barsade, of the Wharton School at the University of Pennsylvania, and Olivia O'Neill, of George Mason University School of Business, "found a clear, positive correlation between compassionate behavior, work satisfaction, and company success." As we've seen, compassion brings meaning to work and, when employees find meaning in their work, they are three times as likely to stay with their company; they "report 1.7 times higher job satisfaction and are 1.4 times more engaged at work."

    Places such as Elite SEM (a search-engine marketing firm), Withum-Smith+Brown (an accounting firm), Orion Holdings (an ad agency), and IDEO (a design and consulting firm that developed Apple's first computer mouse) understand the compassion–success connection and apply it to everything from their mission statements to hiring practices. Orion Holdings' motto is "Work Hard and Be Nice to People," and IDEO's employee handbook—*The Little Book of IDEO*—has guidelines that include "be optimistic" and "make others successful." Is it really any surprise that the retention and productivity rates of employees at companies like Orion and IDEO are as high as their levels of success?

- *Compassion improves academic performance.* A 2011 landmark study of 213 social and emotional learning programs (SEL, programs that help students understand and manage emotions) with a combined sample of more than 270,000 K–12 students clearly demonstrated that students participating in SEL programs make larger improvements with respect to academic, attitudinal, and behavioral measurements than their peers without SEL programs. SEL-taught children, for instance, had an 11-percentile-point gain in their academic achievement over their non-SEL counterparts.

    In a 2015 Columbia University study titled "The Economic Value of Social and Emotional Learning," the authors found that SEL programs produce an $11 return on every $1 spent. Why such an amazing return on investment? SEL-taught students develop the intellectual and social-emotional skills not only to increase academic success, but also to avoid problem behaviors such as alcohol and drug abuse, violence, truancy, and bullying, which reduces costs to the community via lower crime (from misdemeanors to felonies), hospitalization (mental health and addiction services), and school dropout rates.

- *Compassion strengthens the political, civic, and economic health of communities.* Paul Zak, the founding director of the Center for Neuroeconomic Studies at Claremont Graduate University, uncovered oxytocin's role in nurturing the political and economic health of a community. Because compassion activates oxytocin in the brain and oxytocin fosters trust between people, where "trust is high," according to a study by the Pew Research Center, "crime and corruption are low."

Inclusive Success: Success of One Fosters Success of Others

The more competitive you think you need to be, the less successful you will be. Our current default way of thinking about becoming successful—the competitive king-of-the-hill mentality—reduces both the level and likelihood of success. In summing up his research on the effects of competition versus cooperation in business over the last several years, Paul Baard, professor of organizational psychology at Fordham University, said: "The old adage 'Competition brings out the best in people' deserves a proper burial."

When you examine many of the most successful organizations around the world, you find that they capitalize on fostering cooperation, coordination, and collaboration. Companies such as General Mills, Aetna, Target, and Google have buried the competitive culture and resurrected compassion. They have woven compassion into their corporate structure to increase employee satisfaction, boost productivity, and raise the bottom line. Although many people believe that you need to be hard-nosed and ruthless to succeed in business, highly successful businesses not only know better, but also understand how to be better, and it's through compassion.

General Mills, a company with over $17 billion in revenues, has created a mindfulness program that generates compassion and profits. The program, called Mindful Leadership, had the following impressive results after only one seven-week course:

Eighty-three percent of participants said they were taking time each day to optimize personal productivity—up from 23 percent before the course. Eighty-two percent said they now make time to eliminate tasks with limited productivity

value–up from 32 percent before the course. And among senior executives who
took the course, 80 percent reported a positive change in their ability to make
better decisions, while 89 percent said they became better listeners.

A Duke University School of Medicine study of thirty-five hundred Aetna
employees enrolled in a similar program found that the company saved
$2,000 in yearly health-care costs per employee simply because it reduced
stress by a third.

Numerous research studies show the positive effects of a corporate culture of compassion on businesses. James Heskett, professor emeritus at the
Harvard Business School, provides several case studies in *The Culture Cycle*
of the benefits that a culture of kindness and compassion–as opposed to
one of callousness and apathy–generates for a business. Heskett found that
"as much as half of the difference in operating profit between organizations
can be attributed to effective cultures. In addition, an organization's culture
provides especially significant competitive advantages in bad times. . . . All
of this is possible with little or no capital investment, yielding an infinite
ROI [return on investment]." Businesses built upon an effective culture
of compassion were found to have "high levels of productivity resulting
from relatively high worker loyalty, low turnover, and hence low recruiting
and training costs. It translates into closer relationships between employees and frequent customers, thereby contributing to sales and marketing
efficiency."

In a different study on the connection between "intrinsic need" and workplace performance and well-being, Paul Baard, Edward Deci, and Richard
Ryan found that "intrinsic need satisfaction . . . was found to relate to performance." They contend that "the core of the concept" is that managers need
to provide a work environment where "subordinates" feel supported if they
"desire work outcomes of effective performance and employee well-being."
It's also worth repeating the conclusion of Barsade and O'Neill's research
in *Administrative Science Quarterly* that "found a clear, positive correlation
between compassionate behavior, work satisfaction, and company success."

Being a person of compassion also improves your individual potential for
workplace success. A *Wall Street Journal* article outlining tips on how to get
ahead as a middle manager at work concluded: "Top executives are attracted
to people who lift their heads up from their desks and understand the impact
their assignment might have on other departments–not just on their own
teams." Employees who help each other are the engines of successful companies, and the best top executives know it. Understanding what others need or

need to avoid and then acting on that understanding is at the heart of what compassion is and what a compassionate achiever does.

The Dwindling of Compassion

There's a problem with the fuel of success, however: it's dwindling and becoming scarce. Fewer and fewer people are practicing compassion. Evidence of compassion's weakened state is seen in the rising levels of incivility and bullying already mentioned. However, a three-decade meta-analysis of nearly fourteen thousand college students by Sara Konrath, Edward O'Brien, and Courtney Hsing reports additional evidence for compassion's demise. Konrath, O'Brien, and Hsing found that compassion and empathy started to decline in the 1990s and are now at their lowest level since 1979. The research, which analyzed data on college students from seventy-two surveys given between 1979 and 2009, shows that today's university students "are less likely" than the students of the 1980s "to agree with statements such as 'I often have tender, concerned feelings for people less fortunate than me.'" Their research also revealed data from a 2006 survey showing that students have a "get rich" and "not my problem" mentality about life. "Eighty-one percent of 18- to 25-year-olds said that getting rich was among their generation's most important goals. . . . In contrast, only 30 percent chose helping others who need help."

I believe there are several reasons why compassion is dwindling:

1. *Most people don't know or are unaware of all the benefits that compassion provides in their professional, civic, and personal lives.* Some believe that compassion demands sacrifice and is usually without benefit.

2. *Many people think of compassion as weakness, when in reality it is strength.* One of the easiest ways to see its strength is to compare it with water. Both elements—water and compassion—share the quality of "gentle perseverance." Just as the gentle perseverance of water can carve through rock to reach its ultimate goal of the ocean, compassion creates a path to success that is equally fluid and powerful. Their softness—one in the world of nature and the other in the world of human relations—is their strength. As the ancient Chinese philosopher and poet Lao-Tzu famously wrote: "Water is fluid, soft, and yielding. But water will wear away rock, which is rigid and cannot yield. As a rule, whatever is fluid, soft, and yielding will overcome whatever is rigid and hard. This is a paradox: what is soft is

strong." It is this type of strength that powers the success of compassionate achievers.

3. *People don't realize compassion can be taught.* Research has clearly shown that compassion can be taught and learned. We can strengthen our nerve of compassion. Researchers have provided a wide range of insights into how to strengthen the nerve of compassion. Zak discusses successful ways of stimulating the vagus nerve that range from "rubbing your fingers between the ribs" to hugging and massaging. Although Keltner notes that breast-feeding and eating chocolate can trigger oxytocin release, he has focused his own research on "how people might rely on touch to soothe, reward, and bond in daily life." The role of practicing meditation or mindfulness in lowering blood pressure and cortisol levels (stress hormone) as well as in "priming" people "to think more socially in various ways" has been highlighted in both the scientific and popular presses. One study at Northeastern University found that simply tapping hands in synchrony made partners feel more similar and have greater compassion for each other, thereby increasing the desire to help; "it increased the number of people who helped their partner by 31 percent." Another study at the University of Wisconsin–Madison provides evidence that we can strengthen our "compassion muscle" through meditation: "Our fundamental question was, 'Can compassion be trained and learned in adults? Our evidence points to yes. . . . It's kind of like weight training. . . . We found that people can actually build up their compassion 'muscle' and respond to others' suffering with care and a desire to help."

We can each develop skills to restock our dwindling levels of compassion. The next chapter outlines a four-step program focused on developing compassion. Learning to be a compassionate achiever is easy, meaningful, and beneficial. LUCA will show you the way.

2

LUCA: The Four-Step Program for Cultivating Compassion

Doing nothing for others is the undoing of ourselves.

—HORACE MANN

There is no single way to be a compassionate achiever, but there are certain skills every compassionate achiever should master: Listening, Understanding, Connecting, and Acting, or LUCA. LUCA, in biological terms (specifically in evolutionary biology and astrobiology), stands for the "last universal common ancestor," the most recent organism from which all organisms now living on earth have a common descent. Just as scientists can trace the genetic code back to posit biology's LUCA, I use LUCA to facilitate compassion, humanity's most basic and common virtue. Luca (Lucas, Luke) is also a common personal name in several languages: it means "bringer of light."

Developing these skills is a step-by-step process.

Listen to learn about the problem or challenge.

Listening, the first step in cultivating compassion, is a simple act that takes many forms. Listening as a compassionate achiever is less about the amount of information you hear and more about your level of focus on what you are hearing. Listening also involves the art of questioning. The right questions lead us to answers that strengthen our learning. Equally important is listening for what is not being said. The gaps of silence sometimes say more than the words and sounds we hear.

Understand to know what options can help.

The definition of compassion has two central parts, and acquiring understanding is the goal of the first. Acquiring understanding is not simply knowing facts or information, but knowing how the pieces of knowledge fit or do not fit together. To understand is to know concepts and facts by

23

examining and studying them from as many angles, contexts, disciplines, processes, and perspectives as possible. Knowing the context in which an idea occurs matters just as much as the idea itself. Simply using the word "fire" in different contexts changes the meaning (for example, used in a burning building to warn, it could save lives, while used in battle or with a firing squad, it could take lives).

Furthermore, we now know the importance of emotional intelligence in developing understanding. Excluding emotions from problem solving and decision making will hamper your ability to achieve understanding. Finally, being able to make and identify connections between facts, turning factual knowledge into conceptual knowledge, enables you to assess the resources—what I call capabilities—you will need to effectively address the problem or challenge.

Connect to capabilities that can address the problem or challenge.
Sometimes capabilities are hidden in plain sight. Other times, we need to look well beyond our immediate circle. Your ability to develop a wide network of quality connections will determine the resources and options you will have for addressing issues. Finding ways to shift your perspective on a situation leads to unexpected opportunities. Connecting to capabilities generates options for effective action.

Act to solve the problem or challenge.
The second central part of the definition of compassion is action. Finding ways to overcome the fear or reluctance to act as well as developing a sense of responsibility in a community help to foster action. The idea of inaction, however, though paradoxical, is sometimes the best course to follow in solving a problem. When it comes to compassion, acting to solve includes both action and inaction. Sometimes the most compassionate way to act is to follow the passive path of Mahatma Gandhi or the doctor who prescribes "doing nothing" as better medicine than pills or treatment. Compassion's power can take many forms, but it has one effect: success.

There Is a Compassionate Solution to Every Problem

During a recent talk on compassion, I said, "For every problem there is a compassionate answer, and if you haven't found a compassionate solution, you simply haven't thought creatively enough." A male student approached me afterwards and presented the trolley-track dilemma that philosopher Peter Singer and others have made famous as an example of a problem without a compassionate answer. The dilemma goes like this. You are standing on a bridge under which a trolley will pass that is heading toward five people who will die if you don't stop it. There is a big man standing at the edge of the overpass, and if you push him over the edge, you kill him, stop the trolley, and save the five. Should you push the man?

The student said that the choice is simply between a bad and a worse option (I didn't ask him what the bad was as compared to the worse choice— that is for another discussion). "You see Dr. Kukk, there is no compassionate answer."

I responded that there was, but that he wasn't yet being creative enough to see it, because he thought that he had only two choices. "If you don't mind embarrassing yourself," I added, "a compassionate answer is literally and figuratively on you. You could strip off your clothes and toss them over to gum up the wheels of the trolley. Although it may be an embarrassing act, it is definitely a more compassionate solution than the other two options that philosophers like to corner you into choosing."

Most of life's decisions, in contrast to the theoretical situations presented by some philosophers, have more than two options. There is always a compassionate path through our daily dilemmas and problems even when split-second decisions are involved. Split-second decisions occur in the most regular and mundane situations as well as those with life-or-death consequences. When you and another shopper are reaching for that last half-gallon of chocolate milk, you pull back, knowing that you can stir chocolate syrup into regular milk just fine. In 2007, Wesley Autrey was waiting with his two daughters (ages four and six at the time) for a subway train. As the train approached, they saw a man fall onto the tracks into the path of the oncoming train. Autrey reacted instantly, leaping down onto the tracks and covering the man's body with his own in a space between the rails. Several subway cars rolled inches from his head, but Autrey and the man he saved were unharmed.

For every problem there is a compassionate answer, and LUCA helps to uncover it. In the army, we called the soldiers who could find a safe path through or over enemy lines Pathfinders. Compassionate achievers ask what they can do with what they have to help find a safe path through, over, or under a problem. It's worth noting that Pathfinders work as teams, and you'll read a lot about the importance of making connections to others in this book. Compassion is about interactions and interrelationships, not separateness and aloofness. The connections you make can power your success to new heights—heights that cannot be reached independently or individually.

How to Use This Book

Compassion, like love, is a positive-sum game: by giving more, you get more. Your compassion reserves can never be depleted within you. Instead, think of compassion as a muscle. The more you use your muscle of compassion, the stronger it gets; the less you exercise it, the weaker and more atrophied it becomes. This book outlines a daily exercise regimen for compassion.

This book is divided into the four steps for practicing compassion: listening to learn, understanding to know, connecting to capabilities, and acting to solve. In each step, I've highlighted three skills that will help you accomplish that step and move to the next one. In most situations, you'll proceed through the steps in the order presented, but practicing compassion is not a rigid process. And the more you incorporate compassion into your daily life, the more natural it will feel.

PART TWO

THE FOUR STEPS FOR CULTIVATING COMPASSION

3

Listen to Learn

Wisdom and compassion share a first step: listening. Owls seemingly understand this better than we do. Owls are commonly used as a symbol of wisdom and knowledge, but they are also models of altruism and compassion. A study in the journal *Animal Behaviour*, for instance, found that barn owls share food with their "smaller, hungrier siblings." When I told my wife about the study, she immediately laughed, because we use a barred owl call as the main way to let our sons know that it is time to eat when they are out playing or working in the yard. I've been fascinated by owls since grade school, and they can teach us a basic lesson about listening: listen more than you talk, because listening is essential for acquiring wisdom and for developing compassion.

Owls listen to pinpoint any change in their environment. Active primarily at night, they rely on acute hearing to create a three-dimensional map of auditory space and identify prey. "An owl," according to officials at the San Diego Zoo, "can hear a mouse stepping on a twig from 75 feet away." To generate their unique auditory map, scientists have found that the neurons in owls' brains multiply incoming signals rather than simply adding them, as occurs in most animal brains, including ours. We may not have the neural hardware to be able to listen at the extraordinarily high level that owls do, but we do have the capacity to prioritize listening, specifically listening to learn. Compassion grows when we talk less and listen more.

Most people hear, but compassionate achievers listen to learn. Although hearing is necessary, it is not sufficient. Hearing is an unfocused, passive act of detecting sounds. It's a routine mode of monitoring that doesn't necessarily involve understanding. You can hear something without grasping its meaning. A recent lecture I stumbled into on thermodynamics comes to mind. In contrast, listening to learn, also called attentive listening, is a focused activity for detecting *and* understanding the meaning of the sounds being received. It requires awareness and concentrating your thoughts and observations on what the person is saying to you. As a compassionate achiever, you don't simply hear what is being said so that you can offer a knee-jerk reply or reaction; you want to understand the issue or difficulty, so you can figure out what action to take to resolve it.

Attentive listening is crucial for ending many types of problems in compassionate ways. Bernard Mayes understood the power of attentive listening in preventing suicide well before medical experts did when he created the first suicide prevention hotline in 1962 in the city of San Francisco. As a recent article about Mayes and his effort to reduce suicide said, "It doesn't take a Ph.D. or M.D. to save someone's life; what it takes is a willingness to listen." San Francisco's suicide rate has been cut in half since Mayes's hotline was established. "It is most important to listen first, and listen well," says Ronald Diamond, of the School of Medicine and Public Health, University of Wisconsin–Madison; listening can help suicidal persons "decide to live," because they get a sense that "someone understands" their pain. With a 24 percent jump in the U.S. suicide rate from 1999 to 2014 and because more Americans commit suicide than are murdered each year (one American takes his or her own life every fifteen minutes, which includes approximately twenty veterans per day), increasing our capability to listen can help more people succeed at life's most basic task: living.

Listening to learn is also a key step for resolving conflicts. The Compassionate Listening Project, which is located in Seattle, has eased tensions between people involved in conflicts ranging from workplace incidents to the Israeli–Palestinian struggle. The project is based on the idea "that people need to listen, without judgment, to the stories of those on the 'other side' . . . while asking nonadversarial questions that allow them to see the other person's humanity." It's conflict resolution through attentive listening.

Listening to learn is a valuable means for developing understanding that can help you to solve problems and resolve conflicts. It is also a form of engagement that helps you to connect with the person who is speaking. Listening to learn builds a bridge between people constructed out of respect and concern. You show respect and concern when you attentively listen to a speaker, who can see it in your focus and hear it in your silence and later in your questions.

How does it make you feel when people look at their cell phone when you are speaking? What about when they look you in the eye and give you their undivided attention? When individuals feel that you are attentively listening, they know that you are taking what they say to heart, and that simple perception is at the root of cultivating trust and nurturing a strong, productive relationship. A 2012 study in *Technology Innovation Management Review* by Mila Hakanen and Aki Soudunsaari found that "genuine listening" is "required" to build trust as well as "rich and open communication" and is "essential for the building of high-performing teams."

Listening attentively and inquisitively acts to connect people in profound ways. Ursula K. Le Guin, one of the world's most insightful, thoughtful, and award-winning science-fiction writers, states: "Listening is not a reaction, it is a connection. Listening to a conversation or a story, we don't so much respond as join in—become part of the action." The listening connection is not only alive as long as attentiveness and inquisitiveness are flowing, but it literally synchronizes people in a conversation. Le Guin and others explain how the listening connection naturally and organically syncs people in a way similar to the idea of entrainment in physics. Entrainment is when two separate but similar objects synchronize or harmonize their actions. The most common way to demonstrate the concept is to place two pendulum clocks on a wall next to each other and then simply watch what happens. After a while, the pendulums start to swing in synchrony as their vibrations become coupled or harmonized through the wall. Attentive listening is a way that you can get in sync or entrain with another person. A "successful human relationship," according to Le Guin, "involves entrainment—getting in sync. If it doesn't, the relationship is either uncomfortable or disastrous."

Neurobiologists over the last few years have shined a bit of light on how people "get in sync." Uri Hasson and others have used functional magnetic resonance imaging (fMRI) and intracranial EEG (iEEG) in ways that have "revealed a surprising tendency of individual brains to tick collectively" when we are in conversations that connect us to others. A different neuroscience study showed that "the simple act of tapping one's hands in synchrony with another caused participants to report feeling more similar to their partners and to have greater compassion for their plight." Joy Hirsch, of Yale University, uses a technique for measuring brain activity by emitting tiny wavelengths of light or lasers into people's heads called near-infrared spectroscopy. Hirsch describes her neuroscience research as finding out that when we talk with another, "parts of our brains are in synchrony with our partner. . . . Our brains in some sense fuse as we become a unit by sending and receiving" communication signals. The listening or receiving part of the brain, Wernicke's area, plays an important role in our ability to turn dialogue into Hirsch's human fusion. When listener and speaker are in sync, the train of constructive conversation is less likely to derail and more likely to stay on track.

Great achievers in history knew that to reach understanding, they needed to travel the two-way track of communication. Oliver Wendell Holmes's words remind me of Hirsch's research about the sending and receiving parts of the brain: "It is the province of knowledge to speak, and it is the privilege of wisdom to listen." Henry Ford, whose success continues to be acclaimed long after his death, said: "If there is any secret to success, it lies in the ability to get the other person's point of view and see things from his angle as well as from your own." How do you get others' point of view, if you don't listen to them?

The science is clear: only by becoming an attentive listener can you hope to understand another person's problem or challenge and develop a relationship based on respect and trust. The problem that most of us have, however, is that we don't listen as well as we think we do.

Most of Us Hear but Don't Listen

There's a Lake Wobegon effect happening around the world when it comes to listening: almost everyone thinks they are above average listeners even though they're not. The illusion that we think we are effective and efficient listeners begins in our schoolrooms and is carried right through to our boardrooms. In a 2015 study of thirty-six hundred business professionals from thirty countries, 96 percent rated themselves as "good listeners." The catch is that 98 percent said that they multitask at work, and 80 percent admitted specifically multitasking during conference calls. Previous research showed that the average person operates at a 25 percent listening efficiency. *Education Digest* reported the same percentage in the listening rate of students.

Even though it was found in two separate studies that 80 percent of executives and teachers believe that listening is "the most vital skill for accomplishing tasks," most schools and businesses don't teach or train to develop the skill, because they don't think there's a problem. Hey, everyone is an above average listener, so what's the problem? If Garrison Keillor's voice in the closing monologue of *A Prairie Home Companion* came rushing back to you, you are not alone: "Well, that's the news from Lake Wobegon, where all the women are strong, all the men are good looking, and all the children are above average." In the world of listening, we have been fooling ourselves about our above average prowess for a long time.

Developing the skills covered in the next three sections will help you improve your ability to listen to learn:

Skill 1: Focusing your attention with TAR (think, act, review)

Skill 2: Knowing when and how to ask questions

Skill 3: Discovering meaning in silence

SKILL 1

Less Is More: Focusing Your Attention

A wise old owl sat on an oak.
The more he saw, the less he spoke.
The less he spoke, the more he heard.
Why aren't we like that wise old bird?
—ANONYMOUS, FROM THE 1800S

Successful leaders and compassionate achievers know how to maximize their listening capabilities by focusing their attention. By improving your ability to focus your attention, you strengthen your ability to listen while reducing your tendency to fall into the routine of simply hearing. When you are not focused, you are hearing sounds, but are you really processing them for careful and thoughtful understanding?

Hearing is about the quantity of sound you notice, while listening is about improving the quality of sound you process. Think of it as hearing a music concert in an open-air arena where people are talking, the wind is blowing, and traffic noises are heard in the distance (the quantity of sound is enormous) as compared to listening to the same concert in a private studio or intimate music hall (the quality of the sound is amazing). In the arena you can only hear basic rhythms, beats, and vibrations; the music and lyrics become diffuse and incoherent. But in the more intimate setting you can appreciate the nuances; you can feel the emotions of a vocalist or the crispness of strings on a violin.

Being able to focus your attention helps you to find meaning in and better understand whatever is being communicated. There are three basic ways to improve your focus:

1. Thinking about why you are listening

2. Acting to improve listening

3. Reviewing what you heard

Using TAR (think, act, and review) will help you be a more effective listener.

Thinking

Thinking when listening means focusing on taking in what another person is trying to convey to you—*not* about what you assume he or she will say or what you will say in response. It means keeping the speaker front and center throughout your conversation and resisting the urge to "zone out" and craft your response instead of continuing to listen.

You've probably been on the receiving end of a "zone out." There you are, just beginning to explain to your coworker how frustrated you are with a project you are working on, and before you even get to the crux of the matter, she's jumped in with suggestions on how you should handle it. Your coworker has fallen into the trap of thinking she already knows what your trouble is—so why waste time continuing to listen to you? Though trying to be helpful (we'll give her the benefit of the doubt), she's been the exact opposite, which has probably ratcheted up your frustration level even more.

Listening is not about *you*, the listener. It's not about preparing an argument or response. Listening is about focused attention on the speaker in order to build understanding.

When we don't listen to others, even though we may hear them, we inevitably create problems that may eventually snowball into even bigger ones. An example is the children's game called telephone. In this game one person whispers a phrase to the next person, who whispers it to the next person, and so on, around the room. A phrase that starts out as "A big brown cow was milked by a farmer" may become something like "A vegetarian doesn't eat cows" by the end of all the whispers. We usually laugh when we hear the original phrase, but when this happens in the real world of our personal and professional lives, it's usually no laughing matter.

Here are a couple of ways to practice focused thinking:

- *Turn on (and keep on until it's over) a podcast or radio or television show in which someone argues the opposite of what you believe on a specific topic and listen for the speaker's strongest argument.* This helps you to practice silencing your inner voice of preconceived ideas and beliefs.

- *After you exercise and/or commute (public transportation), try to name the songs you listened to in the correct order on your iPod.* It's a way to practice focusing on what you listened to while something else may be happening.

Acting

"Actions speak louder than words" is a common adage, but in listening to learn "Actions make words louder." The simple action of looking at others when they talk to you not only increases your level of comprehension by helping you hear every word being said, but it makes the speakers feel as though you care about what they are saying. Compassionate achievers act in ways that help them become deeply present when listening. They look at the person talking and not at their electronic devices. They lean in and "touch" the speaker with their eyes. They look for a straight line of sight, so that their eyes connect.

Follow these suggestions for ways to act that can help you tune into what a person is saying (one of which seems counterintuitive):

- *Eliminate distractions.* One of the first things I do before listening to another is to clear off the desk or table between us, so that there is nothing to distract me from listening to the speaker. It acts as a physical reset button, reminding me to be attentive to the person in front of me. I've also discovered that the people I've listened to sometimes notice this action (they came back to tell me), and it made them feel as though my focus was exclusively on them. *Yes!* An added benefit of clearing the table is that I can read a person's body language more clearly, which we'll discuss in more depth later.

- *Don't answer your phone, e-mail, or text when listening to another person.* The literature on the limitations of multitasking is broad and deep, not to mention that many people consider it disrespectful.

- *Don't interrupt.* One of the worst things you can do when you are listening is to jump into the middle of a person's words with reassurances or advice. Resist the urge to interject, "Oh, I know what you mean. I . . ." or "You know what you can do?" This also includes restraining yourself from filling in the *silences.* When I regularly practice meditation each morning, I've found that I am much more patient with silence than when I do not. Practicing meditation can help you resist interrupting the silence of others.

- *Close your eyes.* The idea of closing your eyes to listen better may seem counterintuitive. Making eye contact is important, right? But there's proof that decreasing what you see increases what you hear. Depending on the context of the conversation, for example, on the phone, closing your eyes eliminates visual distractions from degrading your level of listening. One analysis of how hearing improved in mice that spent a week literally in the dark has been called the "Not Seeing Is Hearing?" study. Hearing improved because activity in the part of the brain used to process sound increased when visual stimulation was temporarily removed. Have you ever noticed that when you close your eyes when listening to a song, you can hear the lyrics better?

Reviewing

How do you know that you have listened to learn? How do you know that you understand the entirety of an issue after listening to what someone has told you? *Paraphrasing* and *questioning*.

Paraphrasing

Taking the time to ask those you are listening to if you can restate their basic ideas helps you to confirm what you heard and shows them that you care about correctly understanding their problem. Whether you are 100 percent correct in paraphrasing, however, is not the issue; it's about learning. The learning not only happens during listening, but also when the speaker clarifies or corrects your paraphrasing. The act of having your restatement corrected will help you to better understand the situation.

But correcting a restatement can also become a learning experience for the speaker. It can cause an idea to pop into the speaker's own mind that may be a possible solution to the problem—commonly known as the lightbulb effect. Listening to you retell the story, in other words, allows the speaker to understand the situation from another perspective, thereby providing a new or different way out of a problem. Hearing you paraphrase provides a chance for the speaker to listen to learn. "One friend, one person who is truly understanding, who takes the trouble to listen to us as we consider our problem," according to Elton Mayo of the Hawthorne Study, "can change our whole outlook on the world."

Dos and don'ts when paraphrasing:

- *Do begin a verbal paraphrase by saying, "If I understand you correctly. . . ."* This does two things: it places any errors in the paraphrase on you, and it puts an emphasis on what the speaker implied and not what you believe the speaker should be implying.

- *Don't begin by saying, "I believe what you meant to say is. . . ."* With this language, it is too easy to interject your own beliefs and ideas into the speaker's situation, thereby devaluing the speaker's words—which you were supposed to be listening to.

- *Do weave the speaker's words into your paraphrase to show that you listened closely to what was said.*

- *Do steer clear of any judgmental phrases such as, "I think that you're letting your feelings get in the way of really seeing the problem for what it is when you say. . . ."* The purpose of paraphrasing is to review, not rebuke.

Several ways to practice paraphrasing include:

- *The tried-and-true method.* Read a magazine article that is at least five pages long or a long-form piece of online journalism that takes fifteen minutes to read. Describe the main points in 150 to 250 of your own words.

- *Editing: getting to the heart of the matter.* Write a one-page reaction piece to a problem you're having. Include how you feel about the problem, the cause of it, any ideas you have for how to solve it, and anything else that comes to mind when you think about it. Walk away from the document for an hour. Then, read your one-pager and write a new three-sentence description of the problem. Those three sentences will reveal the core of the problem, which is sometimes very different from the thoughts you initially had bouncing around in your head. A complex problem doesn't have to be complicated, and paraphrasing helps to remove the complications.

- *Taking on the world.* An activity that I do with my high-school students each summer in a course called "Taking on the World" is to have them give a thirty-second verbal paraphrase of a news story they have read. The other students then question the paraphraser about the story. With time and as they get to know each other through their questions, the students start to paraphrase their stories with an eye toward the possible questions they might get from their classmates. Although I do the exercise so that they can see how news from far corners of the world affects our little corner, a by-product of the exercise is that they all start to see the world through other people's lenses and anticipate how other people might question what is happening in the world. It's reviewing with an empathetic twist. Try this exercise with a friend or partner.

Questioning

To review by questioning can change an outlook on a problem for the listener and speaker. Questions can be both brooms that sweep away shards of misinterpretation and lightbulbs that reveal unexamined approaches to a problem. However, not all questions can be turned into brooms and bulbs. The alchemy of constructive inquiry lies in insightful questions skillfully asked.

An insightful question is one that inspires answerers to reveal something new and constructive about themselves or about what they said to you. It's a way of bringing your voice into the discussion as a clarifying filter. An insightful question, however, changes depending on the context of the conversation; a question that might be insightful in one situation may be insensitive and even destructive in another. For example, the question, "What do you think triggered your emotional response?" might be insightful for a husband or wife going through a marital problem, but insensitive when talking with a parent who lost a child to gun violence. To skillfully ask a question entails seeking clarification and comprehensiveness without creating consternation and awkwardness. The following questions can help you kickstart the review process (because the next chapter is entirely focused on questioning, we'll concentrate here on only a few questions that specifically help you review):

- "Are you saying that . . . ?"

- "What did you mean about . . . ?"

- "From what you just said there's a lot going on. So what do you think are the main issues that get to the heart of the matter?" If the speaker only provides one issue, then you can say, "That's only one thing, though. What do you think are some others?" Don't hesitate to ask for further clarification. This is where a conversation begins in earnest and querying in this way will help the speaker look at the causes of the problem more deeply, often realizing something new about the situation in the process.

Some believe that in order to hear you have to be quiet, but compassionate achievers know that in listening to learn you also have "to question," which has the same letters as "not so quiet." Allowing uncertainty about what someone has told you to settle into your conversation without asking clarifying questions is like standing in concrete as it hardens: you may as well carve your initials in it, because you've cemented yourself into the problem. Questioning is an act of caring.

Listening to learn is based on focusing your thoughts, actions, and observations on the person speaking to you. It is striving to be attentive and present when listening. Do you have a favorite song? At some point you must have tried to listen so closely that you could memorize the lyrics. In this section, you've learned how to focus your attention to help you listen to people as though their words are the song you want to learn.

As you TAR their words you are creating a gift that is filled with respect and sincerity, for listening is a gift that only occurs when you take another's words seriously. Another way to show someone your sincere interest is to ask great questions that move beyond reviewing.

Open the Closed and Close the Opened:
Asking Great Questions

Judge a man by his questions rather than by his answers.
—VOLTAIRE

One of the key factors in making a great photograph is the same for asking a great question: aperture. Aperture, in photography, is the adjustable opening in the front of a camera that allows the photographer to increase or decrease the amount of light entering the camera. The extent to which that hole is either opened or closed affects what a person sees in a picture. Aperture in questioning has a similar effect. The extent to which a question is either open or closed will affect the scope and detail of the reply. For both photographer and questioner, context determines how open or closed the approach will be. Whether creating a picture or asking a question, the goal is the same: to reveal the essence of a subject.

Questions are the photographs of listening, because they can capture as well as reflect the essence of what is being felt or thought about in a given moment. As we've all experienced, there are bad, good, and great questions. This is especially true when you are trying to address a difficult situation with compassion. A bad question disconnects people from each other and causes hesitancy and reluctance to continue a conversation. The common adage "There are no bad questions" is, well, not totally true.

What happens to a conversation in which you've shared that you're feeling down and the other person asks, "How can you feel that way?" or "What's wrong with you?" Or how about when you didn't achieve what you were going for and you get what I call the Rolling Stones question: "'You can't always get what you want,' right?" (I'm always waiting to hear, "But if you try sometimes you just might find you get what you need"!) The end result is that the conversation breaks down and people disconnect.

A good question connects people and proposes a way to move the discussion forward. A good question with respect to feeling down could be, "What has you feeling down?" A better question than the Rolling Stones inquiry would be, "Why do you think it didn't work out?" In short, a good question connects and a bad one disconnects people.

The words of the famous photographer Ansel Adams provide an excellent framework for talking about good and great questions; we will use several of his quotes throughout this section to guide us in asking them. Adams said, *"A great photograph is one that fully expresses what one feels, in the deepest sense, about what is being photographed."* A great question creates an interpersonal connection and exposes the essence of what a person feels and thinks about a problem. Some examples of great questions for our two scenarios are: "I can see you're feeling down. Do you want to talk about it?" and "What can you do differently the next time an opportunity like this comes along?" Great questions of compassion diminish the sense of loneliness that people feel while also helping them to look simultaneously inward and outward for strength and answers. A great question is reflected in your body language, when you lean in, smile, or even give a hug. When you ask a great question, you get the sense that your question was the key for opening a door of new understanding and realization and that, by answering, the person turned the lock.

Questions act like waves, transmitting curiosity and concern from the person asking the question to the person answering it. If you are asking the questions, you want to create waves that the responder can ride to an answer, not ones that verbally or emotionally wipe them out. Two types of questions— closed and open—provide you with relatively simple ways to avoid wipeouts. A closed question can only be answered in one or two words; the options for answers are limited or closed. An open question has many answers with responses that are more than two words; the options are wide-ranging. We'll dive deeper into when and how to use questions throughout the rest of this section, but the main reason I focus on a combination of open and closed questions is that they are effective yet simple to ask. One of the pitfalls you want to avoid is complicating an already complex situation with difficult to ask or interpret questions, and open and closed questions can help.

Deepening Your Understanding Through Questioning

"A photograph is usually looked at—seldom looked into" (Ansel Adams). Listening is not just quietly collecting thoughts and feelings through close attention; it also involves the not-so-quiet way of looking into a problem through a series of questions. In listening to learn, inquiring is caring.

In the previous section, we covered how to use questions to review what you've heard. Now, we'll use questions to probe in a more comprehensive way. As the questioner, you'll use questions to increase your understanding of a problem by gathering more facts and information about what the responder thinks and feels about the situation. However, you're not on a hunt for specific answers as if you were conducting a deposition. Instead, you're searching for understanding as though you're on an exploration. The responder will immediately feel the difference between the two approaches. It's the difference between being asked where you've been all night by an irate spouse and being asked the same thing by an interested friend.

Are you a deposer or an explorer? A deposer interrogates while an explorer investigates. A deposer searches for specific answers to specific questions as though trying to either prove or score a point. The responder feels trapped in an interrogation. An explorer searches for a broad understanding of the issue. The responder feels as if a journey is just beginning.

Strive to be an explorer rather than a deposer when questioning someone you are trying to help. Not only will you acquire a more comprehensive understanding of the problem, but the answerer will also be less defensive and more forthcoming (if we've learned anything from "enhanced interrogation techniques," it's that they don't work). Looking into a problem doesn't mean getting into its specifics, but seeing its entirety so that you don't miss the forest for the trees. In statistical analysis, for example, you discover problematic trends only when you "zoom out" for a picture of all the data, not when you "zoom in" to specific data points.

"Looking Into" a problem, as Ansel Adams describes it, is key for unlocking understanding when listening. Questions can sharpen thoughts and refine emotions of the questioner and answerer alike. Some of the most interesting research on the dynamics between people who are asking and answering questions has come out of the Computation and Cognition Lab at Stanford University. One study showed "that an answerer's level of informativeness varies with the inferred questioner goal." Understanding, in other words, can be altered by how you ask a question and any prejudices you may have. So how do you use open and closed questions to explore the responder's as well as your own understanding of a problem? Their use largely depends on the answerer's perspective or stance on the problem.

"A good photograph is knowing where to stand" (Adams). A great question is based upon knowing *when* and *what* to ask. Open and closed questions are some of the most helpful and simplest questions to use, especially in combination, when trying to unlock understanding.

A *closed question* can only be answered in one or two words: "Yes," "No," "Up," "Down," "It's true," "It's false," and so on. A closed question such as,

"Do you think that X caused the problem?" narrows a person's thinking and focuses attention on a quick, simple answer. Closed questions tend to yield facts or what the speaker believes to be facts.

An *open question*, in contrast, is one that can have many answers and consists of more than two words. It encourages the responder to think and reflect. An open question such as, "What are the causes of the problem?" widens individuals' thinking and expands their field of attention by prompting them to respond with their opinions and feelings. Open questions usually begin with words like "What," "Why," "How," and "Can you describe."

Compassionate achievers "look into" a problem by blending open and closed questions. You don't ask one type of question rather than another as though it were based on a formula; instead, you ask based on what will help the responder better understand the problem. It reminds me a lot of playing jazz, where the music becomes complexly smoother, the more you listen to others as you play. Questions become your instruments for broadening the understanding of both you and the person answering your questions: your understanding becomes more comprehensive the more you listen to others as you question. There's an improvisation of question and answer, where you play off each other's ideas and emotions. It's this improvisation that can produce an understanding, one that becomes "music to your ears."

Whether you use open or closed questions depends on your subject's position in relation to the problem. For example, sometimes people are so focused on what they perceive the problem to be that they haven't considered other explanations or points of view; their one explanation blocks or removes from consideration any other narrative. Using open questions in this instance, such as "What caused the problem?" followed by "What other causes could have contributed to the problem?" can help people consider other explanations and perceptions if they are locked in to one way of thinking.

When people, however, become deeply lost or adrift in a problem, they can have a difficult time focusing; closed questions help them focus. A question such as, "Do you think one cause is more important than others?" narrows the field of attention.

Although the difference between closed and open questions can be slight ("Are there multiple causes of the problem?" as compared to "What are the multiple causes of the problem?"), their effect on the way people see a problem can be quite different. When you ask people a yes or no question (closed), a problem can seem pretty simple. But when you expose them to multiple causes of a problem through an open question, they start to see the complexity of an issue. This is where the improvisation of listening by questioning comes into play. If you find them lost or adrift, then ask a couple of closed questions to help them focus. If you hear them locked into one idea about a problem, an open question could be helpful. Remember that your central goal is to help them find a resolution to their problem, so if they close themselves off from other solutions, you need to ask questions that open them up to other possibilities.

Closed Question	Open Question
Are there several reasons for the problem?	What are the reasons for the problem?
Does your boss know about the problem?	Why doesn't your boss know about the problem?
Are you looking for another job?	Can you describe your dream job?

Now you try. Write three closed questions and then convert them to open questions.

Closed questions

1. _____

2. _____

3. _____

Open questions

1. _____

2. _____

3. _____

The following conversation between coworkers at a fictitious company is an example of how a responder's replies influence the type of questions a compassionate achiever should ask. Pay attention to the way open and closed questions are used throughout.

JOSEPH: *Good morning. Do you have some time to talk?*

RICHARD: *Sure do. What's up?*

JOSEPH: *Is it okay if I use you as a reference?*

RICHARD: *Yes, of course. Are you looking for another job? (closed)*

JOSEPH: *No, but after what happened yesterday I want to cover all my bases.*

RICHARD: *What happened yesterday? (open)*

JOSEPH: *My loyalty to this country and my job—the sales part of my job at least—were both questioned by a couple of members of my team at lunch. I don't want to get too deep into what they said, but it was pretty bad.*

RICHARD: *Can you tell me the gist of what they said? (open)*

JOSEPH: *They basically said that my sales numbers are down, because I have dual citizenship, Estonia and America. They said that since I celebrate the holidays of both countries, I'm not keeping my sales numbers up. They also insinuated that someone with dual citizenship can't be trusted, because they are unsure which country I love more.*

RICHARD: *Does your boss know about what they said? (closed)*

JOSEPH: *No.*

RICHARD: *Why doesn't he know about the problem? (open)*

JOSEPH: *He doesn't care how we treat each other as long as we make the numbers. He's all about the numbers.*

RICHARD: *We'll get to the dual citizenship comment in a moment. I think they're simply jealous of all your past success. But are your sales numbers down? (closed)*

JOSEPH: *Yes, but it has nothing to do with dual citizenship.*

RICHARD: *What do you think are the reasons for the sales problem? (open)*

JOSEPH: *I've been worried about my mom and dad's health. Since they still live in Estonia, the time difference between here and there makes our "prime time" for sales—as my boss likes to call it—the only time for me to talk with them and their doctors. I'm stuck . . . I'm stuck between caring for either my parents or my job.*

RICHARD: *It sounds, if I'm understanding you correctly, that the people you work with are making you feel stuck or trapped in a couple of either-or problems: parents or job and Estonia or America. Does that sound about right? (closed)*

JOSEPH: *Yes.*

RICHARD: *Okay, bear with me on this question. Do you love both your mom and dad? (closed)*

JOSEPH: *Yes, of course. I thought I just made that clear. What kind of question is that?*

RICHARD: *That's the kind of question you can ask your coworkers when they challenge your loyalty as a person with dual citizenship. It shows them that it's not unusual for someone to love two people, two organizations, or two anything else for that matter at the same time equally. Don't you love your three sons equally as well? (closed)*

JOSEPH: *Sure do. I get what you're saying.*

RICHARD: *Good, because that same type of thinking can help you and this company.*

JOSEPH: *What do you mean?*

RICHARD: *We're looking to increase sales, right? (closed)*

JOSEPH: *Yes.*

RICHARD: *Do you think we have a better chance of increasing sales if we stay local or go global? (closed)*

JOSEPH: *Going global.*

RICHARD: *Do you think you would be a good fit for the global team? (closed)*

JOSEPH: *Yes, you bet, especially with all of my contacts throughout Europe.*

RICHARD: *What do you think would happen to your time difference problem if you became part of our global effort to increase sales? (open)*

JOSEPH: *It would disappear, because I would be on a different schedule, which would . . . ahhh . . . allow me to help my parents as I increase sales.*

I used this scenario not only as an example of how to weave open and closed questions together to increase understanding toward finding a solution, but also to illustrate that too many of us turn problems into either-or scenarios—into black-and-white issues—when they don't have to be. When we make problems into either-or situations, we limit ourselves to only two solutions that usually have the end result of win-lose. A series of great questions can break open the either-or trap to reveal different ways of getting to win-win. The more you practice listening to learn, the more you'll feel comfortable with knowing when to use open and closed questions.

Simply being an active listener will help you. Uri Hasson, a neuroscientist at Princeton University, and his colleagues have shown that the more attentive a listener is, the more in sync the listener's brain waves are with the speaker's. And the more synchronized two brains are ("brain coupling"), the more a listener can anticipate what a speaker is going to say (an example is when someone finishes your sentence), the better "we understand one another," and the "more successful" communication becomes. In short, if you have a clear conception of what someone is saying *and* going to say to you, the better you will be at asking questions that move the conversation constructively along. "Successful communication," in the words of the Princeton study, "requires the active engagement of the listener." An active listener is a connected questioner who knows when and what to ask.

"You don't take a photograph, you make it" (Adams). You don't just ask a great question; you craft it. Someone who's an active listener and connected questioner knows *how* to ask a great question by carefully crafting it. To craft a great question, you need to pay attention to more than just the speaker's answers to your questions. You need to also be aware of the way he or she is responding. Leisurely or hurriedly? Reluctantly or effusively? Confidently or hesitantly?

The responses to your questions are like light sensors in a camera. They tell you how open or closed in your approach you need to be. For instance, whether a defensive person uses short or long responses can help you determine what questions to use. If the person is being curt in order to keep you at the surface of a problem, craft an open question. If the person is being long-winded to avoid having to answer questions that drill down beneath the surface, closed questions will be helpful in furthering the discussion. Usually, though, most people answer with a mixture of responses and that requires using a combination of question types.

Although the funnel model of asking questions, starting with open questions and ending with closed ones to narrow understanding, is a popular approach, compassionate achievers subscribe to the lens, or focus-ring, method of questioning. High-quality cameras have a focus ring on their lenses so that photographers can make their subjects appear with crystal clarity whether they zoom in or out. Skillful questioners use an alternating combination of open and closed questions to acquire a clear focus on a problem. Just as an artful photographer tweaks the focus ring back and forth, a skillful questioner blends or alternates open and closed questions to mirror the speaker's responses. In our Estonian-American scenario, did you notice how, although the questions became more closed as the conversation moved toward focusing on a solution, we ended with an open question, so that the answerer could reach his own understanding of the situation? In other words, compassionate achievers don't follow the formulaic funnel approach to asking questions, but fashion them according to what they hear or don't hear.

Again, simply being an active listener will give you an edge here. Remember that acting compassionately activates oxytocin in the brain. Studies have shown that when oxytocin is flowing, a person becomes better at reading another's interpersonal cues (i.e., voice and facial expressions), being sensitive to the emotions and feelings of others, and fostering a "calming and connecting" reaction. That is also important in how you ask your questions: stay calm and keep your voice measured. Remember that your questions are to help the answerer better understand the problem in a way that is more constructive and calmer than it would be without you. Your caring is important to make a connection with the speaker, but don't let it create an undercurrent of emotion that can take you and the speaker down the path of simply complaining about the problem. If open and closed questions make up the focus ring of a skillful questioner, then the active listening is the lens through which they zoom in on a problem. By developing these skills, you'll have an extra powerful lens for seeing, understanding, and connecting to the world around you.

"To photograph truthfully and effectively is to see beneath the surfaces" (Adams). Compassionate achievers use great questions to get as close to the truth as the responder sees it and to reveal additional truths that lie beneath the surface of a problem. John Medina, the founding director of the Brain Center for Applied Learning Research and the Talaris Research Institute, in a chapter on the brain's sensory integration, writes: "Two people can see the same input and come away with vastly different perceptions. . . . There is no one accurate way to perceive the world." A connected questioner not only strives to understand how responders perceive a problem, but also

helps them to discover what was unseen or what they have hidden from themselves.

An ultraviolet light, or black light, works by picking up phosphors woven into the surface of objects and people. A phosphor is any substance that has the property of luminescence; it absorbs energy and converts it into visible light. Phosphors are used in laundry detergents to make our whites appear "whiter than white," and they naturally appear on the surfaces of people's teeth and nails, which is why our teeth and nails appear to glow when an ultraviolet light is used at parties and dance clubs.

Compassionate achievers use great questions like an ultraviolet light for making hidden feelings and thoughts visible. Great questions highlight the emotional and logical phosphors of people's thoughts about a problem on the surface of a conversation without making them want to shut down or disconnect from you. You want to make others feel as though what you just asked is what they should have asked themselves. Your question, in essence, converts hidden insights into a "visible light" for them to see the problem anew. Some phosphors that "light up," or cues suggesting that you should direct your questioning to dig deeper, appear in specific words or phrases:

- "By the way": This phrase is often used to downplay important information. It's your job to find out why the speaker is treating the information in this way. Fear and insecurity are two common reasons, but use your questioning skills to understand the speaker's unique motivation. It will help you to find an appropriate solution.

- "How did you do it?": People usually ask this question about how you have handled a past experience (transitioned from military to civilian life, moved to a new country, handled a job loss, etc.), because they are going through something similar but aren't ready to tell you about their situation yet. First, share part of your story. Admit to them that the experience was a big moment for you and answer the question about how you did it as best you can and in a way that feels comfortable to you. Then ask, "Are you going through something similar right now?" to redirect the conversation.

- "It's who I am": When people connect a problem or issue to what they believe is at the core of their identity, they feel hopeless. They think, "If the problem is because of who I am, and I can't change who I am, then there's nothing I can do to change the situation. It is what it is." It is impossible to find a solution to a problem by approaching it with a sense of resignation to the status quo. You can help break the loop of resignation by asking people an open or closed question that you know they know the answer to. This approach builds their confidence and capacity to imagine a potential solution.

You are helping them to see that you are listening to them and taking their situation seriously, that you are committed to helping them find a solution, that their situation isn't a dead end but the start of a dialogue aimed at finding a solution, and that they have the capacity to solve their problem. This "It's who I am" sentiment is present in the conversation scenario between coworkers earlier in this chapter and is why Richard asks, "Do you love both your mom and dad?" Richard knows the answer to that question before he asks it because he has listened to Joseph express how deeply he cares about the health of his parents. Richard uses this closed question to "unstick" Joseph and move him toward a solution.

Without listening to the person you're with, the questions you ask will be without meaning.

Great questions generate thoughtful and heartfelt conversations. Just as exposure in photography is about bringing light to what is already in front of you, questioning while listening to learn is about bringing to light what is inside the person in front of you. Great questions expose the essence of a problem's difficulties and a speaker's thoughts and emotions. The silence or gaps in conversations, however, are sometimes just as important as the words we listen to.

SKILL 3

SKILL 3

Mind the Gaps: Appreciating Silence

*In human intercourse the tragedy begins not
when there is misunderstanding about words,
but when silence is not understood.*
—HENRY DAVID THOREAU

On subway platforms around the world from New York to Beijing to São Paulo to London, the words "Watch the gap" or "Mind the gap" appear as warnings to passengers not to step into the space between the platform and train when boarding. It is always easy to tell the difference between veteran riders, who are used to the gap and board as though there is no space, and the "newbies," who step over the gap as though it were a deep chasm of no return.

The silences or gaps in conversations are often treated in a similar "newbie" fashion—as if they were deep chasms of no return that need to be avoided or filled in. In conversations around tables in living rooms, boardrooms, and classrooms, most of us seem to have an overwhelming urge to fill in the gaps or silences in our conversations. One study found that most people break silence within only four seconds, mainly because they're trying to either overcome a sense of insecurity or satisfy the need for social acceptance. Compassionate achievers, however, have learned to read and understand the gaps between words as important parts of the conversation.

Embracing Silence

Listening to learn involves being attentive to what is said and noticing what is being communicated through silence. As a kid, I devoured Sir Arthur Conan Doyle's books about Sherlock Holmes and loved watching the classic black-and-white Holmes films starring Basil Rathbone. After reading *The Adventure of Silver Blaze* for the first time as a seven-year-old, I finally understood the power of silence (at least as well as a seven-year-old can, which is for about two seconds): there is untold meaning in silence. The story's plot revolves around solving the disappearance of a famous racehorse and the apparent murder of its trainer. Holmes solves the case by focusing upon "the curious incident of the dog in the nighttime": the dog didn't bark when the horse abduction and murder were thought to have occurred. Sherlock Holmes was my first model in learning how to solve a problem by paying attention to silence.

A pause or other moment of quiet in a conversation is not separate from the conversation, but an integral part of it. Musicians have known this for centuries, composing songs based on the simple principle of how "sound yields to silence." The importance of silence over sound is acknowledged around the world and echoed across cultures. Silence has been at the heart of music, no matter the place or time. One of my favorite pieces by Joseph Haydn is nicknamed "The Joke" (Opus 33, Number 2), because he uses silence humorously: he uses pauses to repeatedly fool his listeners about when the composition is over. In *Silence: The Power of Quiet in a World Full of Noise,* Thich Nhat Hanh uses a traditional Vietnamese song ("Lute Song") to illustrate how his culture sees the "space between notes [as] very, very powerful, very meaningful."

There are two main reasons for embracing silence in a conversation when listening to learn:

1. Silence offers an opportunity to heighten your awareness of the present moment and assess what's been said and how it's been said.

2. Silence is filled with meaning.

Silences or pauses, according to neuroscience research in music, help to sharpen your attention. Embracing silence provides you, the listener, with an opportunity to refocus your attention. Although the "Mozart effect" (the idea that if children listen to music composed by Mozart, their intelligence will increase) has been debunked in numerous studies, there is a musical effect that Mozart himself sincerely believed in: the "grand pause." Mozart believed, "The music is not in the notes, but the silence in between." Neuroscientists have found that the real Mozart effect on the brain occurs during music's grand pauses and it helps to focus our attention.

Recent neuroscience research has shown that musical pauses have a greater effect on the brain than the sounds emanating from musical instruments. The research of Vinod Menon and his team from Stanford and McGill universities found that "peak brain activity occurred during a short period of silence between musical movements." Their research demonstrates that the brain fires up its activity for maintaining and sharpening attention in the absence of sound. This neural firing of focused attention is experienced in one of the most famous film scores in history: the theme of *Jaws*. Our neural wiring of attention clicks on during the pauses between the "dun-dun . . . dun-dun" of the *Jaws* theme. *Jaws*'s grand pauses build anticipation that focuses our attention; it's the anticipation during the silence of what is coming next that heightens our awareness and "catalyzes our powers of perception," according to George Prochnik in *In Pursuit of Silence*. Pauses awaken the mind in ways that help us to be better listeners and provide an opportunity to slow down, so that understanding can catch up to what we heard and noticed.

Silence itself is also filled with meaning. Conversational pauses have multiple meanings all of which depend on context. Paul Goodman, in his classic book *Speaking and Language*, outlines nine types of silence:

> There is the dumb silence of slumber or apathy; the sober silence that goes with a solemn animal face; the fertile silence of awareness, pasturing the soul, whence emerge new thoughts; the alive silence of alert perception ready to say, "This . . . this . . ."; the musical silence that accompanies absorbed activity; the silence of listening to another speak, catching the drift and helping him be clear; the noisy silence of resentment and self-recrimination, loud and subvocal speech but sullen to say it; baffled silence; the silence of peaceful accord with other persons or communion with the cosmos.

Others have added to Goodman's typology, such as the silence of avoidance, but all types of silence share the same quality: they have meaning and are not void or empty spaces. Even if there is an awkward silence in your conversation, allow it. Treat it with respect. An awkward silence can create the space needed for enhanced contemplation, especially if you're speaking with someone who is introverted. Silence is not a gap, so don't be in a rush to fill it with your own words.

To be an attentive listener, you must allow silence—even encourage it—but allowing silence can be a challenge. Our culture doesn't value quiet. Too often silence is treated as a hole that needs to be filled, usually within four seconds. "If we were supposed to talk more than we listen," Mark Twain is often credited with saying, "we would have two mouths and one ear." Slowing your need to speak speeds up your understanding.

Because I tend to get a little excited about the subjects I teach, I have had to come up with ways to slow myself down in the classroom. This slowing down is especially important because I use the Socratic style of teaching, which depends on my asking a lot of questions to foster learning, and I need to allow time for students to answer the questions. There is some-times an awkward amount of silence after asking a question, and I have had to learn to simply sit with it. And sit with it. And sit with it. I've learned I can endure a much longer Socratic silence than I'd originally thought, and the rewards are worth it. If you break the silence, you miss a valuable opportunity to learn.

In one-on-one conversations outside of the classroom, I have found a few ways that help me resist the inclination to interrupt another's silence. I take a few sips from a cup of coffee or bottle of water, or I look for facial expres-sions. Often I try to notice something about the person that is different from before. And I wait for verbal and nonverbal cues that tell me the person is through with the silence and wants me to jump back in the conversation. A common verbal cue is "I don't know." A common nonverbal cue is a slightly tilted head, shrugged shoulders, or raised eyebrows.

Interpreting Silence

Seeing is a part of listening, especially when sitting in the middle of silence. Until now, we've focused on skills that strengthen your abilities as a listener, improving your focus and using what you've heard to ask great questions. Now it's time to strengthen your skills as an observer. As silence grows, seeing becomes a greater part of listening. Interpreting facial gestures and reading body language, for example, enhance our ability to mind the gaps in conversation. Observing like a robot and watching like a spy catcher will help you to make sense of silence.

Interpreting pauses in a conversation involves *reading microexpressions* and *reading body language*.

Reading Microexpressions

Interpreting silence is all about how well you can "read between the lines" in conversations. There are two basic lines of context that you need to be able to read between in order to understand any type of pause in a conversation: your line of questioning and the verbal response. Taken together as one part of a conversation, they make up the syntax of silence. Your understanding of what happens in between those lines of syntax depends on your ability to read what psychologists call microexpressions. Microexpressions are facial expressions that "last only a fraction of a second" and "occur when a person either deliberately or unconsciously conceals a feeling."

We know more about microexpressions than ever before due to recent advancements in robotics and artificial intelligence. Many researchers and companies in artificial intelligence around the world are working on developing caring and emotionally intelligent robots. Human beings have upwards of forty-three facial muscles, and engineers in the field of affective computing are developing algorithms that can translate their movement into the underlying emotions. Researchers are teaching robots to recognize, depending upon the combination of facial muscles moving, the difference between fake, discomforting, and happy smiles as well as gestures of confusion, disgust, displeasure, and interest. By measuring how far the corners of a person's mouth are raised (engaging the zygomaticus major muscle) and how deep the outer corners of the eyes crinkle (contracting the orbicularis oculi), a computer can determine whether a person is giving a genuine or a fake smile. The following table provides some algorithms developed in the field of artificial intelligence that can be helpful clues when trying to read another person's microexpressions.

The Algorithm/Code	Facial Expression
Eyebrows furrowed, hard stare, and lips pursed	Anger
Lips closed and angled up only on one corner, chin raised	Contempt
Eyes narrowed, top lip flared, and nostrils raised	Disgust
Eyebrows drawn together, upper eyelids arched, and lips elongated	Fear
Cheeks and lower eyelids raised, corners of eyes crinkled, and lips curved upward	Happiness
Eyelids sagging, eyes wandering, and lips curved downward	Sadness
Eyebrows arched, eyes widened, and lips separated	Surprise

Although many people echo the beliefs of business magnate Elon Musk, who called artificial intelligence humanity's "biggest existential threat," it can also help us, paradoxically, to be better human beings. Artificial intelligence offers humanity a technological mirror in which we can uncover messages and signals that we hide in plain sight: the emotions and feelings written on our faces. Learning how to make our technology more human is making us more observant and providing us with the tools to help us be better listeners.

Use your sharpened attention and heightened awareness during pauses to interpret microexpressions. Recognizing microexpressions can be useful for distinguishing the different silences. People often reveal more about themselves and their feelings about a situation through unspoken means of communication. Your heightened awareness and ability to read faces in those moments can help you to better learn about what they are thinking and feeling.

Reading Body Language

Spy catchers, or counterintelligence agents, are specifically taught to see what is hidden in plain sight. They are experts at decoding a person's body language, especially during silence. Some spy-catching practices can offer ways to improve your ability to see what is often overlooked.

To sharpen their skills, many counterintelligence agents used to play a game with each other about telling truth from fiction called "Two Truths and a Lie." The game was made famous in the movie *Breach* (based on the true story of Robert Hanssen—a convicted Russian spy who once led the FBI's counterintelligence unit). All you need is two people: one person tells two truths and a lie and the other person tries to figure out the lie. Two places to watch for clues are the face and hands. If people increase the number of times they touch their face when talking or answering a question, it is usually a sign that they are under stress and therefore lying. Another signal that people may be hiding something happens when they touch their throat as though they are covering it (and covering up what they don't want you to know).

Understanding the context and environment in which body language occurs is as important as the movements themselves. Because people cannot control the size of their eye pupils, an agent is taught to focus upon how dilated or contracted a person's pupils become. The pupils dilate, on balance, when a person is interested in what is being said and contract as the conversation slides into uninteresting. Be careful, however, on being too focused on pupil dilation without taking notice of how bright or dim the lighting is during the conversation; pupils dilate as a room becomes brighter.

A common misconception in body-language reading is that arm crossing equals lying; it can mean a variety of things, such as masking insecurities or self-restraint, as well as being a blocking behavior. It could also mean that a person is simply feeling cold in a fully air-conditioned office or a frigid field environment—context matters. Stiff interlaced fingers or the frigid finger teepee is a pretty good sign that people are distressed or ready to reveal information that is disconcerting about themselves (there is a contextual caveat, however: the distressed or disconcerting finger read does not apply to people who habitually fall into the frigid teepee).

Another contextual caveat applies to reading a person's eyes. A common way to read people's eyes to discern lying is that when they look to their left they are attempting to honestly remember something and when they look to their right they are being more "creative." However, what is commonly overlooked is that such "reads" apply to right-handed people; right and left are reversed if the person is left-handed. Again, context matters when interpreting body language.

Keeping context in mind is especially important if a person has recently experienced a traumatic event. Experiencing a significant loss can affect people in very erratic, inconsistent, and uncharacteristic ways. After a trauma, someone who is usually upbeat and friendly may withdraw and disconnect from people, physically shrinking or moving away from you. Others who are usually generous and helpful may lash out, bully, and present aggressive body language like pointing a finger at you. Keep recent events in mind when interpreting body language.

Learning to read body language and in different contexts will significantly enhance your ability to listen with your eyes as well as your ears. Many of humankind's greatest artists, such as Leonardo da Vinci, knew "how the changing expressions of the face would be the key to understanding the human condition." For a compassionate achiever, it's a crucial part of becoming an attentive listener.

Removing Static

Your preconceived ideas or perceptions can create a noisy static that interferes with your ability to interpret silence. Our preconceived notions of what someone is feeling, thinking, or interpreting can cause us to mishear, misremember, or misperceive what we are listening to. Each one of us sees the world differently, and those preconceived perceptions can twist what you see and hear. For example, when my wife and I saw the picture below for the first time together we saw two very different animals; we had different perceptions of the same image. What do you see? Do you see a duck or a rabbit? We eventually helped each other to see both images, which is what attentive listeners do: they learn to see what the other is seeing.

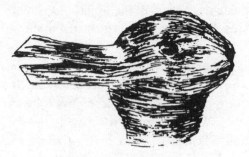

Researchers in psychology and neuroscience have demonstrated in numerous behavioral experiments, and recently on the cellular level, that what we experience or perceive in a given moment doesn't simply depend upon what our senses tell us, but on what we already know and the emotions we are feeling. Our prior experiences and beliefs can cloud our perception of what we think we may have just heard to such an extent that "we cannot easily distinguish between what we recall verbatim and what we construct based on associations and knowledge. . . . People often remember what they expect to remember."

An "expectation calculation" for how we perceive the world may even be something we're born with. Neuroscientists who study expectation calculations in infants call it predictive coding (this contrasts with the idea that children are "sponges" for learning). This is not bad in and of itself, because it can help you navigate the world without always questioning or wondering what will happen next: when you hear the doorbell ring, you expect to see someone at your door. We expect that what has happened before in a specific situation will continue to happen into the future. However, predictive coding can also make life more challenging and difficult if your situation or circumstance changes. How challenging would it be if your roommate or spouse moved the furniture around before you came home late one night and didn't tell you? Besides gathering some bumps and bruises you'll probably also experience some frustration.

Our expectations are formed from a mental framework built from not only predisposed beliefs and ideas but also in-the-moment emotions (like frustration from bumping into moved furniture). Emotions or moods are such integral parts of cognition that they impact how we experience the present moment. Our vision is literally affected by our emotions. Positive and negative moods, according to a 2009 neuroscience study, affect the way we see the world around us by either broadening (positive) or narrowing (negative) our peripheral vision, respectively. The study clearly demonstrates that our moods modulate the activity of the visual cortex "with positive affect broadening and negative affect narrowing the distribution, or scope, of one's field of view (FOV)."

Our feelings about (rather than for) people even determine if we see them as attractive. The more honest we believe people to be, the more likable they are to us, "and the more likable, the more physically attractive" we see them to be (and vice versa). The reason is that "we do not see with our eyes; we see with our brains." Because it is our brains that see and not the eyes, emotions and opinions define our vision of reality. When we have different emotions, we release different neurochemicals that alter our perception. For example, we release dopamine when we're happy and cortisol when stressed; dopamine helps us to focus, and cortisol is linked to creating blurred vision. Emotions and their accompanying neurochemicals help to define not only how we see reality, but how we hear it too.

Your brain processes what you hear and how you remember it differently depending on how you feel about a situation you're in and/or a person you're listening to. One of the key findings of a meta-analysis of scientific studies on language learning by the University of Maryland Center for the Advanced Study of Language was that the feeling of anxiety makes whatever you hear more difficult to understand: the higher your anxiety, the more difficult it is to comprehend what you are listening to. In another study published in the *Journal of Memory and Language*, the authors found that the longer an emotional moment lasts, you increase both "the likelihood that any information (specific or general) will be remembered" and "the amount of specific information." Emotions can either help you hear as though you're wearing an excellent pair of headphones, or they can make your conversation seem as though it's happening through a set of fast-food drive-through speakers.

We tend to default to hearing what we want to hear and to seeing what we expect to see based on our personal emotions and history. When I am working with various types of community leaders in helping them create schools, cities, or towns of compassion, some think I'm a Buddhist. I'm not, but many associate compassion with Buddhism. Similarly, I've actually been asked, "How can someone who is in the military know anything about compassion?" In short, people make an assumption that the military and compassion could not possibly be associated with one another.

Acknowledging and simply understanding the fact that we default to predictive coding and are influenced by our emotions can help us silence our static. We can silence, for example, our stereotypes of others when we listen. Most of us have implicit biases and make judgments about others based on dress, ethnicity, age, and gender every day without recognizing that we're doing it. When a young doctor who doesn't look like he should be out of high school enters the room to perform your surgery, what do you think? Our mental defaults are so strong that neuroscientists have determined that we tend to jump to conclusions or make snap judgments about others in approximately a hundred milliseconds simply based on the look of their faces. If our implicit biases are negative, we tend to "tune out" and discount what someone is saying. I may spend ten minutes with each of my sons on Apple's FaceTime when I'm traveling, but all the face time we need to travel to judgment about other people is a blink of an eye. One way you can keep your implicit biases in check is through mindful listening.

Practicing mindful listening is a simple way to let go of your ideas, feelings, and reactions and focus on the speaker. Mindfulness encourages you to be attentive to the present moment and pay attention without judgment. When you listen mindfully, you let your preconceived perceptions slip away, while giving full attention to the words and body language of the person speaking. You can hear people's feelings and emotions in the tone of their words, and you can see them reflected in their facial expressions. Mindful listening is treating speakers with respect, so that their words become more important than your judgments. If you catch your mind wandering away from what is being said or you notice your focus shifting to what you think or feel about what is being said, bring your attention back by leaning in slightly in an effort to listen better to the words and tone they are using. The more aware you become of your static, the easier it will be to refocus your attention on the speaker.

I find myself practicing mindful listening, or what I like to call "tree searching," a lot when I speak with leaders such as city mayors, school superintendents, and university presidents about how compassion can be helpful to them in achieving their organization's objectives. I realize that I often come to the table with strong feelings about the role compassion should play, and I consciously remind myself of my goal: to put my thoughts and judgments aside and listen to each leader in order to understand the needs involved. Different leaders make and follow different lists of priorities for their organizations. Every leader has a political, economic, social/cultural, or intellectual "tree" that they are focused on cultivating in their community. Mindful listening helps me to understand what issues they consider important and identify what tree we need to nourish in order to help them reach their goal. Some mayors, for example, make reducing crime a priority while others are focused on promoting business development. If I can understand their respective socioeconomic priorities, I can more effectively help each of them to achieve their goals through compassion than if I don't mindfully listen.

One mayor may be interested in having her city become a city of compassion to help heal the community after a tragedy, while another mayor may only become open to the idea when he learns of its economic benefits. I would approach the first type of mayor by explaining how compassion can strengthen the civil society of a community, while I'd approach the second mayor with examples of cities, towns, and businesses where a focus on compassion has increased real estate values and profits. The leaders each have a specific tree that they are concerned with, and I listen to make sure that I've gotten the right tree, so I don't "bark" up the wrong one, one they are not focused on cultivating. When I mindfully listen, I'm searching for the other person's most important tree.

When we quiet our static, we clear the way for understanding.

Silence is the most fragile part of a conversation, because it is when speakers are feeling the most vulnerable; they may be unexpectedly revealing more than they intended. Their silence becomes a way of communicating that they didn't plan on. Sometimes speakers' silence and their own reaction to it reveals more about who they are and what type of character they possess than any sentence they can say. "We can learn a lot about a person," according to the multitalented Anna Deavere Smith, "in the very moment that language fails them, in the very moment that they have to be more creative than they would have imagined in order to communicate. It's the very moment that they have to dig deeper than the surface to find words."

Letting speakers' language fail them opens another path to a solution. Allowing a conversation to yield to silence can also produce an answer that may lie hidden among the words. The problem is that too many of us seek to overcome that constructive failure with our own failure at silence. Compassion, in this instance, is best expressed through silence. To be compassionate achievers, we have to learn to let language fail the people we listen to and be ready to read their silence. Silence is both a form of communication, conveying reluctance, anxiety, uncertainty, or other emotion, and the space that highlights other nonverbal forms of communication, such as facial expressions and body language. When we embrace silence and learn how to use it, we improve our understanding of the people and problems around us.

Is there such a thing as too much silence? Not as long as you are listening and questioning as an explorer and not as a deposer. If you are listening with genuine compassion to learn how to help the person you're talking with, rarely will silence be interpreted as a sign of disagreement or intentional rudeness. And although an extended silence may be uncomfortable, remember all of the ways you can use that pause in the conversation to move closer to a solution for the person you are trying to help.

Listening to learn, overall, involves noticing the spoken as well as unspoken signs of communication. It's about having focused attention, a willingness to explore a problem through questions, and the patience to find meaning in silence. By improving your ability to listen, you have paved the way for a heightened level of understanding.

4

Understand to Know

Did you know what you were going to do for the rest of your life when you were eighteen years old? I had at least a half dozen ideas, and it took me a little too long to figure out how to hit a curve ball. I'm still contemplating what I'm going to do, but I know what I want to be: a compassionate achiever. When students would come to talk with me for help in finding an academic major, I used to ask what they wanted to do. Instead, I now ask what problem(s) they want to understand and solve. They don't need in-depth knowledge of a problem or field of study to answer that question (for those are two reasons why they are in college), but they need an understanding of why a problem is important to them and their world. Their answers give me a better understanding of what I need to know, so that I can ask better questions in an effort to help them discover their own educational and professional path. Their comments and ideas during our discussions turn their education into a quest for meaning and purpose rather than a race for a paper trophy to hang on a wall.

The search for understanding should be your North Star when you journey through the world as a compassionate achiever.

Listening to learn, Step 1 of becoming a compassionate achiever, is focused on attentive information gathering and establishing a meaningful connection. Step 2, understanding to know, is focused on connecting the pieces of information you've collected into a coherent whole. You'll be paying attention to how the people you are speaking with see the world around them—What are the beliefs and feelings that shape their perspective of reality?—as well as how to identify and develop connections between ideas and people, so that you can acquire a holistic understanding of the situation. This understanding sets you up to be a more effective problem solver.

We have a tendency to believe that knowing the relevant facts about a person, thing, or situation leads to understanding—comprehending its meaning, significance, character, or nature—and that the more we know, the greater our understanding. But that's not the case. In fact, the reverse is true: understanding leads to knowledge. Think of it as the difference between completing a jigsaw puzzle with a picture to use as a guide or doing it without one. Aren't you able to solve the puzzle more efficiently and effectively with the picture? Having the picture gives you an understanding of how the different pieces fit together. It's not enough for you to know the facts and figures of a particular situation; they are just pieces of a puzzle or problem. To be a compassionate achiever, you must understand how speakers interpret this information or, in other words, how they picture the problem. It may be very different from the way you do! We touched on this in our discussion of reducing your own static, minimizing your own feelings and thoughts, when listening. We all frame reality a bit differently, no matter what the facts are. There are times that we see the same thing differently, as my wife and I did when we looked at the "duck or rabbit" drawing.

Below is another example. Look at the picture. How many columns do you see?

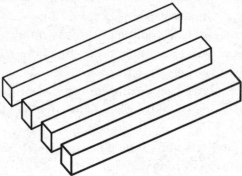

While I immediately saw four columns in the picture, my wife saw three. My understanding of the picture, after listening to my wife's perspective, has changed; now I fluctuate between seeing three and four columns.

Context also factors into someone's perspective. What if I told you that I had "sanctioned" a student? What would that mean to you? Either answer, that I had approved of the student or that I had punished the student, could technically be correct. Only by understanding the context would you be able to determine the right meaning. Or what if a friend said to you, "I saw a man in a blue fedora hold up a man with a flat cap"? Without understanding the context, you would have no way of knowing whether your friend meant that he saw a man in a blue fedora support a man wearing a flat cap or steal from him.

Paying attention to perspective and context builds understanding. We all know the aphorism about where good intentions and ideas can lead without understanding. "The evil that is in the world," according to Albert Camus, "almost always comes of ignorance, and good intentions may do as much harm as malevolence if they lack understanding."

A lack of understanding was the difference between China's and South Korea's recent approaches to decreasing traffic accidents in their respective countries. Both countries decided to use countdown clocks at traffic lights in an effort to reduce the number of accidents. South Korea experienced a dramatic decrease in traffic accidents, but China saw a significant increase. Why the difference? South Korea installed countdown clocks for red lights while China set them up for green lights. South Korea understood the difference between the placement locations: people are more patient waiting at a red light if they know its duration, but people speed up to get through a green light if they know its time is about to end. Understanding the context in which an idea is going to be used matters just as much as the idea itself. In this case, the context changed the effect of a countdown clock. This is a problem of knowing without understanding.

An important part of understanding is not allowing your understanding to become fixed. Understanding is the search for meaning, and that meaning, whatever it may be, can change as situations evolve, new information comes to light, or different challenges are introduced. You can find success in situations where your understanding may not be fully developed as long as you have an adaptive response: an approach that can yield appropriately different answers in diverse situations. Success—from the evolution of humanity to overcoming our individual everyday problems—is about adaptation, specifically about not having a fixed or rigid understanding of the world around you. Although we'll discuss at the end of the next chapter a couple of ways to mentally practice changing perspectives so that you can avoid cultivating a fixed mindset, my effort in learning to hit a curve ball offers an example that I think is also relevant to life outside of baseball.

I eventually succeeded in hitting curve balls, but it wasn't until I adapted my understanding of how to hold a bat (and after ACL reconstruction while playing in an adult baseball league; as I said at the beginning of the chapter, it took me a while to figure it out). I used to squeeze the handle and choke up on the bat, but then I noticed how the great hitters in baseball would sometimes lose their bat into the crowd, because they were holding it so loosely when they swung. As soon as I stopped squeezing and choking the bat and held it loosely, my swing easily adjusted to the curve of the pitch, so that I made constant solid contact. Creating consistent success in life is uncannily similar to hitting a baseball. Life throws plenty of curve balls, and if you are too rigid or fixed with your bat (your understanding), you will never be able to adjust your swing (your knowledge), so that you can hit the ball (overcome the problem).

By listening to learn, you've built a solid foundation of mutual respect and essential information. Now, as you use the skills that help you to understand to know, you'll be able to interpret this information:

Skill 1: Recognizing the mindset of the person you're trying to help

Skill 2: Developing your emotional intelligence to strengthen comprehension

Skill 3: Making connections between people, facts, and ideas to help you see a problem more fully and clearly

With these skills you'll be able to develop a holistic understanding of a problem and feel confident about what you need to do and not do to be effective in solving it.

SKILL 1

Flight, Fight, or Freeze: Recognizing Mindset

To understand the things that are at our door is the best
preparation for understanding those that lie beyond.
—HYPATIA

Discovering how people frame what they already know and how they
respond to incoming information, what psychologists call "mindset," is the
first step in understanding to know. How do they respond when you make
a comment, answer a question, or provide a suggestion? What is their reaction when you propose a possible solution to their problem?

Recognizing people's mindset is important at the beginning of a conversation, because it enables you to better communicate with them by tailoring
your approach to their style of thinking. They'll be much more receptive to
your insights, suggestions, and questions if you frame your ideas so they
mesh with their way of perceiving the world.

My wife and I simply adored her Noni (her Italian grandmother), and
we always tried to help her get the best out of everything in life. She did
that for us as well. In one instance we tried to help her but almost failed,
because we didn't understand and respect her way of thinking. Noni had
a savings account at a bank that had a very low interest rate, and we knew
that her money could earn more if she moved her account to a different
bank. We showed her the facts and figures about the interest rates at various banks, but we failed to convince her. About ready to give up, we asked
her why she decided to have her account at that specific bank, which provided the lowest interest rate in the area. She said that her favorite actor
made advertisements for the bank, and if the bank was good enough for
him, then it was good enough for her. After a little investigation, my wife
and I showed Noni that he actually banked somewhere other than the
one he advertised for. That was all she needed to know, and she moved
her money to a bank with higher-paying interest rates. We eventually succeeded because we reframed the issue according to her priorities and manner of thinking. If you cannot understand how other people think about a
problem, how can you know how to help them find their way through to
a solution?

I found that in graduate school, where the acquisition of knowledge was more intense than any other place I've experienced, people tended to follow one of three paths: they either thrived on learning, believed that they already knew everything, or became overwhelmed with information and didn't finish their degree. The three paths are very similar to the different ways we all physiologically respond to fear, stress, and anxiety: flight, fight, and freeze. I identify people who walk the three different paths as knownauts, knoxers, and kneers.

Knownauts Fly Toward New Information

My sons and I are longtime fans of Dr. Seuss books and love his book *Oh, the Places You'll Go!* My name for a flight-response person is inspired by Dr. Seuss's boundless enthusiasm for learning new things and exploring new places: knownaut, for "knowledge astronaut," someone who is willing to explore the vast cosmos of knowledge. The flight response to knowing is the polar opposite of the flight reaction to fear. While the well-known flight response to a fearful situation is running away from the danger, the flight response to knowing is flying toward more knowledge. A person with the "flight toward" mindset is looking to launch into more learning and is usually not afraid of whatever change new information might bring. Psychologist Carol Dweck calls this way of thinking a "growth mindset," because people who subscribe to it seek to increase their learning for improving their understanding of the world. They desire to learn more simply for the sake of learning and understanding. They embrace the idea that there is no final frontier of knowledge and set out to explore its vastness.

How to Identify Knownauts

- Knownauts are willing to admit that they don't know something.

- Knownauts lean toward you when talking about something that they admit not knowing about.

- Knownauts ask the question: "What do you mean when you say . . . ?"

- When confronted with an idea or perspective that opposes theirs, knownauts respond by saying, "I didn't see it like that, but I understand how and why they see it that way now."

- Knownauts don't see much in life as black or white. They feel comfortable in the gray areas of life, where there isn't "one way" to live or only two sides to an argument.

- Knownauts embrace the Siddhartha quote: "The opposite of every truth is just as true!" They find such ideas exciting, and you'll even hear them say that contradictions and paradoxes "tickle their brain." They consider such complexities thought provoking.

How to Help Knownauts

Helping knowledge astronauts is relatively easy: keep asking questions. Lots and lots of questions. Knownauts will be enthusiastic participants in the conversation, eagerly answering your queries. This dynamic will help move you toward a solution in two ways. First, it helps deepen your understanding of the situation. Second, it provides knownauts with the opportunity to understand their problem in a new way or come up with their own solution.

Even when they don't have an answer, knownauts treat a failure as a learning experience and will usually respond by saying something like, "I don't know, but I'll find out," or "I hadn't thought of looking at it that way." They live by Nelson Mandela's dictum: "I never lose. I either win or learn."

Knownauts	How to Help
Those who love to learn new things	Ask questions

Knoxers Fight New Information

Knoxers are those who fight against new information. These folks have what Dweck labels a "fixed mindset." They believe that they already possess what they need to know, and they treat new knowledge as a boxer treats an opponent in the ring—as something to knock down. New information could not only weaken their current understanding of a problem but also, in their eyes, make them look like a failure.

How to Identify Knoxers

- Knoxers believe and act as though they already know all that they need to know. They are afraid to admit that they don't know something.

- Knoxers tend to fold their arms close to their chest when learning something new.

- Knoxers ask the question: "What does that have to do with what we're talking about?"

- When confronted with an idea or perspective that opposes theirs, knoxers try to distance themselves from it by saying, "That doesn't apply to me because. . . ."

- Knoxers tend to see everything in life as black or white and avoid the gray areas.

- Knoxers carry Occam's razor to cut through all of life's difficulties. Occam's razor is the idea that the simplest answer is always the best answer. Complexity, in the view of knoxers, is something to avoid.

- Knoxers embrace the dictum: "It's my way or the highway."

How to Help Knoxers

The key to helping knoxers and getting them to see a different perspective is to make any new idea part of their mental framework for understanding. Every person has a default framework that they fall back on when evaluating options and making decisions. Having a clear picture of their default perspective allows you to frame your help so that it will be effectively received. Linking knoxers' default perspective to an idea that you believe can help softens their resistance and makes them more receptive to hearing it.

Although many city and business leaders are a mixture of knownaut and knoxer, most have a laser focus on economic development, sometimes to the extent that they become economic knoxers. Because some city and business leaders have difficulty seeing how compassion nourishes the civic soil in which the economic trees of every city, town, and village grow, I usually begin every discussion with the economic benefits that a compassionate city or business generates, such as an increase in real estate values. If I am talking with school leaders, I will start our talk about how a compassionate classroom increases test scores and deepens learning while decreasing levels of violence and bullying. Because they are experts in their respective fields of economic and educational development but may not have yet learned about the socioeconomic and cognitive benefits of compassionate communities and classrooms, I try to fit compassion into their concerns and understanding.

Inserting ideas into the mental framework of those with a fight response to knowledge is one of the most effective ways in helping them to see different paths to success. You simply frame ideas and help according to their way of understanding an issue, topic, or problem.

Helping knoxers is a lot less simple, but still achievable, when the situation is more fluid, spontaneous, and contentious. The following scenario about helping a very religious Christian friend to accept his daughter's lesbian relationship represents one of those times.

I was out to dinner with a friend when he told me that he was very concerned about his daughter's personal choices; in fact, he was thinking about cutting her off from the family "until she didn't sin anymore." That was when he leaned in and whispered that she was gay. It wasn't a secret to anyone who knew the family, but he always treated it as though it was.

I tried to explain that science, especially neuroscience, has clearly shown that being straight or gay isn't a choice, but is hardwired into our neurocircuitry.

He didn't listen to any of the science I tried to cite, and when I ended, he simply shrugged and said, "What did you tell me about a popular saying in graduate school? 'When all else fails, manipulate the data.' You all can spin a good story with parts of your science, so I'll stay with the words that can't be manipulated: the Bible."

I asked him what he meant by that.

He said that the Bible was clear about homosexuality being a sin and cited Leviticus 18:22 and 20:13, which say, "You shall not lie with a male as with a woman; such a thing is an abomination," and "If a man lies with a male as with a woman, both of them shall be put to death for their abominable deed; they have forfeited their lives." He then added, "You can't be any clearer than that."

I agreed that his statement was clear: "You're right. That is clear, and so is the rest of Leviticus." This was where all my years of Sunday school paid dividends. I didn't know my Bible as well as he did, but I did know it better than most because of those weekly classes.

"What do you mean by that?" he asked.

"There are a lot of things that you did today that Leviticus clearly says you shouldn't have done, but I still love you anyway, man!"

He laughed and said, "What the heck are you talking about?"

"Let's start with the Captain's Platter that you and I had for dinner just now. According to Leviticus 11:12, 'Anything living in the water that does not have fins and scales is to be regarded as unclean by you.' So basically we shouldn't have eaten the crab, shrimp, and lobster . . . you know, the lobster we dipped in butter."

"Come on, that's just fish," he replied.

"Okay, then what about your job?"

"My job as a bank manager?"

"Yes," I replied. "It clearly says in chapter 25, verse 37: 'You must not lend them money at interest or sell them food at a profit.' It's pretty clear that banking goes against Leviticus, not to mention the obvious problem with grocery stores."

He had a cautious laugh, but remained silent.

"If we are to follow Leviticus," I continued, "then we'll have to repeal the Thirteenth Amendment to the Constitution, which abolished slavery. Leviticus 25:44 states: 'Your male and female slaves are to come from the nations around you; from them you may buy slaves.' If you are going to live your life according to Leviticus, then it's more than okay to own slaves."

"Yeah, but that doesn't apply to me," he said. "I will never own a slave."

"Okay, but what about your wedding vows to your wife?"

"What does that have to do with what we're talking about?" he asked.

"Did you know that the Bible reading you chose for your wedding ceremony over twenty-five years ago—which is one of the most popular readings in the country, so I'm not singling you out here—are words of love and loyalty that were said between two women? The reading is from Ruth 1:16–17, and it is part of a discussion between Ruth and Naomi."

Right after he said he didn't realize that, he asked, "What's your point?"

"If we all pick and choose what to follow in the Bible every day," I said, "and it's obvious that we all do—you're using a credit card with interest to pay for our dinner (by the way, thank you) and I'm going grocery shopping right after this—why don't we pick and choose the things that help support others, especially our loved ones, and not the things that hurt them? We seem to draw arbitrary lines about what to follow and not follow in the Bible."

He asked where I drew the line.

I said, "I make the line out of compassion, which I think Jesus did. He didn't discriminate against anyone, and he helped everyone. If something in the Bible helps people, I follow it, but if it leads to hurting people such as slavery or discrimination of any kind, I do not and will not follow it."

As we said our good-byes, he asked, "Could you e-mail me some of that science you were talking about?"

The important part about helping knoxers is using their mental framework of understanding the world, especially if your help requires the introduction of new ideas and concepts. One of my close friends gave me a T-shirt that said, "If you stand for nothing, you'll fall for anything." Knoxers tend to take that principle to the extreme: they'll stand and fight for their ideas even when they have no ground left to stand on. If you provide new ground for them to stand on that is not threatening to their mental framework, they'll likely step in your direction for help rather than fight it off.

Knoxers	How to Help
Those who feel threatened when faced with learning new things	Incorporate new ideas into their perspective

Kneers Freeze in the Face of New Information

When faced with new information, kneers freeze like a deer in headlights. Stunned and confused, they feel overwhelmed or unsure about how to use what they just learned. Kneers lack confidence in deciding what to do or where to go with new information. Kneers have a fear of being overwhelmed or swept away by what they've learned. You know the feeling. It's as if you are standing in thigh-high water and out of nowhere you see a fifteen- to twenty-foot wave heading your way, and there isn't time to reach the beach. It's a hopeless feeling when the wave breaks over on you; you don't know whether you should ride over or dive through the wave. The problem for kneers is that they just stand there in indecision, where they will inevitably get knocked over if you don't help them move.

How to Identify Kneers

- Kneers sit silently and withdraw from the conversation.

- Kneers tend to look down a lot and touch their throat often, which is a sign of fragility and insecurity.

- Kneers don't ask questions. Rather, they want you to make decisions for them.

- Kneers are not sure if they should oppose or absorb the information they just learned, so they ignore it or pretend it doesn't exist.

- It's hard for kneers to see an issue in black, white, or gray terms because everything is a blur. Everything is too complex for them to deal with.

- Instead of addressing life's problems with the motto "Seize the day," kneers follow the dictum "Freeze, and it'll go away."

How to Help Kneers

In order to help kneers, you must build their self-confidence. Since they feel frozen in the moment, your job is to help them start moving toward a solution to their problem.

Be subtle. Your objective is to make kneers feel better about themselves without their knowing that is what you are trying to do. If they know that is your purpose, they are likely to question the veracity of what you're saying. They'll think you're only pumping them up just to be nice. Don't make it obvious that you're boosting their confidence. One way to do that is to offer praise with specific examples, for example, "You showed excellent critical thinking skills at last week's meeting."

Remind them of times when they have overcome the odds. Find a way to bring into the conversation an example of how they overcame a previous difficult situation. It may have no specific relevance to the issue at hand, but ask what they did to overcome the past problem. Their answer helps them to reflect on a time when they conquered an issue. You're building their self-confidence by having them remember their own successful actions. It is the beginning of helping them to see that they have the capability within themselves to overcome any issue that is in front of them. You can see their body language change: they will sit up straighter and make more eye contact with you as they are reminiscing. You're reminding them that they had the strength to get through a difficult situation before, so they can find the strength now.

Help them move forward by showing them a path through their problem. The feeling of being stuck or frozen in place, which kneers feel, is emotionally exhausting. It's like treading water; they're going nowhere but getting tired and drained of energy anyway. They feel as though they are struggling just to maintain the status quo while everything else is passing them by. Use questions to encourage them to determine a first step, and then a second, and then a third to move them along a path that will help them navigate their problem. Choose easy steps so that one success leads to another. The idea is to get them moving, to get them to take that first step.

Focus on their strengths. Reiterate the qualities that you believe to be their strengths. When asking them to talk about an instance where they overcame the odds, listen for the strengths that they relied upon and highlight one or two that pertain to the current issue.

Let go of your ego and share your failures. Have enough confidence in yourself to use a difficult time that you went through to show that failure is not the opposite of success, but simply a detour on the path to success. How many times have you failed at something or had difficulty achieving it, only to have it turn out better than you could have ever imagined? I failed the practical part of the lifeguard test the first time I took it, and I still felt embarrassed even after I passed the retake a few weeks later. If I let the embarrassment of failing the practicum stop me from becoming a lifeguard—I seriously thought about giving up and finding work that avoided the beach—who knows what would have happened to the fourteen people I saved that summer. Failure can breathe new life into the people you're helping if they know that you went through something similar.

One of the most difficult times I had in helping a kneer was when a fellow veteran came to me with news that his wife and son were both in the hospital on life support. He was a student of mine at the time and someone we all regarded as "tough as nails." He survived military tours in Afghanistan. His son had had a serious medical condition since birth and it had gotten worse; his wife had just been in an accident. He was significantly falling behind in all his classes. He came to my office to inform me that he was leaving school (with only two semesters left before graduation) and that he didn't know when he would be able to return.

His words and demeanor were all saying "I'm giving up" without his ever actually saying the phrase. As he sat down, I could see a bulge under his jacket that I assumed was a gun, which he had a permit to carry. It occurred to me that he probably came to my office as one last attempt to find help without asking for it.

After he talked about his wife and son, I mentioned his tour in Afghanistan. He said that the way he felt then was the way he felt now: hopeless. I knew, however, that he was able to find his way through the hopelessness he had experienced in Afghanistan, and I was looking for a way he could build on that same strength now. I also knew that I needed to find professional help for him as soon as I could.

Knowing that he didn't give up on the men in his unit during a particularly horrific battle, I asked him why he appeared to be giving up on himself and his family now. I explained that this was just a different type of battle and that, as warriors, I thought that we were supposed to engage.

He looked at me sideways, as if to indicate he knew I was up to something, and said, "I knew what weapons to use over there, but I don't know how to fight this battle."

"I know of a way," I replied. "Just as your men trusted you over there, you need to trust me right now, right here."

He paused and asked, "What way?"

The short story is that I walked him to the counseling center, where he received the help he needed and deserved. He graduated from college the following year with both his wife and son in attendance.

There are times where even the strongest among us become kneers, where we lose sight of our own strength and power to understand and process what is happening around us, where we become overwhelmed by the information that hits us. The best thing we can do during those times is to help each other find the inner strength to ride over or dive through the problems that can feel so overwhelming. Sometimes we need help in finding our own strength.

Kneers	How to Help
Those who feel overwhelmed when learning new things	Build their self-confidence

Recognizing Your Mindset

Identifying where you fall on the knownaut-knoxer-kneer spectrum at any given moment is just as important as recognizing the mindset of the person you are trying to help. Your mindset plays a large role in determining the information you gather and how you frame that information. Being a knownaut helps you remain open to all ideas. As a knoxer, you are closed to ideas that don't fit your perspective. When you're a kneer, you're confounded and unsure about the meaning of what you've learned. "Thinking about our own thinking," according to Dietrich Dörner in *The Logic of Failure*, "can make us better problem solvers." The best problem solvers are knownauts, because they have more ideas to draw on when trying to overcome difficult issues.

Although most of us would like to believe that we are knownauts all the time, in reality we tend to move in between the three depending upon the topic and emotion we're experiencing (emotions are the focus of the next section). You know you're being a kneer on a certain topic when you avoid conversation and feel yourself shutting down. When you feel defensive about something you just heard and are finding it difficult to listen, you're becoming a knoxer. The more questions you ask, the more you are becoming a knownaut.

I was clearly a knoxer when it came to sleep. I subscribed to Benjamin Franklin's dictum "There is plenty of time to sleep when you are dead" through all of my schooling up until the first years as a professor. I felt as though I had something to prove to my professors and peers, so I didn't investigate the matter or look into any research about reducing sleep. I just did it (four hours was my average). I used to think of sleep as something that was inefficient and, evolutionarily speaking, made you vulnerable. In other words, my frame of mind was similar to the way that some people think of compassion today. All through my counterintelligence and student experiences I believed that if I reduced sleep for efficiency reasons, I could achieve more. The problem is that reducing sleep reduces effectiveness. Researchers have found that sleep effectively strengthens your brain by removing toxins from it. Additionally, the brain is very active when you are sleeping, in some ways more active than when you're awake. For example, sleep is when the brain consolidates memories. I was even more stupid than I thought back then, and I did it to myself!

It's pretty easy to assess whether you're a knownaut, knoxer, or kneer in hindsight, but how do you know if your mindset is helping or hindering in addressing a problem when you are going through it? A knownaut solves, a knoxer complicates, and a kneer ignores a problem. The difference between the three approaches can be seen in three scenarios that ensue when you find out someone stole $100 from you. When you catch the thief, you follow one of three very different paths:

- Knownaut: You ask the thief the reason for stealing the money, which effectively goes to the root of the problem. The answer is that the money was going to be used to buy food for the family's children. You ask to see the children and then take them all grocery shopping.

- Knoxer: You consider the stealer a bad person, a simple thief, and you call the police. Anything the person says seems like an excuse to escape punishment for the crime, so you don't listen. You have just complicated the situation by sidestepping the root of the problem (hunger), because you addressed its symptom (stealing). The children are not only hungry, but also alone now, and you have no idea about their predicament.

- Kneer: You do nothing; you ignore what happened. The person thinks it's okay to steal again, but next time the person tries to steal from someone who has a gun and ends up getting shot.

The above scenarios were based on the true story of a Tarrant, Alabama, police officer who caught a woman stealing food from a grocery store. Instead of immediately arresting the woman, he asked her why she stole the food. After finding out that her children were going hungry, the officer bought her the food she was trying to shoplift.

It's the knownauts' flexible perspective of not making assumptions and adhering to them that helps them address problems more successfully than knoxers and kneers. There are a couple of ways to practice such mental flexibility that are both fun and creative. I mentally practice changing my perspective by challenging myself with anagrams and ambigrams (AA). It's my AA for breaking the habit of having a fixed or unadaptable mindset.

An anagram is a word made out of the rearranged letters of another word; for example, "silent" is an anagram for "listen." In a less strict form, not all of the letters need to be used and are sometimes chosen from a random set of letters. For example, how many words can you make out of the following letters?

A, C, E, I, M, N

My boys and I quickly "came" (which is one word that can be made from the letters) up with eighteen.

An ambigram is a word that, when it's turned upside down or looked at from a different perspective, spells either a completely different word or the same word. They are much more difficult than anagrams. Here are two examples:

1. Turn the book upside down, and you'll see that the words "hope" and "faith" remain the same.

2. This is how "easy" it can be to go from sinner to saint!

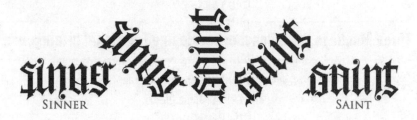

SINNER   SAINT

A knownaut mindset is important for solving problems, because no two problems are exactly alike. If you're closed to different perspectives like a knoxer or feel overwhelmed by new information like a kneer, how can you understand different problems in ways that produce novel and appropriate solutions? One definition of insanity states that it is "doing the same thing over and over and expecting different results." Knownauts rarely do the same thing over and over, because their understanding changes with the context of a problem. A knownaut's understanding is more likely than a knoxer's or a kneer's to produce results that are insanely ingenious.

Have you ever heard people say that they can sense fear in another person? I've been told that dogs can smell fear, so we should act with confidence around them. We've all used our different senses of hearing, sight, smell, taste, and touch to better understand the world around us. However, scientists at the Max Planck Institute for Chemistry in Germany have found that smells can alter our perceptions of faces and therefore our understanding of what we think others are experiencing. Equally amazing, the same scientists have reported that people's emotions can be detected on their breath. The lines between the physical, intellectual, and emotional worlds of people seem to become more and more blurred with each year of scientific research. It is the world of emotions to which we turn now. The next section explores the role emotions and feelings play in our ability to understand to know.

SKILL 2

Three Monkeys and a Bonobo: Developing Emotional Intelligence

I would rather feel compassion than
know the meaning of it.
—THOMAS AQUINAS

Do you know the difference between a monkey and a bonobo? There are really two differences. One is that monkeys have tails and bonobos don't. The other is that monkeys are mostly ruled by violent and aggressive behavior, while bonobos have a "make love, not war" mentality. The bonobo's brain is structured to make it capable of compassion, altruism, empathy, and kindness, and it can better regulate and control emotional impulses than that of its primate cousins. Being aware of emotions and feelings—your own and others'—is essential for a compassionate achiever. It's why I add "feel no evil" to the traditional Three Wise Monkeys maxim, "See no evil, hear no evil, and speak no evil," as the path to wisdom and success. Our traditional way of thinking needs to be updated to include the bonobo way of "feel no evil."

Elie Wiesel, Nobel Peace laureate and Holocaust survivor (he endured evil that no one should experience), wrote that none of his literary works could be "understood if one has not read" his "very first" book, *Night*. Emotions are people's "very first" piece that you need to read if you are going to help them. You can't understand people if you don't know where they emotionally stand on a problem. Their emotions filter how they perceive any situation they are in. We instinctively know this when we ask individuals who are angry, or "seeing red," to step away until they can think about the situation more calmly and clearly.

When you try to understand others' emotions and feelings about a situation, you get to know them better. The idea that you have to get to "know" people before you can "understand" them is backwards, especially if we want a more caring and compassionate world. If you don't try to understand others, you will never get to know them. It's the reason why foreigners seem so alien and why strangers are able to do such evil things to people: we think we know others even though, more times than not, we haven't even tried to understand them. Developing your emotional intelligence is key for building your capacity to understand to know.

The Importance of Emotional Intelligence

Your capacity to understand to know is based not only on how fixed or flexible your mindset is, but also on how emotionally intelligent you are. In his groundbreaking book *Working with Emotional Intelligence*, internationally renowned psychologist Daniel Goleman defines emotional intelligence as "the capacity for recognizing our own feelings and those of others, for motivating ourselves, and for managing emotions well in ourselves and in our relationships." The less you are able to regulate your emotions and feelings as well as read other people's, the weaker your understanding of any situation becomes.

What would you think if a coworker whom you were competing with for a promotion came to you and, without any emotion, said, "The big boss decided to toss out my name for the promotion in front of all the company's executives"? If you couldn't read whether your coworker was excited or depressed when telling you the news, you wouldn't know if your coworker was either suggested or rejected for promotion by the big boss. Reading and regulating emotions and feelings are at the heart of your capability to understand to know.

Most psychologists believe there are seven universal emotions: anger, contempt, disgust, fear, joy, sadness, and surprise. This general consensus is grounded in Paul Ekman's work over the last four decades. Although some researchers believe that we can interpret just four of the seven emotions and others argue that there are at least twenty-one recognizable facial expressions representing the complexity of emotions, most of the studies in the field are based on Ekman's work. Because the same can be said of Daniel Goleman's work in emotional intelligence, I've based my discussion about emotions and feelings on the writings and findings of these two psychologists. We'll leave the debate about how many emotions there are to others.

Before we discuss ways to develop your skills for emotional intelligence, we need to iron out the difference between emotions and feelings. Understanding the difference is the foundation for the ability to manage your emotions. If you understand the difference, then you have a better chance of not allowing your emotions to cloud your judgment or dictate your action; you will be able to respond to problems instead of simply reacting.

Emotions produce, or "spark," feelings. However, the way you think about your feelings can affect your emotions. Emotions are instinctual, physical reactions that originate in the subcortical regions of the brain and are woven into our genes. They create biochemical reactions in the body that lead to physical changes, which can be measured by blood flow and brain activity as well as seen in microexpressions and body language. Emotions generate feelings.

Feelings are the mental reactions you have after experiencing emotions and arise in the neocortical regions of the brain. They are the results of your brain assigning meaning to emotions by using your personal beliefs, thoughts, temperament, memories, and experiences to define them. Each feeling is a subjective interpretation of an emotion, and it is difficult to measure. Feelings are like pictures in a coloring book whose theme is exclusively you: the outline of every picture is drawn by an emotional pencil and the crayons that you use to color it are your beliefs, thoughts, temperament, memories, and experiences.

An emotion is a physical experience and a feeling is a mental experience. Here are some basic differences between emotions and feelings.

Emotions	Feelings
Physical reactions (body)	Mental reactions (mind)
Initial attitude toward reality	Long-term attitude toward reality
Easy to measure	Difficult to measure
Intense but temporary	Moderate but continual
Anger	Bitterness
Contempt	Indignation
Disgust	Sickened
Fear	Worry
Joy	Happiness
Sadness	Depression
Surprise	Amazement

Being emotionally intelligent means that you can manage your emotions and feelings so that they are positive and constructive rather than negative and destructive factors when making judgments and taking actions. Although emotions generate feelings, your feelings influence your emotions, so that the two are in a never-ending cycle of interaction. As a basic example of this interaction, think of a time when you were sad (emotion) and a friend told you to think of your favorite person or place that makes you happy (feeling); you did, and you used the feeling of happiness to bring you out of your sadness.

The interactive cycle is where your conscious thinking about feelings plays an important role in whether you simply react or consciously respond to any problem or situation. When you react, you are acting on the instincts of your emotions. When you respond, you're making a conscious choice to act in a particular way based more on your feelings. So how do you manage your emotions and feelings to help you respond instead of react? It's all about controlling the gap between your emotions and associated feelings (see the accompanying diagram). If you want to control your behavior, you need to manage the interaction between emotions and feelings, for behavior is born out of that interaction.

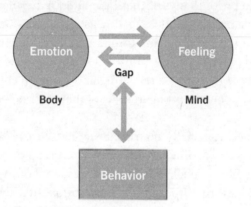

You manage the interaction by reflecting on the problem, your feelings, and your behavior. By taking a moment to simply think about what you're feeling, your behavior becomes an act of reflection, not of instinct. During that moment of silence you are filling the gap with reflection and self-awareness. When you leave the gap unfilled, you're letting your instincts dictate your behavior. How much understanding are you allowing yourself if you are instinctually reacting to what you hear and see? If you take time to consciously understand what feelings you're experiencing, you can respond with actions that are better than off-the-cuff reactions.

An additional benefit of focusing on the gap is that your behavior can, in turn, influence the way you're feeling. Let's use the emotion of fear as an example. Fear can generate the feeling of panic, which can cause a person to cower. Thinking about how we cowered can create the emotions of sadness and disgust, which generate the feeling of shame. It's a cycle that I don't think anyone wants to go through. What, on the other hand, causes a person to act courageously in the face of fear? (And courage does not happen in the absence of fear but in its presence, by overcoming it.) It begins by thinking about the gap between fear and the associated feelings of panic or anxiousness. You can change the way you feel about your fear and its resulting behavior (cowering) by turning it into a feeling that can build your courage.

We all can choose what feeling is associated with an emotion in any given moment. I try to assign the feeling of "focused excitement" when confronted with fear. When I rappelled from a fifty-foot tower the first time in the military, for example, I had to overcome my fear of heights. Instead of allowing the feeling of panic to wash over me, I "focused" on the steps I was trained to do while on the ground and saw it as an opportunity (I get "excited" about opportunities) to prove to myself that I could do more than my fears would allow. By focusing on the emotion–feeling gap, you can change your mindset from one that can cause problems to one that solves them. You never have to act on a feeling if you don't want to, as long as you take time to reflect on the gap. The simple moment of reflecting about your feelings and emotions helps you to comprehend a problem in ways that can lead you to successfully overcome it.

Modern science, especially neuroscience, has clearly shown the importance of emotions and feelings for attaining a rational understanding of any problem. Commander Spock, of *Star Trek*, was one of my heroes growing up. I always believed that if I had his logic, rationality, and understanding, I could overcome any problem that I or my "crewmates" of the "starship" known as Huckleberry Hill Elementary School could possibly face. One of my problems, however, was that I was never any good at excluding my emotions from decision making. I was more like Captain Kirk in that regard, and the irony is that neuroscience has recently shown that understanding and rationality are actually based on emotions. From studies on people who lost part of their brain's frontal cortex to studies on how emotion influences vision, neuroscientists are constantly showing that emotion affects every aspect of cognition. Indeed, without emotion you and I would find it difficult to be rational.

Historically, from Plato to Descartes to most modern economists, it has been assumed and argued that logical decision making excludes emotions and feelings. The work of neuroscientist Antonio Damasio upends that historical assumption. Damasio's research on people with damage to the frontal cortex of the brain clearly demonstrates that emotion plays an important role in logical reasoning. In the preface to his seminal work, *Descartes' Error,* Damasio writes:

> The reasoning system evolved as an extension of the automatic emotional system, with emotion playing diverse roles in the reasoning process. . . . When emotion is entirely left out of the reasoning picture, as happens in certain neurological conditions, reason turns out to be even more flawed than when emotion plays bad tricks on our decisions. . . . I see emotion as at least assisting reason and at best holding dialogue with it. . . . I view emotion as delivering cognitive information, directly and via feelings. . . . The brain systems that are jointly engaged in emotion and decision-making are generally involved in the management of social cognition and behavior.

Logical decisions are made when emotions are a part of the reasoning process. If emotions are taken out of the reasoning process, as occurred for Damasio's patients, irrational behavior increases.

Isn't high intelligence without feelings a significant part of what defines a psychopath? My reverence for Commander Spock is now tarnished after reading Damasio's various studies, for how would Spock respond to Damasio's finding that *"reduction in emotion may constitute an equally important source of irrational behavior"* (emphasis in original)? On the other hand, Kirk's belief that "sometimes a feeling is all we humans have to go on" appears to have more science supporting it as a path to success than Spock's logic.

The inability to feel is confounding researchers in the areas of artificial intelligence and cognitive science who are attempting to build computers that can understand people's emotions by connecting pieces of information gathered from wearable technology and video cameras, information such as blood pressure, facial expressions, and body language. You, as a good old-fashioned human being, can easily connect pieces of information to one another, but you make those connections through emotion and meaning, which creates an understanding that artificial intelligence lacks. Connecting pieces of knowledge may be necessary for developing new ideas, but it is not sufficient for building understanding. Understanding is more than simply combining ideas, information, and knowledge; it is about gluing those pieces together with meaning and emotion. This gets to the heart of our "understanding advantage" over computers, and it is what neuroscientists call affective intelligence (it's also why I am not too concerned about a future of robot overlords), a new view of intelligence in which emotion and feelings of emotion-related bodily reactions are critical to steering thinking and decision making. . . . It is the emotional dimensions of knowledge that allow people to call up memories and skills that are relevant to whatever task is at hand. Without the appropriate emotions, individuals may have knowledge, but they likely won't be able to use it effectively when the situation requires. Emotions are, in essence, the rudder that steers thinking.

A computer's intelligence may be more efficient than yours, but yours is more effective at understanding why the world around you works or doesn't work, and that is essential for translating your understanding into useful action, for developing your ability of "understanding to know" what steps would be effectively needed next. Emotions—no matter what classical economists or Commander Spock might argue—make understanding clearer and easier to attain. Improving your understanding to know is about strengthening your emotional intelligence.

How to Develop Emotional Intelligence

Articles and full-length books on the subject of emotional intelligence are as numerous as they are varied. A review in a popular academic database reveals that there are over fifty-six thousand articles, and Amazon lists over five thousand books on emotional intelligence; they cover everything from debating what emotional intelligence is to whether you can tell if a person has it. We'll narrow our focus to the five areas Goleman identifies in his definition: recognizing your own emotions and feelings, managing your emotions and feelings, motivating yourself, managing relationships, and recognizing the emotions and feelings of others.

1. *Recognizing your emotions and feelings:* This is, in a word, self-awareness. This area is about being able to detect and categorize physical sensations as emotions and mental thoughts as feelings. I added emotions to this part of Goleman's definition, because they are where feelings are born. Let's use anger as an example. Can you sense and acknowledge your pulse quickening and your face reddening when the emotion of anger comes upon you? Are you aware that you're feeling enraged, which can lead to retaliatory behavior? The first step in building your emotional intelligence is to be able to recognize your own emotions and feelings.

   An easy way to do this now is to use technology. If you have an Apple

Watch, Fitbit, or other device that monitors your vital signs, you have access to data that can help you learn to recognize different emotions. Review the data on your vital signs when you went through an angry episode and compare it to your usual measurements. See the difference? "Self-awareness," according to Goleman, "is the keystone of emotional intelligence."

2. *Managing your emotions and feelings:* This area of emotional intelligence is all about controlling the gap between emotions and feelings. Give pause to reflect upon how and what you are feeling and redirect your feelings about an emotion, so that they result in a positive rather than negative behavior. I did this by redirecting my fear into focused excitement in order to rappel from that fifty-foot tower.

3. *Motivating yourself:* This area is where you learn emotional self-control. Can you, for example, remain listening to someone even when you want to react to what's being said? Can you persist in striving to attain a goal in the face of adversity and failure? Can you delay gratification? According to Goleman, "Emotional self-control . . . underlies accomplishment of every sort." One way to practice this skill is to listen to podcasts—in their entirety and silently—by hosts whose opinions you know you disagree with (you might also be able to test your Apple Watch software regarding anger!).

4. *Managing relationships:* The aim here is to build rapport, which is a close and harmonious relationship in which people communicate well. Do you find ways that create healthy as opposed to distressed connections with others? Does what you say and how you act help to resolve conflict or fuel it?

   One of my most important relationships is with my wife, and we've been following a rule since we began dating that helps us to manage our emotions when we disagree: we have to hug while arguing. It's hard to get and stay angry with someone you are hugging. When we hug, it also provides me with another way to read her feelings, because I can physically feel when she tenses up and calms down.

5. *Recognizing the emotions and feelings of others:* You want to be able to read another's mood, sentiment, disposition, and temperament. This ability can but does not have to include empathy. We'll discuss some difficulties with empathy in the next section, but the point I am making here is that emotional intelligence is concerned with recognizing what

another is feeling, but not necessarily feeling what they feel. You can read someone's emotions and feelings through facial expressions, body language, and speaking tone. New research has shown that it is possible, by simply using the vocal patterns—whether the tone of language is either negative or positive—between spouses, to "predict whether a relationship was going to get better or worse with an accuracy of just under 80 percent."

Many times in a discussion it is not what is said, but how it is said that can tell you what the speaker is feeling. Say you have given a presentation to an important client, and your boss is meeting with the client now. Your boss comes out of the meeting and says, "You killed it." If your boss says it in a low, depressed, or angry tone, you know you lost the account, but if the tone is a high, excited one, you know you nailed the presentation. This is a fairly obvious example. At other times it may be harder to read another's emotions.

Let's be clear: emotional intelligence involves building and not destroying relationships. Several research teams, however, have recently argued that emotional intelligence has a "dark side," because some people can "manipulate" the emotions of others for "personal gain" and "nefarious ends." Summing up a survey about the "dark side" in different types of jobs, one author penned a cautionary note: "In suggesting that emotional intelligence is critical in the workplace, perhaps we've put the cart before the horse."

Even if you were to grant their research a pass, a central problem with the manipulation critique of emotional intelligence is that it only focuses on one small part of the emotional intelligence cart: recognizing and manipulating other people's emotions. A nefarious person can be good at one or two of emotional intelligence's five areas, but still be considered weak in emotional intelligence. If you're good in math but cannot read or write and know little science, can you be considered cognitively intelligent? If you focus upon strengthening only your legs when you work out and neglect your upper body, are you considered physically strong?

Having strong overall emotional intelligence includes helping and not taking advantage of others for "nefarious ends." When the "social competencies" of emotional intelligence include "handling emotions in relationships well . . . interacting smoothly . . . and using these skills to persuade and lead, negotiate and settle disputes, for cooperation and teamwork," how can manipulating the emotions of others for uncompassionate ends be a sign of heightened emotional intelligence? Other social competencies that Goleman includes in emotional intelligence are "facilitating rather than interfering with the task at hand," "being conscientious," and "cultivating rapport and attunement with a broad diversity of people." Goleman clearly states that when such "people skills ripen" through maturation, they help a person become someone who tends "to mobilize and inspire others, to thrive in intimate relationships, to persuade and influence, to put others at ease."

Although the "mean-spiritedness" of manipulating others for personal gain "bespeaks an *emergence* of a crucial emotional aptitude" (emphasis mine), it is definitely not the sign of an evolved form of an emotionally intelligent being. Emotionally manipulating others "to act against their own best interests" and in the manipulator's self-interests signals an infantile level of emotional intelligence. This should not be surprising, for when we see people acting selfishly, a common refrain is to tell them "to grow up." I don't consider people emotionally intelligent if they are using and manipulating others for their exclusive and personal ends. Such people tend to "burn bridges" with others in their personal and professional lives simply because their actions are eventually exposed over time. People with high levels of emotional intelligence lead themselves and others to constructive rather than destructive ends; they build up rather than tear down other people; they settle rather than instigate arguments; and they overcome instead of being overwhelmed by emotional distress.

Another potentially strong "dark side" argument against emotional intelligence is its emphasis on empathy. Goleman focuses on empathy as an important part of "recognizing emotions in others." In his *Working with Emotional Intelligence,* he singles it out as one of his "five basic emotional and social competencies." The problem is that empathy can lead to feeling emotionally overwhelmed and burned out. If you replace empathy with compassion, however, you'll strengthen your emotional intelligence by avoiding empathy fatigue. Knowing the difference between compassion and empathy can help you avoid being overwhelmed by emotions.

The Difference Between Compassion and Empathy

Compassion and empathy are commonly confused as being synonymous, but they are very different. The difference is more than semantic, for the consequences are pragmatic. Understanding the difference can help you build resilience and avoid burnout.

Empathy is feeling the same emotion as someone else, and compassion is feeling kindness toward another person. Empathy is about stepping into the shoes of others to understand and share their feelings, but compassion is about acquiring a 360-degree understanding of the suffering or problem that a person is experiencing and taking action to resolve it. Compassion involves understanding *and* acting, but empathy is singular in purpose: to emotionally absorb the feelings of another. It's the difference between "I feel your pain" (empathy) and "I understand and will do something about it" (compassion).

Our brain knows the difference between compassion and empathy, even if we aren't aware of it. As I mentioned in the Introduction, research shows that when we think compassionately, we "light up" the same regions of the brain as love, but empathetic thinking lights up regions associated with pain.

The effect on our brain of having compassion at the forefront of our thinking is positive for each of us as individuals and organizations. The effect, in very basic terms, is that when we think from a compassionate mindset, we release the peptide hormone oxytocin, which, as mentioned earlier, then activates the neurotransmitters dopamine (brain reward) and serotonin (anxiety reduction), which facilitate happiness and optimism—two characteristics that contribute to success.

Compassion's strength as a power source for fostering individual and organizational success stems from the fact that it not only is derived from the same neural networks as love, but is also centrally focused on the concern and care for others. When empathy is used as the source for helping another, the central motivation is to alleviate your own pain and stress. Matthieu Ricard, Buddhist monk and cellular geneticist, explains that he and Tania Singer found in their research that "empathy can also provoke a distress that focuses our attention on ourselves and diverts us from the other's needs." And that egocentric motivation is, I believe, one of the keys for understanding why burnout occurs much sooner when we think empathetically. Emotionally absorbing another's feelings, which empathy entails, is physically draining and can make you feel metaphorically stuck in quicksand. This has been commonly mischaracterized as "compassion fatigue"; if anything, it's "empathy fatigue," as Singer, Ricard, and Rainer Goebel conclude in their research.

Compassion, on the other hand, keeps you away from the emotional quicksand by using a more cognitive understanding of a person's suffering when attempting to alleviate the pain: it's understanding without absorbing. If our society's caregivers, such as nurses, paramedics, doctors, social workers, and police and fire personnel, could learn how to harness the power of compassion, they would be helping themselves just as much as they are helping others. Their resilience is an important source of every community's strength.

You can help yourself, especially your resilience, by recognizing when you are feeling overwhelmed and burned out. When you think empathetically, for example, and begin to absorb the sadness that the person you're helping is experiencing, you have the tendency to feel depressed. Some signs that you are either heading toward or already in burnout include:

- You are physically tired, emotionally exhausted, and cognitively slow.

- You are acting cynical, negative, and discouraging.

- You think of yourself as ineffective, inadequate, and worthless.

Some ideas to help you move out of empathy fatigue and into a compassionate verve:

- *Walk:* Take a five- to ten-minute walk around your neighborhood or on your favorite walking path. Although walking in an area with trees is best (leaves emit phytoncides, which help you feel less fatigued), walking outdoors has been shown to reduce stress, irritability, and impatience while restoring your mood and cognitive function. I've noticed that it makes me feel calmly rejuvenated, which helps me see problems through a more composed and clear lens. It has helped so much that I created a walking trail on my property called the Pondering Path.

- *Imagine:* Ask yourself about what your favorite literary characters would do in your particular situation. When I encounter some difficult problems, I think of how Atticus Finch, Siddhartha, or Bernard Rieux would act. It helps me to momentarily break free from my emotions to reflect on ideas that are outside of my situation, but still helpful for thinking of ways to resolve it.

- *Read:* Keep a place in your desk where you hold on to thank-you notes that people have given you, so that you can read a couple of them when going through self-doubt. It's a quick pick-me-up that is all about you: it shows how effective you can be through something you've already done.

- *Listen:* Give yourself a moment to listen to a favorite song that gets you pumped and feeling positive. My go-to song is "Superheroes," by The Script.

When you need to reorient yourself to a more compassionate state of mind, try taking a WIRL (walk, imagine, read, and listen).

Being able to recognize and manage emotions as well as feelings are at the heart of understanding to know. Emotions frame how you and everyone else see and perceive the world. Without understanding emotions and feelings, how can you holistically and realistically understand the world around you? "Emotions," according to Mary Helen Immordino-Yang in *Emotions, Learning, and the Brain,* "are not add-ons that are distinct from cognitive skills. Instead emotions . . . become a dimension of the skill itself." Emotions not only are a part of your cognitive ability to understand others, but also play a part in your being understood.

If you don't speak with some emotion, it becomes difficult for people to understand what you are saying. My family recently went through this in what we now refer to as "the Alexa moment." We have the closest version of a mass-produced artificial-intelligence machine that you can currently get: the Amazon Echo. We enjoy using it every day and love its ever-increasing abilities from spelling, to playing music, to shutting off our lights, to finding local times for movies, to even ordering a pizza or an Uber ride. It does a lot and has been a very helpful addition to our home.

We thought she (her preprogrammed name is Alexa) was "all that" and then some. But then came time for Alexa to fill in for me during the nighttime family read. I tend to read with emotion and sometimes act out the half-hour nighttime reading, but one evening I finished a book with ten minutes still to go on the clock. I decided to be a "cool dad" and queued up a new book series in Alexa's reading application just for the occasion.

After about four or five sentences, my three boys—almost in unison—said that they couldn't understand what Alexa was saying, and my youngest said, "The way Alexa is reading is making me scared." None of us could understand her because she read with no emotion and without inflection. That is what we call an Alexa moment, a moment without emotion. She simply couldn't connect with either the book or the words on the page as you and I can.

If you don't listen to and speak with emotion, you will have difficulty understanding and connecting to others. Creating and establishing interconnections and interrelationships are the subjects of the next section.

SKILL 3

Only Connect: Turning Facts into Concepts and Relationships into Networks

The main part of intellectual education is not the
acquisition of facts, but learning how to make facts live.
—OLIVER WENDELL HOLMES JR.

Your ability to understand to know also depends on your capacity to identify and develop connections between facts, ideas, and people. Facts are the building blocks of understanding, but they are not sufficient for it. It is only by connecting different aspects of factual knowledge that you generate understanding. It seems very similar, to me, to rubbing two sticks (facts) together to start a fire (understanding). Understanding comes from "warming" the cold hard facts by connecting them or, in the words of researchers who study the science of learning, turning "factual knowledge" into "conceptual knowledge." The difference between factual and conceptual knowledge is the difference between being acquainted with an idea and understanding it.

And when you are able to connect people, you increase the likelihood of igniting creative solutions. Connecting is important for not just acquiring understanding, but succeeding in life. This is where we'll drop the sticks and look to the trees. Why? Because trees seemingly understand the importance of connections in a successful life—yes, the trees outside your window—better than some of us do. Trees are living proof of the importance of connections. Trees in a forest are deeply interconnected to such an extent that biologists call them "social beings." As a result of their connectedness, "they can count, learn and remember; nurse sick neighbors; [and] warn each other of danger by sending electrical signals across a fungal network known as the 'Wood Wide Web.'" A forest is not simply an untapped natural landscape, but an electrically charged social network of beings continuously learning and understanding one another and their environment.

Your brain depends on connections to thrive. Neuroscience is crystal clear on this point. According to Olaf Sporns in *The Future of the Brain:*

> Take away a neuron's connections, and it becomes deaf and mute; cut it off from inputs, and it becomes unable to exert any influence whatsoever. The power of

neurons derives from their collective action as part of brain networks, bound together by connections that allow them to interact, compete, and cooperate.

Your capacity to think, sense, and behave lives or dies according to the connections occurring between neurons in your brain. Our connections, or interactions, with others are equally important.

Just as trees succeed because they are "social beings," our social relationships affect the level of success we can reach. George Washington Carver, a scientist and inventor who was born into slavery, instinctively knew what neuroscientists have only recently proven: "All learning is understanding relationships." In his book about the "social brain," Matthew Lieberman shows that when we "socially encode" information, when we learn through interactions with others, we acquire a learning "advantage" that "leads to better retention of the information than the traditional memory system." Lieberman, who is considered a leading researcher in the field of social neuroscience, argues: "Social motivations—the need to avoid social pain and the need to experience social connection—are basic needs that can impair learning when unmet." The basis of life—whether we are talking about the lives of trees or human beings—along with all of its possible problems and solutions, lies in connections. Every branch of life is interconnected, even though we may not see it, and those invisible and visible connections allow us to succeed.

Identifying and Developing Connections

We've seen the technological prowess of computers grow at an exponential rate over the last few decades, which Moore's law predicted. Moore's law contends that computers will double their processing speed/power every two years. Their power has grown to such an extent that computers have beat the best humanity has to offer at chess, Jeopardy, and even Go, which is a twenty-five-hundred-year-old game heavily dependent on intuition and strategy and much more complicated than chess (there are approximately twenty legal moves in a typical chess turn but two hundred in a turn at Go). As humanity steadily keeps losing to machines with seemingly ever-increasing levels of artificial intelligence, some of the world's leaders in business, computers, and science have voiced concern that humanity is sliding into a technological abyss of no return.

Bill Gates, Stephen Hawking, and Elon Musk all have warned of the threat that artificial intelligence poses to human existence. Musk characterized its development as "summoning the demon," and Gates posted the following answer to a question on a Reddit forum: "I agree with Elon Musk and some others on this and don't understand why some people are not concerned." Hawking told the BBC in December 2014 that "the development of full artificial intelligence could spell the end of the human race." With technology companies now pursuing a "More than Moore strategy" (an approach to increasing the power of computers that is software rather than hardware led), are we doomed?

Computers are undeniably becoming faster, smaller (we hold more computer power in our hands walking around every day than the astronauts of Apollo 11 had on their way to the moon), and more intelligent, but their intelligence is superficial when compared to ours. Their intelligence is based on connections like ours, but the links they make are simple associations between knowledge and facts. Computers know a vast amount of information and can recall it efficiently, but computers don't have an understanding of anything that they know. You, in contrast, may not know as much as a computer, but you have more understanding than it does. Michael Strevens compares IBM's Watson, a natural-language question-answering computer, to you and me in order to explain the difference between knowledge and understanding:

> Watson knows a lot of things . . . but it has little or no understanding of the things that it knows. . . . Watson's problem is that it does not understand the world. . . . It gives answers, but it has no grasp of what makes its answers correct. . . . There is something about Watson's statistical ways of knowing that is incompatible with understanding. Watson and you both answer questions by seeing connections between things. But they are different kinds of connections. Watson picks up from things it reads that there is a correlation. . . . You grasp *why* this correlation exists. . . . For you the statistics are a byproduct of what really matters, the physical and causal relations between things and people and what they do and say. Grasping those relations is what understanding consists in. Watson lives in a world where there are no such relations: all it sees are statistics.

The kind of connections you can establish are the key to unlocking understanding.

You could read or even speed-read all the facts you want about any place on earth, but you will never effectively understand it until you connect with it by experiencing the place. Connecting, not examining or testing, builds understanding. What is the best way to learn another language? Is it from a book or even in a classroom? The most effective way of learning a foreign language is to travel to a country in which it is spoken, so that you can connect the words, ideas, and expressions to the people, places, and events that make them come alive every day. It's an experience in turning factual knowledge into conceptual understanding.

Learning to tell time in Estonian, for example, helped me to better understand what I felt and saw as a prominent part of the culture, but couldn't quite explain before living in Estonia for a year. Estonian life is fast; it's a culture of speed, and the way Estonians understand time reflects that. While Americans say 5:30 as "half past five," Estonians say that it is "thirty minutes to six." Estonians are always looking forward, whether it's telling time or inventing new technology. From developing Skype and Li-Fi (it's basically Wi-Fi through lightbulbs—yes, Wi-Fi at the speed of light) to speed walking everywhere and on any surface (even cobblestone streets), Estonians have created a fast, forward-moving culture that is reflected in their life and language.

When I was teaching in Estonia I asked my class of 119 University of Tartu students a question one of my sons asked me: "Why do Estonians walk so fast?" As a class, they seemed to revel in talking about the Estonian trait and came to a consensus on two answers: (1) because it is cold, and (2) because "walking is a waste of time"; they just want to "get it over with as fast as possible; it is a rational use of time." The first answer can be seen as a reflection of the country's geography, but the second answer seemed to me to reflect a cultural perspective. It is as if Estonians are trying to make up for the lost Soviet era by going as fast as they can.

A few weeks after we discussed Estonian speed walking in class, several students stopped me on the street (as they were ready to pass me) to tell me that they discussed my son's question with friends at a party and that the two answers given to me "were good." I find it ironic that I have a better understanding of the Estonian culture of speed and efficiency, because I slowed down to make effective connections. Even in a country famous for its speed-of-light technology, connections are the keys for unlocking basic understanding.

How do connections turn facts into concepts? Let's start with the difference between the two. A *fact* is an isolated piece of information, and a *concept* is a large idea that shows the relationship between facts: facts are hyponyms of concepts. Facts are memorized, and concepts are understood. While facts are concrete and narrow, concepts are abstract and generalized. Here are some examples differentiating facts and concepts:

Facts	Concepts
Flowers	Bouquet
Latitude and Longitude Coordinates	Location
Sun and Planets	Solar System
Bricks and Stones	Wall
Numbers	Math

How do you turn facts into concepts? Think of a fact as being subsumed by a concept. A fact is simply part of a larger whole. And a fact becomes a part of that larger whole when it's connected to at least one other fact. When you connect facts, you turn them into concepts. And concepts can be applied in multiple contexts to understand different problems and situations. Math is used, for example, in a wide array of contexts ranging from architecture to economics to science to sports, all depending on how you connect the numbers through the formulas you use. The concept of a solar system can be applied to the estimated one hundred to two hundred billion galaxies in the universe.

The facts you use and the ways you connect them determine how you understand the world around you. Let's use a simple driving scenario to illustrate the point. You are on the road, there is a large SUV in front of your vehicle (fact), and you both stop at a red light (fact). Before you stopped at the red light, you noticed that the person driving the SUV was on a cell phone (fact). After the light turns green (fact), the SUV doesn't move (fact). You connect the facts and reach the conceptual understanding that the driver is distracted, which leads you to feeling angry. There was one fact, however, that you didn't see and therefore didn't use to help you understand the problem: there was a small car in front of the SUV that was broken down. Wouldn't that one fact change your understanding of the situation and how you were feeling? The facts you use and don't use affect your conceptual understanding.

Different combinations of facts can also lead to different interpretations of a concept. Let's take the concept of a wall as an example. A wall is most commonly thought of as a solid structure made up of any combination of bricks, stones, wood, and plaster. However, if you are talking with someone who loves science about a wall, she could be thinking of the porous, not solid, outer layer of an organic structure, such as a cell wall. If you are talking with someone who is having a hard time adjusting to a new environment, such as a new school, he may think of the transparent wall that he believes separates him from others because of the way he acts, looks, or thinks. Understanding is largely a product of the facts that people experience and use in their daily lives.

Learning to connect facts differently than we normally do can lead to new and effective ways of solving everyday problems. This is partly how a new treatment for muscle cramps was discovered. We were told to eat a banana or down an energy drink to treat a cramp, because we thought it was a result of dehydration of the muscle. However, because one Nobel Prize–winning scientist, Rod MacKinnon, had severe muscle cramps while kayaking when he was fully hydrated, we now have a different and more effective understanding of why muscle cramps occur: the facts of his experience led him to a unique conceptual understanding of a problem that affects all of us. His research has found that "it's your neurons and not your hydration" that matters. The problem of muscle cramps arises from the excessive firing of the motor neurons in our nervous system. The suggested treatment now is to drink spicy or pungent liquids, which calm the nerves by shocking the nervous system.

Your understanding of a problem or situation changes according to the connections you make between facts and ideas. Sometimes the most effective way to understand a problem is to connect facts and ideas whose combination seems counterintuitive, such as calming nerves by shocking the nervous system. Connecting counterintuitive ideas helps you to see problems and people from new and unique perspectives.

Embracing Counterintuitive Connections

What would you think if I told you that you could connect two failing strategies to achieve success? This is exactly what happens in Parrondo's paradox. The paradox, named after Juan Parrondo, a physicist who discovered it in 1996, states: "There exist pairs of games, each with a higher probability of losing than winning, for which it is possible to construct a winning strategy by playing the games alternately." Basically, the paradox shows that you can combine two ideas that are considered losers to create a winner.

One of the most commonly cited examples of the paradox in real-world action is the way in which the combination of sparrows and insects helps crops grow. The paradox is that, although sparrows and insects can—independently of each other—devour an entire crop, their combination creates an ecological balance that produces healthy crops.

In mathematics, researchers use the BABA game to show how the paradox works. Consider two games (A and B) in which you start with $100. In Game A, you simply lose $1 every time you play; losing all your money in 100 rounds is obvious. Game B is a bit more complicated, but you also lose all your money in 100 rounds. After each round, you need to count your money and then determine whether the amount is an even or odd number. If it's even, you win $3; but if it's odd, you lose $5. If you play A or B independently of each other, you will reach the same losing outcome in 100 rounds. If you play Game B and then Game A over and over, however, you will continuously win a total of $2 every two games until you decide to stop. The combination of two losing games becomes one winning game.

My students in *"The Science and Art of Learning"* course found the paradox at work in the growth of plants: if it is too cold, plants die, and if it is too dry, plants die. However, in winter the combination of cold dryness causes dormancy in plants, so that they not only survive but also thrive when spring arrives.

There is also a Parrondo's paradox at work in the science of learning. Psychologists and neuroscientists have shown that some forgetting and confusion are keys to successful learning. According to the authors of *Make It Stick: The Science of Successful Learning,* not only is "some forgetting . . . often essential for new learning," but "interleaving," the mixing of two or more subjects or skills in one learning session, creates more "durable learning." The funny thing, however, is that I don't remember any teachers encouraging confusion or recommending forgetting when I went to school. I do remember, however, too many teachers who ignored students who forgot what they were supposed to remember and brushed aside students who didn't "focus on the single task at hand."

Parrondo's paradox shows that when you cast aside what you might think are losing ideas, you are literally throwing away possible paths to success. Although effective strategies to many problems seem elusive, the elusiveness may be simply caused by our own exclusive thinking. We may be excluding answers to problems simply due to the fact that we haven't enlarged our scope to include ideas considered to be losing propositions. The way that the state of Utah is successfully addressing homelessness shows how incorporating what others think of as losing propositions can lead to effective solutions that challenge "conventional wisdom."

Many state politicians around the country will not even contemplate building "brand-new houses" for their homeless (some perceive the homeless as "lazy" and therefore not worth the expenditure of effort and resources needed to house them), but the leaders of Utah have been doing exactly that over the past decade. They call their program Housing First, and it has resulted in lower crime and hospitalization rates as well as, of course, a significant decrease in the number of chronically homeless (a 91 percent drop between 2005 and 2015), making it the country's leading program in the effort to reduce homelessness.

The economic effect of Housing First, according to Gordon Walker, director of the state's Housing and Community Development Division, is that the state is saving "$8,000 per homeless person in annual expenses" since its implementation, with a total savings in the millions of dollars. The human effect is that Utah is "approaching a functional zero" of chronically homeless, who "are no longer tallied in numbers [but] tallied by name." By valuing the very people that other states devalue, Utah has raised its overall standard of living while lowering annual spending. Utah's approach is also being used with success in several cities in Alberta, Canada.

No matter what state we live in, we all know the value of paramedics. They are not only compassionate first responders, but also effective problem solvers. They come to our rescue no matter where we are. I want you to think of yourself as a Parromedic: someone open to creative insights and counterintuitive solutions to problems that conventional wisdom may have difficulty solving. Only a Parromedic will be able to innovatively address what may seem like unsolvable problems.

Taking an Effective Ax to Efficiency

Although innovative ideas may be *effective* at addressing difficult issues, some may not necessarily be *efficient*. Do you believe that innovative solutions should be more concerned with efficiency or effectiveness? I'll answer with another question: Don't you want to solve the problem—be effective—more than anything else? Parrondo's paradox provides another way of understanding the danger of prioritizing efficiency over effectiveness: combining two failing strategies, which some equate with inefficiency, can often create a successful effective approach to solving a problem. Sometimes we have to prioritize between efficiency and effectiveness; when we have to make a choice, we should be looking for effective connections rather than efficient ones. This is exactly what Utah did. The state spent resources to house the homeless even though it took several years to experience the positive effects of the effort. It prioritized effectiveness over efficiency.

"Give me six hours to chop down a tree, and I will spend the first four," said President Abraham Lincoln, "sharpening the ax." The importance of effectiveness relative to efficiency wasn't lost on President Lincoln. Effectiveness is about achieving the desired result, and efficiency is about the process of doing things in a way that is optimal according to a preset standard, such as the fastest way or the least expensive way. Effectiveness is about achieving the right goals (i.e., learning), and efficiency is about doing something optimally (i.e., standardized tests), which can be right or wrong. If you do something wrong but you do it optimally, you are efficient—just efficiently wrong. The problem is that many people think that they can find effectiveness through efficiency. It's similar to trying to quench your thirst with a fire hose; you'll get some water, but you'll get more than your desired result.

I wish that effectiveness and efficiency always went together, but they do not. And because they don't always go together, we have to sometimes lean toward one at the cost of the other. When it comes to learning and understanding, our default setting should be effectiveness. We, however, have been focused on improving efficiency through mechanized learning approaches such as standardized tests. When you combine teaching with standardized tests, the result is pretty obvious: you get "teaching to the test" rather than "learning for the student." The irony is that international test scores, the Program for International Student Assessment (PISA), for the last ten years demonstrate a problem with our education system's effectiveness, but we are focused on efficiency. Albert Einstein's 1929 words on standardization are as true now as when he wrote them: "I believe in standardizing automobiles. I do not believe in standardizing human beings. Standardization is a great peril which threatens American culture."

Standardized tests may be an efficient form of finding out how many facts are remembered, but researchers in the science of learning have proven that they are the least effective means of improving conceptual understanding and overall learning. Scholars and reporters have shown that the problem with standardized testing is that there is too much information being tested too infrequently for learning to "stick" in the brain. The most effective way of making information "stick" in students' minds is to institute a "regimen of regular low- or no-stakes" testing (a.k.a. quizzing) timely spaced with another activity so that they begin to forget. As counterintuitive as it sounds, forgetting supports learning.

If forgetting is also made an emotional experience, learning is deepened even more. The reason is that an emotion creates "a chemical Post-it note" on whatever you are learning by "releasing the chemical dopamine into your system," and "dopamine greatly aids memory and information processing." Allowing space to forget and creating an emotional connection, however, all need time to develop. Effective learning and understanding lean toward inefficiency. When it comes to problem solving, I'd rather be inefficiently effective than efficiently ineffective.

I also prefer to be inefficiently effective with people. This way of understanding is important not only for problem solving, but also for relationship building. It takes time to get to know someone. How do you want to be understood? Is it by the simple, obvious facts that people can see or guess at when they first meet you? I don't know about you, but I don't want to be simply known as the five-foot-ten, blue-eyed guy with dirty blond hair who lives in town. I hope that people get to understand the person I am: husband, father, and teacher who lives out loud! Trying to understand the world around you also includes making an effort to understand the people in that world.

The Power of a Social Network

You have a power that is used every day for understanding the people around you, but you don't think you use it (or that your ability to do so can be improved). It is commonly referred to as the "sixth sense," and it is defined by social psychologist Nicholas Epley as your ability to read or "reason about the thoughts, motives, attitudes, beliefs, and emotions of others." He adds, "This ability is one of your brain's greatest, because it allows you to achieve one of the most important goals in any human life: connecting, deeply and honestly, with other human beings." Your sixth sense, which is a part of your emotional intelligence, is useful for developing social networks that are helpful in deepening and broadening your understanding of the issues, problems, and people around you.

Epley devotes his entire book to improving your sixth sense, and one way that is directly tied to becoming a compassionate achiever is the skill of intrinsically listening. By listening to learn simply for the sake of learning and listening, you can more easily connect with the people around you through information that strengthens your understanding of them and their problem. And as Epley and others point out, because you and I "inhabit the largest social groups of any primate," we "must have the ability to understand other people's minds . . . if [we] want to get along or get ahead." The combination of our large social networks and our interest in understanding other people's minds creates two by-products according to Epley: greater brain size (our cerebral cortex actually grows) and success. In short, your brain and successes grow as you grow your social networks. It is these networks of connections in which compassionate achievers live, survive, and thrive every day. Never underestimate the power of networks, especially social networks.

A social network consists of a set of connections between individuals that are created through interpersonal relationships. The networks can be established in both the virtual and the real world. The most common networks that we build are our professional networks, such as when we join a professional association, but they tend to be narrow in scope and have a vocational focus. You can build broader networks, however, out of what you are already doing in other aspects of your daily life:

- *Hobbies and interests:* Sharing your hobbies or interests with colleagues at work can connect you to others throughout your organization in broad and productive ways. Some of us at my university have turned our common love of the New York Mets into a "Metwork" (a network of Mets fans) throughout campus. The Metwork has fostered several projects across academic disciplines and university departments simply because we wanted to work together. The projects, which have nothing to do with the Mets, have increased mutual understanding of how we each approach and manage our work to such an extent that our students are now practicing interdisciplinary thinking when setting up and scheduling their own events.

- *The virtual world, on social media:* Do you broaden and deepen your connections in social media? Most people deepen without broadening their connections. Many people, for example, "unfollow" people on Facebook who disagree with their political ideas and remain "following friends" with those who share their political ideology. They deepen their understanding of one political ideology without broadening their understanding of political perspectives. Who you include and exclude in your virtual world either limits or expands your connections.

- *Recreation and sports:* Your extracurricular activities such as sports can establish (or reestablish) a wide range of connections. When I joined a bowling league, I had no idea that it would broaden my network of friends and colleagues in just one year to include motorcycle mechanics and company CEOs, while also reconnecting me with high-school friends whom I hadn't seen in over ten years.

Your success at building social networks that strengthen your understanding is dependent upon how you answer the following question: Do you reach out to people or do you withdraw from them? The more diverse your connections are, the broader and more holistic your understanding becomes. Alexandra Horowitz's *On Looking* is a very innovative and readable example of how a diverse social network (Horowitz's social network) strengthens understanding of the people and places we interact with every day: our neighborhood. *On Looking* is based on eleven walks Horowitz took with eleven very different people through her neighborhood. Each walk gave her an entirely new perspective of the New York City block on which she lives. By the end of the book readers have a holistic understanding of not only her neighborhood, but also the importance of appreciating the ordinary aspects of our everyday lives. If you strive to develop a holistic understanding in all that you do, then you will constantly look for and build diverse connections, even between ideas and people that others may give up on. The success of addressing homelessness in Utah and Alberta is proof positive of this. Diverse connections nurture understanding and are the mothers of innovative ideas.

Social Networks Strengthen Understanding and Foster Creative Solutions

If connections are the mothers of innovative ideas, then the Medici family should be considered the most influential midwife in history. The Medicis are famous for creating a business, learning, and artistic environment in Florence, Italy, from the thirteenth to the seventeenth century, that fostered invention and innovation to such a degree that historians credit the banking family with starting the Renaissance. The way they fostered creativity was through connections, or what Frans Johansson calls intersections. Johansson's book, *The Medici Effect,* explains "the elements" that create the effect and "what happens when you step into" it. The Medici Effect refers to the phenomenon in which diverse groups of people and multidisciplinary perspectives and knowledge "intersect" to produce innovative ideas and concepts. The Medicis created an environment where ordinary life yielded extraordinary opportunities for innovatively solving problems. The Medici "intersection" of facts, ideas, and people provides a social-network model that all of us can follow.

"By stepping into the intersection," according to Johansson, "you will have unleashed an explosion of fresh, intriguing idea combinations."

A strong social network is at the heart of the Medici Effect. Including a diverse range of people increases the number of "idea combinations" that can produce innovative solutions. It's about inclusion, not exclusion. Do you reach out to different kinds of people and ideas or do you withdraw from them? How do social networks strengthen your understanding to help you find creative solutions? Social networks can help to strengthen your understanding by increasing:

- *Diversity:* Having a network with numerous and varied connections offers a multitude of different perspectives and ideas to consider when solving a problem. Who is going to have a more holistic understanding and better chance of working through a complex situation, someone with a diverse network of ideological perspectives or an individual with a network in which everyone thinks alike?

- *Trust:* The more your network is constructively used (i.e., the more people find success in overcoming their problems), the more trust is built between its members. The more trust there is, the more information is shared, because people feel that they will not be betrayed by other members in the network. They feel safe to offer honest appraisals and comments. The more information you have to work with about an issue, the stronger your understanding of it usually becomes. A social network that is feeble or damaging to its members weakens trust and understanding.

- *Questions:* A diverse social network makes you think of questions you may not have thought of before joining. New ways of questioning a problem provide you with potentially new ways of understanding it. If you're looking at securing access to a building, for example, and only have human resource managers as part of the discussion, you will probably focus on personnel answers, such as security guards, and overlook technological answers, such as card readers. Diverse social networks help you to avoid what I call "hammer time." You know the proverb from which "hammer time" comes from: "If all you have is a hammer, everything looks like a nail."

There are more, smaller versions of the Medici Effect in every community than most people know. I'm not just talking about the universities and think tanks that are found around the country. Several new companies are trying to turn spaces in hotels and dinner-only restaurants into shared workspaces.

Businesses such as LiquidSpace, which uses hotel conference rooms, and Spacious, which uses restaurants, liken themselves to being the Airbnb for people who need office space instead of sleeping quarters. The idea of getting different types of workers together in one space is very Medici!

Similar efforts are being made on the local community level to bring different types of thinkers and doers together in a shared space. In our university's local community of Danbury, Connecticut, Mike Kaltschnee has created the Danbury Hackerspace on Main Street, where entrepreneurs, techies, manufacturers, inventors, and "idea guys and gals" share a large working area where anyone can "tinker" on their projects and get advice in areas ranging from 3D printing to copyright and trademark law. Kaltschnee schedules a networking event every first Wednesday of the month to prime the pump of local innovation.

Although I'm more a proponent of diversifying than deepening social networks, I am not against deepening, as long as you don't ideologically narrow yourself in the process. In other words, deepen your network while broadening your ideological perspective on the world and avoid any deepening that narrows your philosophical stream of understanding. Don't just follow or listen to, for instance, one stream of political ideology in your virtual or real worlds. Diversify those you listen to and what ideas you think about on a daily basis. If you live the Medici Effect, you unlock a world of understanding that has numerous "idea combinations."

Turning facts into concepts—turning knowledge into understanding—is about learning how to make connections. Thinking differently and interacting with diverse groups of people open you up to new ways of understanding. With this understanding, you are now in the best possible position to start problem solving.

I like to keep the words of Ralph Waldo Emerson in mind when I start searching for solutions: "The creation of a thousand forests is in one acorn." Each acorn represents a new way to look at an issue and therefore a thousand new possible solutions to any given problem. Are you willing to pick up every acorn of possibility (even those that others discard) to help another? A compassionate achiever is, and in the next chapter, Connect to Capabilities, you'll learn how to zero in on those acorns and access the human potential, resources, and ideas to develop compassionate solutions to any problem.

5

Connect to Capabilities

I was locked in a room with six people, no windows, and one light. A key for helping the seven of us to escape the room was right in front of us for about thirty-five minutes, but we didn't see it until the room went pitch-black. We decided to turn off the light after deciphering a code that revealed a message strongly hinting that we would be better off in darkness. This was not part of my counterintelligence life, but a team-building exercise with the Jesse Lewis Choose Love Movement in the Great Escape Room in Washington, D.C. If you like to solve puzzles that are wrapped in enigmas that then lead to clues for determining numbers that open combination locks that are parts of a larger puzzle, then the Great Escape Room experience is for you. Finding the key (an ultraviolet key) and others like it during the escape made me think and question how many times a day we simply walk past answers to puzzles, issues, and problems—even people—without seeing, noticing, or recognizing them. The previous chapter showed the importance of connecting to the world immediately around us in order to understand it, but we also need to connect to its capabilities if we want to solve problems and achieve success.

Connecting to capabilities means finding individual links to resources that have the potential to solve problems. The resources can be people, places, ideas, or things (i.e., money or technology). Your social network is an important source of connections. The more diverse and numerous your connections are, the greater the number of potential sources of solutions you have access to. The opposite is also true: as you lower the diversity and number of connections, you decrease access to potential sources of solutions. People who are good at connecting to capabilities are very similar to Malcolm Gladwell's "Connectors" in *The Tipping Point*:

- They "know lots of people." They have numerous contacts.

- They see "value and pleasure in a casual meeting." Everyone is seen to have importance and worth.

- "They manage to occupy many different worlds and subcultures and niches." The diversity of contacts is as equally valued as the number of contacts.

- "By having a foot in so many different worlds, they have the effect of bringing them all together." They see everyone and everything as linked in a giant web of interaction. They foster cooperative rather than competitive relationships.

- They "are masters of the weak tie." Acquaintances are developed and cultivated as friends.

Where Gladwell believes that "Connectors" are a "special few . . . with a special gift" and consist of only "a handful of people . . . sprinkled among every walk of life," I believe that we all can learn how to improve our ability to connect to capabilities. Will some be better than others? No doubt, just as in every area in life, but connecting is not the purview of a "special few." We all have the potential to be good connectors. Three skills essential to developing the capacity to connect to capabilities are:

Skill 1: Tapping into the human potential hidden in plain sight

Skill 2: Expanding your reach

Skill 3: Shifting your perspective

Since you've listened to learn about a problem (Step 1) and acquired a solid understanding of what you need to do so that you can effectively help address it (Step 2), now you will learn how to connect to capabilities that offer potential ways of solving problems.

SKILL 1

Take No One for Granted:
Tapping into the Human Potential Hidden in Plain Sight

Some people feel the rain. Others just get wet.
—ROGER MILLER

Too many of us discount what is right in front of us because it is familiar; we begin to see the familiar as an automatic part of daily life. You may not even be aware that you overlook or discount the people you see each day—family, friends, classmates, coworkers—because you've become accustomed to them in an everyday, "taken for granted" way. It's as if we've forgotten that each person brings a unique set of ideas and resources to the table of life. Being a compassionate achiever means eliminating the "daily discount" perspective and recognizing the value and potential in everyone, especially those you interact with every day. This community of people is one of your most valuable resources when you are trying to solve a problem or open up new doors of opportunity. "Everything in this world," according to Nikos Kazantzakis, an author nominated nine times for the Nobel Prize in Literature, "has a hidden meaning."

A simple nudge of kindness is sometimes all that is needed to tap into the compassion in a community. A nudge that we do in the Danbury, Connecticut, area is to engage in pay-it-forward acts of kindness and generosity. It started with the area's Department of Children and Family Services, and it keeps reappearing in different forms and in different places, including grocery stores, coffee shops, and gas stations. A common way of paying it forward is to pay for the coffee order of the person behind you and then see how long others will continue to do so as well (it really is a pay-it-behind idea). The longest one I participated in lasted three hours (I've always wondered about the kind of day the people who stop the kindness chain may have been having and hoped that they received an extra compassion nudge or empathy bump to help them along).

Seeing the familiar in a different light is challenging. Use the approaches in this section to help you tap into the talents, ideas, resources, and perspectives of those around you that may otherwise go largely unseen. When you see familiarity through a compassionate lens, you will more easily find the capability to address a problem and achieve success.

The compassion a mother has for her children is second to none, and when Helen Egger's son Sasha began showing symptoms of dementia almost overnight when he was only thirteen years old, she did what every mom would do: she took her son to the hospital. After only five days of being misdiagnosed with bipolar disorder and prescribed antipsychotics, Sasha deteriorated to such an extent that he was placed in an "intensive-care unit, heavily sedated, and fed through a tube." The doctors believed it was mental illness, but Egger, being a child psychiatrist at Duke University, challenged their diagnosis, noting that Sasha's psychiatric conditions appeared overnight (such conditions appear gradually in a person with mental illness) and he had symptoms of neurological dysfunction (slurred speech and dilated pupils), which can be caused by a weakening of his immune system. A colleague of Egger's, a neurologist named Mohamad Mikati, found out about her son's situation and offered to "conduct a few low-tech tests" to examine the strength of Sasha's autoimmune system. The short story is that Mikati provided "an infusion of antibodies that can quell autoimmune attacks, and the boy improved almost immediately." Sasha's improved health is a testament to the power of being able to connect to capabilities. In the words of Egger, "If I was not my son's mother, with my connections, my son would be dead. That's just horrifying."

Being adept at connecting to capabilities can even help you overcome a series of "expert excuses" that some may use for not supporting you in ways that you need to resolve a difficult situation.

Looking Beneath Excuses

Excuses are everywhere. We hear them every day. *"That's not my problem." "I don't have the time." "It's too expensive." "No one will ever agree." "It'll take too long." "It's not worth it." "It's always been this way; this situation will never change." "I'm just doing my job."*

When you are trying to complete a project, instigate change, or simply get something done, it can be so frustrating to be stonewalled by an excuse. But what can you do? You could get angry, but that usually gets you nowhere with the person giving the excuse and can make you feel guilty later on for raising your voice and showing your temper. You could accept the excuse, walk away, and try to find another way to get the information or resources you need. Or you could try a third way: dig beneath the excuse to try to find out what the speaker's reservation or limitation *really* is and address it. An excuse rarely tells the full story; it's shorthand or a knee-jerk reaction. To tap into as much human potential as possible, you'll need to see beneath excuses to the real issue.

In some cases, you'll be able to challenge those reservations. You'll have to assume responsibility for something others will not, because they are too afraid (afraid for their career if the idea doesn't work) or believe they have too few resources to achieve what needs to be done. For example, when several students asked me if we could start a debate team, I said I didn't know why we couldn't and asked the university's administrators if they would be willing to support such a team. I was told by the administration: "It's a great idea. We would be willing to support a debate team if we had the money, but we simply don't have the resources."

Having a group of first-generation students want to intellectually challenge themselves outside the classroom was something I couldn't let pass by, so my wife and I assumed responsibility for the first two years of funding by taking out two credit cards for each year. Although it took us a little over five years to pay them off, it was definitely worth it: the students have built professional careers with the skills they've learned; the library offered permanent office space for research; secretaries and administrative assistants around campus donated all types of resources; the statewide higher-education office donated money the second year; and the new administration that eventually came in decided to fund the team. Once people saw what was possible, their fears and reservations melted away, and a flood of help came rushing in.

In other cases, finding common ground or making a human connection can be enough to move things forward. Recently, my wife and I had to deal with the "just doing my job" excuse when we were talking with a health-insurance representative about denial of coverage for the only known treatment for my son's rare medical condition. The representative kept saying the same line over and over again, in the same monotone voice, as though she was a computer reading to me: "Because there is no recognized code for the treatment, we are not authorized to cover the medical procedure."

Even when I asked different questions and pointed out that the leading doctors in the field at Yale–New Haven Hospital documented the treatment as the only known way to address my son's medical problem, she restated the same exact sentence word for word. When I asked to talk to her supervisor, the representative simply said that there wasn't anyone higher than her. After a very brief discussion about how I thought everyone had someone to report to (even the president), I told her I sincerely hoped that she would never have to be in the situation that my wife and I were in as parents. She finally went off script and connected with me by saying, "I completely understand your situation, Mr. 'Kook,' because I have a child with a severe medical condition; so I do understand your situation."

Throughout the conversation, I could feel myself getting angrier and angrier, but I knew that would get me nowhere—plus it would make me a worse person than her and I would regret it later—so, once I found out she was a mom, I appealed to her parental side. I wished her child well and then asked her if she really did understand the situation by saying, "If you do understand our situation, then why won't you talk to me like a fellow human being instead of like a robot reading a script? That is all that I am asking for, to be talked to with simple human decency and possibly as parent to parent. Can we please do that?" She promptly transferred me to her supervisor (yes, the person who didn't exist a few minutes ago), who told us how to remedy the "code problem."

When interacting with excusers, try to connect with who they really are (mom, dad, brother, sister, son, daughter) and where they are really coming from. Sometimes people hide behind an excuse, because they don't want to understand your situation or don't want to know how to help. However, if you can use all of the skills you have as a compassionate achiever to look beneath the excuse, you'll connect to a capability and a way out of your problem.

Sometimes, however, an excuse can be an impenetrable brick wall. In that case, I try to think of the different ways water works. For example, the first thing I think of is how water finds a new path when it's temporarily trapped. In other words, I find a "work-around" when one person or department becomes a wall. I immediately look toward other people for help and advice to get through the problem (it's helpful to have a deep and wide social network in this case). Water always finds its way to flow over, around, or through the obstacles in its path. When one boss was attempting to block a program I was building, I found a way to change the person I was reporting to, so that the program had a chance to grow. The new boss not only allowed it to develop, but found new resources to nourish its growth.

Because I also think of water as a basic element that has the power to nourish as well as extinguish all life (I've seen firsthand what happens when people don't respect the water around them: they drown), I try to treat everyone—including the person who becomes a "brick wall"—with respect and kindness. Acting with common courtesy and respect toward those who are blocking you sometimes even leads them to reconsider what they are doing.

Acting with Human Decency

In news and TV stories about those who did something heroic, they usually say that they were just doing their job or they did what anyone else would have done in the same situation. From the school aide in Ohio who saved a ten-year-old girl from being mauled by a dog, to the "nursing home hero" in North Carolina who stopped an active shooter, to the law enforcement personnel responding to the 2015 San Bernardino, California, rampage, they all uttered similar refrains: "I was just doing my job" or "I did what any other person would do." None of them did it for recognition or to receive a plaque; they did it because it was the right thing to do. It was, in their minds, what any decent human being would do. Acting with human decency—in every situation and interaction—is another way to connect to human capabilities hidden in plain sight.

We have met two types of people who say "I'm just doing my job": those who use it as an excuse to do nothing to help others and those who use it to downplay credit for heroism. A book I turn to again and again, however, highlights a third type of person who uses the phrase: an individual who ordinarily and routinely acts with kindness, civility, and respect in normal daily life. Albert Camus's main character in *The Plague*, Bernard Rieux, illustrates the point that you don't have to perform heroic acts like saving lives; you just have to "do your job" with common decency—meaning civility and respect.

I call this way of everyday thinking and acting Rieux's Routine. In one of my favorite passages in all of literature, Rieux reflects:

> I know now that man is capable of great deeds. But if he isn't capable of great emotion, well, he leaves me cold. . . . However, there's one thing I must tell you: there's no question of heroism in all of this. It's a matter of common decency. That's an idea which may make some people smile, but the only means of fighting a plague is—common decency.

Rieux's words point to the idea that basic common decency is all that is needed to overcome and even avoid problems in every aspect of society. Rieux is asked to define common decency by another character in the novel: "I don't know what it means for other people. But in my case I know that it consists in doing my job." It's acting in ways that prioritize kindness, courtesy, and respect for each person you encounter. You befriend and never belittle. Common decency is about honoring and respecting the human dignity of every individual.

Following Rieux's Routine is the middle way between the excuser and the unsung hero; it's something that each of us can follow without ignoring (the excuser) or risking (the hero) anything. It's about acting on our common belief in basic decency. Recent national surveys on civility show that 95 percent of us believe in common decency, but are concerned about its decline in our political, communal, and personal lives. At the beginning of 2016, 70 percent of Americans polled said that incivility in their country has reached "crisis levels, up from 65 percent in 2014."

The "crisis" begins and ends within each one of us—meaning that if we each choose to act with civility, we can avert problems that eventually create crises. This isn't hard to see throughout modern history in the crises that arose in communities where people were treated without dignity: when individuals weren't allowed to sit in certain seats or drink out of specific water fountains because of the color of their skin; when sons and daughters were disowned by their families and places of worship because of their sexual orientation; and when fellow human beings were tracked and monitored because they spoke a different language and followed different customs and religions.

There seems to be a societal default to differentiate between rather than associate with people. As Jane Elliott famously illustrated with her "blue eyes and brown eyes" discrimination exercise with third-grade children in 1968, we can too easily fall into a pattern of treating others with condescension and callousness based exclusively on highly superficial and meaningless differences. One of Elliott's clear and concise observations about the human condition that we all need to heed is: "We see different races when there is only one race: the human race."

When I think of the way we differentiate between people through the ordinary use of language, I am reminded of a line in the novel *To Kill a Mockingbird*. In it, the young protagonist, Scout, is advised by her father, Atticus, how to tease out truth from opinion: "Atticus told me to delete the adjectives and I'd have the facts." Adjectives and other labels have a way of predisposing the way we perceive others.

Early in my academic career, at a social function, I was asked by another professor why I had introduced our coworker Sally as a "colleague" when she was our "secretary." That professor's question and apparent feeling of distinction from our secretary is partially derived from the way we categorize people, in this case at work. At the university we have administrative staff, custodial staff, faculty staff, and secretarial staff. We are all staff and part of the same organization contributing different types of value to our students as well as the university, and if we didn't emphasize the adjectives, we would recognize that each type of staff is equally important.

When trying to connect to capabilities, drop the adjectives and labels. The goal of dropping the labels is to connect to the person you're talking with—the whole person, not just a part of them that you see superficially. When you drop the labels, you pick up the essence of who someone is. Several ways that can help you drop the adjectives and labels are:

- *Remember and use a person's name.* "A person's name," according to Joyce E. A. Russell, vice dean and director of the Executive Coaching and Leadership Development Program at the University of Maryland, "is the greatest connection to their own identity and individuality." Using and remembering a person's name is a sign of courtesy and respect.

- *Subscribe to "mind over matter."* Focus on how and what people think rather than their physical attributes. I strive to explain a person's mind or way of thinking in ways that have nothing to do with superficial characteristics like eye and hair color.

- *Concentrate on what makes people unique as individuals rather than on what makes them part of some group.* For example, what are they passionate about? What stands out about them?

By dropping labels, you help yourself to eliminate preconceived ideas and misperceptions about people that can be demeaning and belittling. We've all heard jokes based on stereotypes. At their core, those jokes are based on labels that foster crude differentiation and division.

Fostering Cooperation

We usually speak of a "culture" as the beliefs, social norms, and physical traits of a people or nation, but every institution, organization, or environment has a culture as well—a set of shared attitudes, values, goals, and practices that characterize it. Which is more likely to foster connections between people and groups of people, a culture of cooperation or a culture of competition?

I have never believed that this is a trick question, but I've experienced more bosses and teachers who created a culture of competition between workers or between students, because they thought that they would push each other to become better or stronger. In short, they took the misinterpreted pop-culture version of Charles Darwin's "survival of the fittest" idea and tried to implement it in the workplace or classroom.

The problem with cultures of competition and confrontation is that they cannot ever be more than the sum of their parts. The main reason is that a competitive environment doesn't promote connections between people or groups of people. Because nearly everyone is focused on individual achievements in such an environment—doing their "own thing"—colleagues hesitate to share ideas. It's as if the organizational climate creates invisible fences that separate coworkers.

Climates of collaboration, in contrast, are productive and effective, and they yield results that can be much more than the sum of their parts. An organization that seeks to be more than the sum of its parts can only grow in a work environment where employees willingly share ideas and cultivate rather than cut down one another. The most productive and effective learning and working environments foster cooperation rather than competition and nurture collaboration over confrontation.

The anecdotal and empirical evidence for the power of cooperative cultures and collaborative groups in producing success—from my experiences in the military and academia to new research in the field of organizational behavior—is strong. The story of MediConnect Global, Inc., a cloud-based health-information exchange, demonstrates how a cooperative culture creates success. Amy Rees Anderson, founder and CEO of MediConnect, reflected on her company's 1,500 percent growth between 1996 and when she sold it for $377 million in 2012 by explaining that its success was built on employee-centered compassion and cooperation. Anderson wrote in *Forbes* that the "ripples" of compassion between employees eventually turned into waves of profit:

> As employees were involved in this showing and receiving of compassion from one another, the entire morale of the company began to improve. People were happier at work, they were kinder to one another, and then suddenly that ripple effect began spreading beyond the walls of our company, . . . [and] the clients were thrilled by this level of compassion being extended to them. And over time we saw these clients begin to go the extra mile for us as well. . . . As a result, our company began to grow and flourish in ways we couldn't have imagined and the impact to our bottom line was amazing.

The more cooperative and compassionate your environment is, the more success it produces. Anderson defines success by building upon Winston Churchill's quote, "We make a living by what we get, but we make a life by what we give." She goes on, "But I would also submit to you that what we give by showing compassion not only makes our lives better; it can make our livings better as well. And that is what I call a success." It also increases success in the classroom.

Making cooperation a prominent feature in classrooms increases academic and the future professional success of students. A pedagogical method called "learning for teaching" not only increases cooperation in class, but also improves cognition. Studies show that when students learned "material in order to teach it, [they] performed better on what to them was a surprise memory test [as] compared to those who knew the memory test was coming and had studied it." The reason, according to psychologist Matthew Lieberman, is that such a cooperative environment creates a social encoding advantage in learning: when students believe their actions are helping others, they learn more efficiently and effectively. Learning to cooperate in school provides children with the social skills needed to achieve their personal and professional goals later in life. Richard Rende, a developmental psychologist, has shown that an excellent "predictor of professional success and of developing strong, meaningful relationships throughout life" is how well a child learns to cooperate with other kids. It's never too early or too late to learn how to cooperate.

Fostering a cooperative over a competitive working environment is a key for unlocking individual and organizational success. Here are a few ways to do so:

- *Provide equal time for talking and listening.* A group of psychologists from Carnegie Mellon and Massachusetts Institute of Technology researched the question of whether "there is a collective I.Q. that emerges within a team that is distinct from the smarts of any single member." One of the two main answers they found was that "as long as everyone got a chance to talk, the team did well, but if only one person or a small group spoke all the time, the collective intelligence declined."

- *Promote a psychological safe zone.* The other answer that the researchers found about effective groups was that they were populated with members who could emotionally connect, read, and understand one another; the members of less effective groups had "less sensitivity toward their colleagues." Both characteristics are part of what psychology researchers call a "psychological safe zone." Psychological safety, according to Amy Edmondson, "describes a team climate characterized by interpersonal trust and mutual respect in which people are comfortable being themselves."

- *Populate with non-zero-sum people.* Surround yourself with people who believe that there are win-win solutions to most problems; such thinking is called "non-zero-sum" in psychology and the social sciences. Zero-sum people believe that life is mostly made up of lose-win scenarios in which, if you win, someone else has to lose. Enroll, hire, and recruit people who approach problems with an absolute- rather than relative-gains mindset (win-win versus lose-win). One of the questions I ask people who interview with me, which discloses their thinking about absolute and relative gains without directly asking about it, is: Is it better to be perfect and late or good and on time, and why? It's the "why" part of the answer that usually reveals which way they lean with regard to zero-sum thinking.

A cooperative rather than a competitive working or learning environment is more likely to produce thoughtful insights, innovative solutions, and dynamic results. Foster cooperation, and you will discover new paths toward success and uncover resources you didn't realize you had access to.

Expressing Gratitude

Expressing appreciation releases hidden resources within yourself. Being grateful has been shown to provide a wide range of benefits from building resilience to improving sleep. One of the most effective ways to increase happiness and decrease depression, according to Robert Emmons, is to adopt an "attitude of gratitude." Emmons, who is regarded by many as the world's leading scientific expert on gratitude, considers it "a relationship-strengthening emotion because it requires us to see how we've been supported and affirmed by other people." It's made my marriage stronger in ways that others have found surprising.

Elly and I have found that cultivating an "attitude of gratitude" in our daily life is an easy way to strengthen our marriage. However, a work friend of Elly's stayed over one night and was shocked and disappointed in Elly when she thanked me for taking out the garbage in the morning. Elly's friend thought she was being weak and subservient and asked her in a very sarcastic tone, "Does Chris say 'thank you' to you for doing the laundry every time?"

Elly said "Yes, every time. We thank each other for the little things, because we don't want the other to feel that we ever take them for granted."

Elly's friend believed her thanking me was an act of vulnerability, but it's really an act of strength: it makes our marriage stronger. By saying "thank you" for the ordinary occurrences in life, you build extraordinary relationships in your personal and professional lives.

An office with a disposition toward gratitude fosters a greater work ethic and a healthier workforce. For example, studies and surveys have shown that 81 percent of Americans "would work harder for a more grateful boss" and either receiving or expressing gratitude "decreases pain and depression, and boosts happiness." In a general summary about gratitude studies over the last decade, Susan Pinker writes: "Whether the feeling or the behavior comes first, we do know that gratitude is tied to conscientiousness."

A 2012 survey, however, found a gratitude gap at work. While 88 percent of Americans believe that "expressing gratitude to colleagues 'makes me feel happier and more fulfilled,' only 10 percent expressed gratitude to their colleagues every day [and] 60 percent say they either never express gratitude at work or do so perhaps once a year." The simple but sincere gesture of saying "thank you" can have a significant impact, creating not only a cooperative climate, but also a productive office. Dale Carnegie made a similar argument over eighty years ago by showing when we create "little sparks of gratitude," they tend to "set small flames of friendship," which "rise" to become "beacons" that guide us to success.

Developing a disposition of gratitude will expose you to an undercurrent of power that can guide you to success in any workplace. My grandmother had always told me that the most important people for getting anything done in any organization were the secretaries, and she couldn't have been more right. The one thing she didn't tell me about was the wide-ranging network secretaries create that is the substrate of executive power. I learned about it early and often in all of my different careers by following my grandmother's one edict: always say "thank you." (And if I didn't when I was growing up, I always received a light tap on the back of my head.)

Following the common decency route of saying "thank you" made me a receiver of support when I tried to build programs that others were either against or indifferent toward. Secretaries convinced their bosses to move monies earmarked for holiday cards into a student debate team I cofounded, and secretaries and other staff successfully guided me through the maze of academic politics that led to the creation of the Center for Compassion, Creativity and Innovation. Somewhere along the line, they all noted how grateful I had been to them. I didn't think anything of it, because I thought everyone said "thank you." After reviewing the studies and statistics on the gratitude gap, however—unfortunately it's rare to receive a thank-you in the work world—I finally understood the sincerity of their comments and the power of gratitude.

We need to bridge the gratitude gap, and it's as easy as saying "thank you" for what anyone does for you. By bridging the gratitude gap, you heighten the potential levels of individual and organizational success that can be attained. By giving gratitude, you receive success as a byproduct.

You could argue that there are callous and uncaring people who have become very successful in every field. I can't and won't deny that such people do succeed, but my argument is that they would have been much more successful than they were, if they had been compassionate and caring. A compassionate leader receives more support from employees than a callous one. The authors of the 2012 survey about the gratitude gap made the following conclusion about executives:

> Executives who withhold gratitude thinking it will make people work harder and give them an aura of strength may be mistaken. The survey found that gratitude could be a key to success: Ninety-three percent agree that a grateful boss is more likely to be successful because people would support her. . . . While many bosses withhold gratitude hoping it will make them appear stronger, they may be undermining their own success.

Leaders who treat their staff with "common decency" can expect uncommon success.

Avoiding Expectations

Expectations frame the world you see and structure your experiences. Expectations have also been proven to cause people to become "inattentionally" blind, lower their intellectual potential, and make them less resilient. When we expect people to fail, for example, they often do, and when we believe people can achieve more than they think they can, they often surpass their self-imposed limits. Expectations, whether conscious or unconscious, can prevent you from recognizing the potential in those around you.

In a famous study known as the "invisible gorilla" experiment, psychologists Christopher Chabris and Daniel Simons demonstrated that when most people fix their attention on something they are told they are supposed to see, they tend to overlook anything outside their scope of focus. Chabris and Simons asked their study participants to watch a fast-paced video of people passing a basketball and count how many times specific players within that group received the ball. (Go to the note on page 219 giving the website to see the two-minute video before reading further if you want to experience the effect without the spoiler.) The problem was that at least half of the observers didn't see the person dressed in a gorilla suit pound his chest in the middle of the video; their (and possibly your own) focused or selective attention on counting caused inattentional blindness. Most people see only what they want to see or are looking for.

Many people tend to "judge a book by its cover" or judge people by what they look like. At each university I have taught at as a professor, I have initially done some fieldwork on this tendency and hopefully raised awareness about it, to the benefit of my students. Before the first week of classes, I dressed as a student and pretended to need help to see how I would be treated at places ranging from the library to the financial-aid office. I did this to find out which places on campus were truly student centered and friendly. If I was treated well, I immediately thanked the person, explained who I was, and asked for the supervisor, so that I could describe how helpful and professional the person had been. If I wasn't treated well, I came back the next day dressed in a tie and sports coat, formally introduced myself, and asked for the supervisor, so that I could describe why I would never send a student to that office for assistance.

A compassionate mindset requires that you keep an open mind. See the people around you for who they are and not who you think they are. In counterintelligence, the worst agents were those who went into the field with expectations, because they missed what they thought shouldn't be there, and the best were those who perceived each field experience as something unique and something to learn from. Treat each individual similarly: as unique.

In two famous studies about expectations in the 1960s and 1980s, researchers investigated whether teacher or supervisor expectations have an influence on student or worker performance. The 1960s study showed that positive expectations about specific students influenced their performance positively, calling it the Pygmalion or Rosenthal effect; the 1980s study demonstrated that negative expectations of students or workers negatively influenced their performance, calling it the Golem effect. In other words, the studies found that self-fulfilling prophecies are real, because "when we expect certain behaviors of others, we are likely to act in ways that make the expected behavior more likely to occur."

Quieting expectations increases the likelihood of success. One of the most powerful examples of this for me happened when my family was living in Estonia. It's taken a while for Estonians and Russians in Estonia to trust one another since the end of the Cold War, when Estonia gained independence from the Soviet Union. Both Estonians and Russians have ethnic jokes and slurs about one another that are unflattering in every way possible. In general, both ethnicities have expectations of the other that are relatively low.

When a young Russian man stole a lambskin blanket from our baby stroller that was parked on the ground floor of the apartment building we shared, my wife and I decided to appeal to his kindness and his new identity as a father. (He didn't know that I knew he had stolen it.)

When I met the young Russian man on the stairwell the next day, I congratulated him on being a dad and then asked, shaking my head, "How can someone steal from a child?"

"What do you mean?" he asked.

"We had a lambskin in the carriage," I replied, "to keep our three-month-old warm when we walk, and someone took it. Can you believe that someone would steal from a baby?"

"Whoa, I don't know who could have done that," he said.

He showed up, later that night, at our apartment door, crying, with the lambskin and said that a couple of his friends had taken it. We looked out for each other for the rest of our stay in Estonia.

When you change your expectations of people, it has the power to change the dynamics of any problem or situation that you may find yourself in.

When trying to connect to the capabilities of the people around you, strive to be a leader and not a boss.

> A boss drives others. A leader coaches them.

> A boss uses people. A leader develops them.

> A boss takes credit. A leader gives credit.

> A boss says, "Go." A leader says, "Let's go."

A leader creates a supportive, respectful environment that cultivates productivity and overall teamwork. In the service, we followed leaders anywhere and duct-taped bosses to their cots (it was a sign to a unit commander that the duct-taped officer did not have the respect of the soldiers and that officer was then transferred to another unit).

Discovering and acknowledging the "hidden potential" in everyone around you, especially the people you may take for granted, is an essential part of being a compassionate achiever. By doing so, you will find yourself summiting whatever professional and personal mountain you seek to conquer. The wider your reach, the easier it is to summit any mountain. Expanding your reach with regard to connections is the focus of our next skill.

SKILL 2

The Web of Connections: Expanding Your Reach

---

*There are two ways of spreading light: to be
the candle or the mirror that reflects it.*

—EDITH WHARTON

Marley Dias, an eleven-year-old girl from West Orange, New Jersey, was tired of reading books at school that were, according to Marley, all about white boys or dogs, or white boys and their dogs. She wanted to diversify her school district's reading list to include books with a black girl as the main character. Marley tweeted #1000blackgirlbooks and within a matter of months received donations totaling more than $5,500 and over four thousand books. She appeared on *Charlie Rose* and *The Ellen DeGeneres Show* to talk about her experience. When Marley was asked what was next, she replied, "Although this might be for black girls, I think next year I can do it for Latino guys or Latina girls or something that I'm not. I can still help people who are feeling that same way about their voice."

With one tweet, Marley successfully connected to capabilities well beyond her immediate circle and found a solution to her problem that exceeded her expectations. And as a true compassionate achiever, Marley plans to share her success to continue to help others.

Although it's important to tap into the often overlooked human potential surrounding you, it is also important to consider opportunities outside of your immediate community. Great ideas can come from anywhere, but innovative solutions are often found by going outside your comfort zone of people and ideas. Social media has made it easier than ever to connect to capabilities in every corner of the world. Anyone, even those with bedtime curfews, can transform a problem into a constructive solution with the help of connections made through the Web.

The Web of Connections

Connecting to capabilities is easier now in the Internet age. Finding assistance for problems before the Internet was about gaining access to the right person's Rolodex and its web of contacts, but now it's about using the right search words or a provocative hashtag. The options for overcoming problems went from exclusive to inclusive access with just a few keystrokes—although "http" stands for *hypertext transfer protocol*, it could also mean a way of finding *help to transform problems*.

Companies and nonprofit organizations are trying to get help with their problems by posting them on the Web. Websites such as InnoCentive, which is considered the world's largest problem-solving marketplace, or the "eBay of innovation," host problem-solving competitions on topics ranging from creating a biomarker that identifies people who might be at risk for suddenly dying from epilepsy ($150,000 prize) to developing a plan for "increasing civil society's influence on nuclear-weapons policy" ($10,000 prize). A study of InnoCentive competitions found that "outsiders, rather than those within a field, tended to hit on the best answers." The website connects people with problems to "solvers" all around the world. This can be done on the micro level in communities and organizations, for example, by having different departments in an organization crowdsource solutions for each other.

The idea of crowdsourcing has a very successful track record in organ donation; approximately eighty people a day receive life-benefitting transplants. Although we all know organ donation happens every day but not as frequently as it is needed (approximately twenty people die each day waiting for organ transplants), most of us haven't really taken notice of how the system of connecting strangers to help one another could be used as a working model for finding ways to help people with other types of issues. Good matches are vital not just for donors and recipients of organs, but also for "solvers" and those with "lesser" problems, and the more we open our networks to outside people and ideas, the more likely we are to find great matches.

Social media is another powerful tool for connecting to capabilities. Guiding emergency assistance to the hardest-hit areas of a disaster can mean more lives will be saved. In a recent study, social media's, specifically Twitter's, ability to help assess the damage of a natural disaster was found to be "a better measure of local damages than federal emergency estimates"; social media is now considered "an increasingly useful tool for emergency managers and insurers." The prospective ability of social-media services to be highly effective and efficient in helping to save lives is so strong that disaster-relief experts and responders are trying to "crowdsource" their potential.

One article reported: "Twitter reactions can be so swift that federal seismologists are experimenting with the service to crowdsource earthquake warnings. When a magnitude-5.8 earthquake hit Virginia in 2011, for example, the first Twitter reports from bystanders at the epicenter reached New York about 40 seconds ahead of the quake's first shock waves." All that may be required for connecting to the help you or someone else needs is a tweet. Nearly two-thirds of Americans own a smartphone and over three-quarters use social media, so most of us have the capability to connect people to the assistance they need.

Using the Internet, and especially social media, to connect to capabilities reminds me of the butterfly effect. The term "butterfly effect" was coined by Edward Lorenz to help explain his findings in meteorology, but the concept is commonly used to represent the idea that small actions can have large effects. Lorenz argued that the simple fluttering of a butterfly's wings in one part of the world can alter weather patterns in another region; the tiny winds of change that a butterfly's wings make can alter atmospheric conditions that influence tornadoes and hurricanes. I see this every day online. A Facebook post from a nonprofit, a tweet from an eleven-year-old, or another quick virtual-world interaction has the potential to affect tremendous change in the world.

How to Expand Your Reach

You can extend your possible connections much easier through the virtual world of the Internet. You can extend your connections to capabilities online if you:

- *Participate in a couple of social-media platforms such as Facebook and Twitter, but be selective in who you follow.* Do seek diversity in your virtual world, but avoid connecting with people who use their social-media platform to denigrate others. I follow not only people I admire, but also people who think very differently than I do in an effort to keep a balanced perspective on issues.

- *Subscribe to news alerts such as Google News Alert.* You can receive news from around the world on any topic of your choosing, and it is very easy to set up. I find unique compassion initiatives all over the world that I would have missed, if not for the news alert service.

- *Create your own website.* When it comes to building websites, today there are software programs that are "plug and play": you plug in the information you want to publish on the Internet and the software posts it so that it can be "played" and shared with anyone in the world. Many of my connections to universities and other organizations are made through my website.

Extending your reach through the virtual world is simple to initiate, but problematic to maintain. You can get drawn into checking your updates so often that it becomes a source of distraction rather than a tool for making connections. Limit your activity to actions that build personal and professional contacts and unplug from the platform when you see yourself clicking on the infamous "cat video."

Real World and Virtual World

If you see or have a problem in real life, you can take it online to find help in addressing it. But remember that what you do online has an impact on real life. If you act with compassion online, you can help spread compassion in the real world. If you act with disdain or anger online, you help spread disdain and anger in the real world. If you intend to broaden your network and extend your reach in the virtual world, never forget the power you have to effect change, both positive and negative, in the real world.

The fabric of life, from the quantum to the cosmic levels, is woven from strands of interconnections. Quantum physics is famously associated with the idea that an object can be in two places at the same time, and that concept can be helpful to us when we think of the interplay between the real world and the virtual world: we can interact within and between the virtual and real worlds simultaneously. Practicing compassion in the virtual or real world creates its own kind of quantum event: one compassionate act can occur at two places at the same time, in both actual and virtual realities.

Compassion can go viral online in many different ways, so that it can spread to not only everyone's URL (uniform resource locator, which is a website's unique Internet address), but their IRL (in real life) address. One of the most prevalent ways this occurs is through the "rehoming" of dogs, which is about finding a new home for pets. Since I have a Vizsla puppy named Kalev, I joined a few of the online Vizsla groups, so that I could find guidance and ask for assistance when I need help. What I noticed right away was that people use such social-media groups not only for everyday help in raising a Vizsla, but also for the heartbreaking process of rehoming a dog. Within a day of posting the need to rehome a Vizsla, there are usually at least a handful of different people offering assistance in matching a pet with a potential adopter or adopting the dog themselves. Although dogs are considered "man's best friend," the virtual world has helped make many people best friends to dogs in the real world.

Animosity can spread from the virtual world to the real world just as easily. This hit close to home—my hometown—a few years ago when a friend and colleague of mine lost her teenage daughter to suicide, which was mainly caused by cyberbullying. Bullying can now be felt relentlessly for twenty-four hours a day via the Internet. One in four teens admit that they have been cyberbullied at least once, and the rate of cyberbullying increased from 6 percent in 2000 to 11 percent in 2010. For all of its benefits, the virtual world can have a negative impact on life in the real world as well.

Because social media also has its downsides, such as cyberbullying and digital stalking, some companies have recently created teams of engineers, designers, and psychologists for the explicit purpose of building compassion on their respective sites. Facebook is one of the companies taking the lead in addressing social concerns on its digital platform through compassion teams. "The Compassion Team," according to the *New York Times*, "is devoted to making Facebook's interactions more human, and more humane." There are compassion teams composed to address specific issues ranging from eating disorders to suicide prevention.

Practicing compassion in the virtual and real worlds helps to reinforce the practice in each reality. Exercise your compassion muscle online or in life to keep it healthy.

The Web has made it easier than ever before to connect to capabilities outside of your circle of direct experience. Life-saving rescues can be started by simple tweets. One of the world's leading theoretical physicists, Carlo Rovelli, the head of the Quantum Gravity group at the Centre de Physique Théorique of Aix-Marseille University, has argued that "we must accept the idea that reality is only interaction. . . . [It is] a world of happenings, not of things." The Internet has provided us with an entirely new world, the virtual world, that has the potential to either strengthen and deepen our "happenings" with each other, or weaken them. The path you choose depends on the perspectives you use when you interact with others in both the virtual and the real world. The importance of perspective is what we turn to next.

SKILL 3

Walk This Way: Shifting Your Perspective

There are always flowers for those who want to see them.
—HENRI MATISSE

"Who do you think you are?" We hear this question a lot in pop culture, whether it is in songs or on television shows, and the question usually carries a negative connotation. It's usually asked of those who are acting as though they are more important or know more than the people they are with. I'm using the question, however, in two very different ways: to show that it is a more complex (not complicated) question than we acknowledge and to highlight how that complexity can be a guide to finding ways of helping each other.

You and I each have multiple identities, and we use them more than we believe. We "call up" our different identities depending upon the context or environment we are in and the interactions we are having at any given moment. I do the following exercise with my 100-level students to illustrate how we change identities based on context.

I say to a student who I know lives in Brookfield, Connecticut, "Hi. I live in Danbury. Where do you live?"

The student responds, "Brookfield."

I then say to the student, "Now imagine you and I are in California. I'm a native Californian, and I ask you where you live. What do you say?"

"Connecticut," says the student, beginning to smile, because the idea is starting to come to life.

I conclude the brief exercise by saying, "Now we are in France, and I, as a Frenchman, ask you where you live. And you say . . ."

"The United States."

We change our identities depending upon the context we are in and the interactions we have with others. Within each of us we have multiple identities; in one we are many. The idea of "in one there are many" is a fundamental principle for how we experience life in all its forms. Take, for example, our basic experience of sunlight. We feel its warmth and see it as a single white light. The warmth we feel is the rapid vibration of many molecules (an elementary principle of thermodynamics) and what we perceive as one white light is actually made up of seven colors (nature provides us hints of the colors when we see a rainbow). Shining light through a prism separates the colors so that you can see them individually. In short, sunlight is one made up of many.

Recognizing your perspective in a given situation and then shifting or combining it with others will help you to see new solutions to your problem. When dealing with challenges at the university, shifting my perspective from professor to administrator to parent has helped open up my thinking in new ways and with very positive results. When working on increasing honors enrollment at the university, for example, we were much more effective when I shifted from my professorial focus on teaching and took the advice of our Vice President of Enrollment to start engaging with prospective students more. The same year that I started closely aligning my efforts with the university's admissions department, I also started thinking more like a parent and considering what policies or practices a prospective student's parents would want to see in place in order to feel their child was receiving the best experience possible. With that in mind, I worked with the university's security team to increase safety at the Honors House, so that all parents would know that while their daughters and sons are getting a high-quality education, they would also be protected by the latest security technology and strategies. The end result of approaching enrollment from the administrative and parental perspectives? A 160 percent increase in registration in one year.

Calling up your different identities is one way to shift your perspective. Another is to empathize with a perspective outside of your experience. Seeing a problem through the eyes of others can reveal resources and solutions that you would otherwise overlook. In addition, there are different ways to look at a problem that can impact your ability to find the resources and ideas needed to complete the path to success. By becoming a divergent thinker, seeing opportunity in "failure," banishing fear, and revising the language you use to describe the problem, you'll increase the likelihood of connecting to the capabilities you need.

The Power of Perspective

We've talked about the role of perspective in building understanding. It also plays an important role in connecting to capabilities and problem solving. Sometimes we don't see the resource or path we need to take to address a problem, because we're looking from a perspective or understanding that blinds us from seeing it.

Before I began lifeguard training, for example, I believed that one of the primary objectives was to save any and every person from drowning as fast as possible. But that perspective is dangerous if the person you're rescuing starts to grab onto you. Sometimes you have to take a paradoxical perspective in order to help someone: to rescue some drowning victims, you may need—as strange as it may sound—to let go of them. Every lifeguard is eventually taught that the first action you do to save the person who struggles by grabbing you is to go underwater, so that the person lets you go; the last place a drowning person wants to go is below the surface of the water. As you submerge yourself, you angle your body behind the other person's, so that you can lock it into a position to be carried to safety. My superficial thinking about how a lifeguard approached drowning persons (take an efficient and direct approach to rescue them) changed as I learned and studied to become one: helping someone is more about effectiveness than it is efficiency.

Nicholas Epley, in his book *Mindwise,* makes a point that aptly describes my lifeguard lesson. He says we should "try harder to *get* another person's perspective instead of trying to *take* it" (emphasis in original). The difference between getting and taking a perspective in this case is the difference between learning (getting) what lifeguards do and assuming (taking) what they do, which was what I did before being trained. Epley also notes that *getting* someone else's perspective can also be a source of inspiration and inner strength.

Sometimes the daily grind can wear us down to such an extent that we have difficulty seeing and acknowledging the positive aspects of life. And "getting" another person's perspective, especially someone who may be going through the same experiences as you, may be the only prescription you need to start looking up rather than down.

Our kids gave my wife and me a lesson on "getting" a positive perspective when we lived and traveled in Estonia for a year. We encountered many challenges, including airport connections that tested our agility and time management techniques, and experienced a fire across the hall in our apartment building that seemed to be a test in courage and language skills. Our three little ones helped us to see traveling and living overseas as a world of wonder rather than as a world of problems and obstacles. It was the questions that our children didn't ask that really highlighted this perspective. They didn't ask "Why is it cold?" or "Why is it dark?" in the middle of a Baltic winter. Instead, they said, "Wow, the cold makes you do things faster. That's pretty cool!" and "I like it here, because I like walking around in the dark with all the lights." They turned a cold and dark Estonian winter into a faster and brighter place for their mom and dad.

There are several entertaining ways to practice shifting and combining perspectives without having to have kids:

- *Jokes:* Make up jokes in which the punch line or main question uses different roles in life. One of my favorites is: "How do you tell the difference between a plumber and a chemist? Ask them to pronounce unionized."

- *Riddles:* Devise riddles that are based on perception. A fun business example is: "Who earns a living by driving customers away? A taxi/Uber driver."

- *Radio:* Listen to radio shows such as *Ask Me Another,* which is a National Public Radio show that features puzzles, word games, and trivia.

- *Books:* Read books, such as *The Diving Bell and the Butterfly* (the memoir of a man who could only communicate by blinking one eye), that provide you with a new and different perspective on life.

- *Movies:* Watch movies that place very different perspectives at the center of the plot. A good example is *Mindwalk,* a story about a poet, a politician, and a scientist physically exploring the castle at Mont Saint-Michel, France, while intellectually exploring the problems of humankind.

- *Games:* Play board and electronic games, such as *Dungeons and Dragons,* that allow you to become different characters with very different skill sets in the same imaginary or virtual world.

Understanding how different types of people perceive the world can also help you to unlock the different perspectives that are inside of you.

Making Use of Multiple Identities

Who you think you are affects how you act and the results you achieve (positive and negative). Using your different identities can be like a Swiss army knife for solutions: when it's difficult to find an answer with your current mindset, simply take the perspective of another identity and look at the problem from that angle. Too many times we become stuck in the role we assume in a specific context and forget how many different identities are within each one of us. They are empathetic tools that, if used constructively, can connect us to new ways of seeing solutions to problems.

At a minimum each day, I'm a dad, husband, pet owner, friend, professor, runner, director, entrepreneur, and employee. I've noticed that the way I listen varies in different contexts. For instance, while listening as an employee is focused upon learning how I, as an individual, can make the organization stronger (i.e., What can I do to help?), listening as a director is targeted at learning how to make the individual employees stronger from an organizational perspective (i.e., What can the organization do to help?). The difference between listening as a spouse and listening as a parent is that there is more focus on what is *not* said in the latter than in the former; I pay more attention to the words being said by my wife, but tend to listen more for the gaps in what is being said by my sons. In short, the skill of compassionate listening changes in direction and form according to the interpersonal context that we find ourselves in from moment to moment.

There are five basic stages for effectively shifting perspective by changing identities: recognizing your identity in a current situation; understanding that identity's limitations in solving a problem; considering other roles you can assume that might overcome the limitations; making the shift to another identity; and connecting to capabilities for addressing the problem.

1. *Recognizing your identity:* Acknowledge the role you are assuming in a specific situation. This stage is very straightforward, because it is usually the job, task, responsibility, or position you chose or assumed. When I was a babysitter in middle and high school, for example, I knew that I had specific jobs to do in that role, such as feed the kids, change their diapers if need be, protect them from imaginary monsters, get them to bed on time, and, most important, keep them alive until their parents came home! I was their protector, provider, disciplinarian, and bedtime storyteller (all skills that helped prepare me for my most important role in life: dad).

2. *Understanding the limitations of one identity:* Every role you assume in life is limited by the fact that it is a single identity. Although that single-minded identity is needed to perform the role well—in order to do my job as a babysitter I needed to be a babysitter and not a bike rider—when novel situations or problems occur, new perspectives are needed. Acknowledging the idea that every identity you become in life is inadequate by itself is important for overcoming problems that require an "outside the box" solution. Your acknowledgment of the limitations of a single identity is a key for unlocking the identities that can help you approach problems in extraordinary ways.

I did pretty well, according to my savings account, as one of the few male babysitters in the area where I lived, but when I was babysitting a three-year-old and we lost power at his house, all my babysitter tools—from Red Cross training in first aid and CPR to being a skilled diaper changer at fourteen years old—couldn't get him past his fear of the dark to go to sleep. He always went to sleep with his "sleepy light" on, and with the power outage he didn't have it. He wouldn't settle down even when I tried to use a flashlight as the "sleepy light." I felt stuck and anticipated a long night of crying. I then asked myself what calms me down when I'm upset or brings me up when I'm feeling down. The answer was and still is music. But with no power, I couldn't turn any music on.

3. *Finding a new identity:* Because we all have many identities and roles in life, we all have options for handling any problem that may arise, but we tend to restrict our thinking to the role we are engaged in within a specific context. I had limited myself to traditional babysitter solutions such as flashlight storytelling, but it wasn't until I thought about my "budding career" as a musician that music came to me as a potential answer. I had sung in an all-kids choir since I was seven and learned to play guitar when I was ten. It was my identity as a musician that offered a way to help the little guy stop crying.

4. *Making the shift:* After finding a different identity that you think can help, become it and act the part. In my babysitting case, I started singing, and it helped to settle my charge down a little. Then I realized he needed to hear the sound of a musical instrument. I needed my guitar.

5. *Connecting to capabilities:* Once you have shifted perspective and understand what is needed to address a problem, finding what you need is usually as simple as looking within and around you. Adding my guitar, which was still attached to my bike, to my voice did the trick. He stopped crying with the first strum of the guitar. It was the most gratifying performance of my young "career."

Using your multiple identities on a daily basis makes overcoming problems easier and daily life more fulfilling.

Combining the perspectives and skills of your different identities broadens your ability to help. By combining listening skills from different identities, for example, I'm more likely to connect my students and employees to resources that are better equipped than I may be to help them address issues and solve problems. Combining is different from shifting in that you weave identities together rather than move between them to connect to capabilities to solve the problem. Instead of dropping one role for another, you weave different identities together to find a way forward through a problem.

By the time the second week of every semester is over, I am fortunate to know not only my students' names, but some of their characteristics and daily habits. It was obvious that one of my students was not himself during the fourth week of class. He was coming late to class, sat slumped at his desk, didn't contribute during discussion, and avoided all eye contact—actions that were the opposite of those he had displayed during the first three weeks of school. As he was leaving the classroom, the last student out the door, I simply asked if there was something wrong and if I could be of any help. The next moment he was holding back tears as he explained that his mom was dying of cancer.

After listening to his family's story, I knew that he needed more help than I could provide and asked if I could walk him to the counseling center. He said he had another class after mine and was worried about missing it. After walking him to his next class and talking with the professor, he and I walked to the counseling center, where I knew he would be in great hands with people I trust. His mom died six weeks later, but my student completed the semester and is finishing his degree. By simply combining the listening skills from different identities (counterintelligence agent, teacher, and dad) and understanding that I didn't have the necessary background to comprehensively help him, I was able to connect him with people who could help him work through his loss while staying on the path to academic success.

Listening to my student as a parent helped me to "hear" what he wasn't saying, such as "I feel all alone because my mom and dad divorced." Listening based on my counterintelligence work allowed me to call him out when I knew he wasn't telling me everything. Many weeks later he told me: "When you called me out for not telling you everything, I knew you cared so much because you were carefully listening. So many people find excuses to stop listening, so that they could be rid of me, and you kept finding ways to keep me talking." Weaving my professor's identity into the mix was an important step to keep me from getting in over my head. When operating in the "dad" mode, I could have become emotionally overwhelmed into thinking that I had to protect him or that I could have solved all his problems. From a professor's vantage point, I knew that his problems were much bigger than I was trained to handle; the counseling center had given seminars to help us recognize when we should bring students to their offices. Combining identities helps you to help others in ways that open up potential resources for solving a problem, while also keeping you from being overwhelmed by circumstances.

Looking Through the Eyes of Another

We tend to become locked into our perspectives about issues, problems, and people by what we know, feel, and experience. By a normal process of human development—not through any malice or callousness on our part—we as individuals acquire a set of thoughts and feelings about the world that forms a boundary beyond which we cannot normally "see." Yet by going beyond this boundary, by exploring how others perceive the world, *we can unlock our perspective* and broaden and deepen it. As mentioned above, it's what Epley calls "getting" rather than "taking" another's perspective. There are several ways to unlock your perspective by getting someone else's:

- *Reading:* Reading a nonfiction book centered on experience and perspective, such as a biography, can provide an entirely new understanding and appreciation of the world around you. After reading Temple Grandin's autobiography about living an autistic life, *Thinking in Pictures,* you more fully understand the importance of what she meant when she said, "The world needs different kinds of minds to work together." Reading fiction also puts you in another place and time. A recent paper published in *Trends in Cognitive Science* argues that reading fiction can improve your "understanding of others." Keith Oatley, the University of Toronto author of the paper, goes on to show that "this effect is especially marked with literary fiction, which also enables people to change themselves." Reading has the power to unlock your perspective and possibly alter the person you become.

- *Discussing:* Ask a person who opposes your view on a specific topic to meet over lunch or coffee for the explicit purpose of discussing the issue. Challenge yourself to listen more than talk and question more than argue.

- *Debating:* Find a couple of friends willing to debate an issue with you and choose to debate for the side you personally disagree with. In other words, take the role of "devil's advocate" against your own perspective.

- *Asking:* Near the end of Nicholas Epley's book about how we can better understand other people, he sums up his argument: "The secret to understanding each other better seems to come . . . through the hard relational work of putting people in a position where they can tell you their minds openly and honestly." In other words, ask questions that help you "get" an understanding of another's perspective by their actually telling you their opinions, ideas, and perceptions. Two of the first questions I ask people when trying to get their general perspective on life are: What is your favorite book and why? Who is your favorite artist (musician, painter, poet, etc.) and why? You can learn a lot about a person's perspective on life from these two questions alone.

Unlocking your perspective is about acquiring new insights, perceptions, and understanding about your world.

David Foster Wallace's 2005 commencement address at Kenyon College is one of the most highly regarded as well as viewed speeches of this century because of its insights about the human condition and way of thinking. Wallace was well known as a "hyper-anxious chronicler of the minute details of a certain kind of upper-middle-class American life." He opened his address with a short story about two young fish meeting an older fish. As the older fish comes upon the younger ones, he says, "Morning, boys. How's the water?" The two young fish don't answer and swim on. One of them eventually asks the other, "What the hell is water?" Wallace explains to the graduating class: "The point of the fish story is merely that the most obvious, important realities are often the ones that are hardest to see and talk about."

Our everyday *socioeconomic environment*, I suggest, is our "water." Many of us are blind to its importance and effect even though we live in and depend on it for daily life. Recognizing and understanding how your socioeconomic environment shapes and molds you is another way to unlock your perspective.

We all identify with a socioeconomic class in our everyday lives, and it too has an effect on perceptions and actions. What Paul Piff, a social psychologist at the University of California–Irvine, and other researchers have found is that, as people become monetarily richer, they become poorer in compassion. Piff and his colleagues also discovered that lower-income households are proportionally more generous to charities than higher-income households. "The findings across dozens of studies and thousands of participants is," according to Piff, "as a person's levels of wealth increase, their feelings of compassion and empathy go down, and their feelings of entitlement, of deservedness, and ideology of self-interest increase." Their research found that high-income people live, work, and travel in ways that detach them from socioeconomic diversity: living in the suburbs rather than in the city, driving a car rather than riding the bus or subway, and being an "overseer" rather than a leader at work. There are simpler ways to avoid the "class crash of compassion" than moving or giving up your car or your job, and that is through small nudges.

Recent studies at the University of Zurich have found that altruistic behavior increases in selfish people when the brain's connections for compassionate motivation ("the desire to help a person for whom one feels empathy") are more active than the connections for reciprocity motivation ("the desire to reciprocate an individual's previous kindness"). When you replace a tit-for-tat strategy in life with a compassionate lifestyle, altruistic acts increase in a community, especially by those considered to be self-centered. Piff's work has also shown that "little nudges of compassion and bumps of empathy" increase the "levels of empathy, compassion, and generosity" in wealthy, selfish people.

The "nudges" and "bumps" can occur through "simple reminders," such as a minute-long video (this is what Piff used), inspirational posters, a brief discussion at the end or beginning of a meeting about the importance of compassion in whatever is being done or planned, providing incentives for those who are acting as compassionate achievers, and inviting customers to talk with the team about how the product has helped them. The customer-talk idea has also been shown to significantly increase worker productivity, because it validates in a very real way the intrinsic motivation for doing the job. Workers are not just doing a job; they are also helping people with real problems.

Walking a Divergent Path

The way you approach and think about problems determines the number of options you can connect to for solving them. It all depends on whether you are a convergent or divergent thinker. People who primarily use convergent thinking perceive problems as though they are multiple-choice tests: there are only a limited number of solutions immediately in front of them to choose from and they need to figure out the right one. In contrast, divergent thinkers look for options that connect them to solutions that are beyond the immediate choices in front of them. Divergent thinkers don't just look in front of them for connections to solutions, but also to the left, right, above, below, and behind. Divergent thinking not only helps you to unlock your perspective by opening your mind to possibilities coming from every direction, but also strengthens your interpersonal interactions.

Although problems in interpersonal relationships are divergent issues, we often try to manage them through a convergent thought process. Convergent thinking is using logical and linear reasoning to arrive at a solution that "can be written down and passed on to others, who can apply it without needing to reproduce the mental effort necessary to find it." Divergent thinking, in contrast, occurs in a nonlinear manner as a solution emerges out of the interaction between free-flowing ideas. All issues in "human relations" are "divergent problems which have to be lived" or experienced, according to E. F. Schumacher, but when we view them through the lens of convergence, we begin to create a meaningless automated existence, or "living death":

> If this [convergence] were the case with human relations—in family life, economics, politics, education, and so forth—well, . . . there would be no more human relations but only mechanical actions; life would be a living death. Divergent problems, as it were, force man to strain himself to a level above himself; they demand, and thus provoke the supply of, forces from a higher level, thus bringing love, beauty, goodness, and truth into our lives. . . . All divergent problems can be turned into convergent problems by a process of "reduction." The result, however, is the loss of all higher forces to ennoble human life, and the degradation not only of the emotional part of our nature, but also, as Darwin sensed, of our intellect and moral character.

I add compassion to Schumacher's list of "higher forces" that "ennoble human life." When we try to handle our interpersonal relationships through convergent thinking, we cut ourselves off from those ennobling forces, to the detriment of our emotional nature as well as our intellect and moral character. How do you begin to walk on and then remain on a divergent path? One way is sincerely *listening to learn* and not *listening to reply* to what someone is saying. You stay focused on those you're with and not cheat on them by sneaking a peek at your electronic device. The paradox of working through divergent problems is to practice focused attention, so you can freely flow with the conversation and ideas, which you need to understand so that you are capable of constructively helping.

My hometown of Brookfield, Connecticut, has been actively trying to walk its own divergent path of compassion in an effort to strengthen communal ties. From a monthly compassion club where theories of psychology and practical advice are discussed, which was created by a loose-knit group of independent citizens, to an organized citizens' group called Brookfield

Cares, which hosts a community forum about mental health, addiction, and suicide prevention, our town has demonstrated that communities and organizations don't have to wait for their leaders to foster divergent thinking. It can start with any individual in any context.

After participating in the forum called "A Courageous Community Dares to Discuss" and listening to a wide array of townspeople, including high-school students, parents, grandparents, and local officials, I couldn't help but feel a bit of pride for, but also amazement at how many different ways we live, think, and work in our relatively small town. Sometimes you don't see the possibilities for divergent thinking until you create the conditions that allow it to blossom—the group of women and men of Brookfield Cares did exactly that by organizing the community discussion.

A main objective of the forum was to uncover as many problems as we could while also building a list of possible action steps to address them. The problems were similar to those in other suburban communities (alcohol and drug addiction as well as bullying and suicide, to name a few), but what was different was the variety of ideas that people brought from their groups into the one large meeting at the end (there were a total of 130 people divided into 12 groups, which were eventually combined into one group for the last hour and a half).

We were sincere not just in our effort to figure out how to marshal resources within our community, such as connecting high-school students with senior citizens on projects that are mutually beneficial to both age groups, but also in trying to reach out to neighboring towns and organizations so that we might pool our capabilities as a region. By "daring" to walk toward the problems in our community, we found ways to connect to capabilities hidden in plain sight on our town's streets (i.e., businesses) and in our neighbors' houses (i.e., professional expertise and networks).

Seeing Only Opportunity

Walking into problems is not usually considered a good thing, but that is only one perspective: problems and failures, from a scientific point of view, offer new ways of thinking that can lead to helpful discoveries. National Public Radio annually bestows the "Golden Mole Award for Accidental Brilliance" to scientific discoveries that are born out of mistakes, coincidences, confusion, or problems.

For instance, one 2016 nominated scientist's failure in medicine has turned out to be an important advance in the field of agriculture. He was attempting to create "a molecule that would light up in the presence of chloride," which would be useful to "scientists studying cystic fibrosis, a disease that disrupts the movement of chloride across cell membranes." Instead, he produced a molecule that lit up when nitrate was present. The discovery is now being used to build nitrate sensors that could help farmers all around the world fertilize their fields more efficiently.

A science lab trying to find a way to determine what fossilized viruses might look like today under a microscope inadvertently found a way to preserve vaccines without refrigeration. By accidently leaving out a flask of the solution containing the viruses overnight, the scientists may have found a way to make sure that no one gets left out from receiving vaccines for deadly diseases.

Such scientific discoveries show that problems and failures are not just sources of angst; they can also be solutions if we can look at them from a different point of view and understand how they connect to other areas and issues in life. Although neither of the "failures" mentioned above walked away with the Golden Mole award, they both succeeded in bringing to life James Joyce's words in *Ulysses:* "Errors . . . are the portals of discovery."

Shifting your perspective on failure from one in which you see defeat to one in which you see opportunity can connect you to capabilities that have the ability to increase your business profits, academic achievements, and personal health. David Kelley, who is the founder of Stanford's highly successful d.school (Institute of Design at Stanford), teaches his students: "If you keep making the same mistakes again and again, you aren't learning anything. If you keep making new and different mistakes, that means you are doing new things and learning new things." Stanford's d.school is all about unlocking perspectives to achieve success, even through failure.

One of the most famous failures turned successes in modern business is Post-It notes. Spencer Silver, a scientist at 3M in 1968, was trying to create a superstrong adhesive, but created a "low-tack" adhesive instead. Silver continuously attempted to get 3M officials to consider his low-tack adhesive as a "solution without a problem," but he kept being rejected for five years. It wasn't until Art Fry, a product development engineer for 3M, saw the practical use of Silver's adhesive notes to mark his choir book at church. After years of rejection and even more years of development, Post-It notes are arguably one of the most widely recognized office supplies in the world.

Numerous research papers and books in the field of education and parenting demonstrate the importance of framing failure as an opportunity to learn rather than as evidence of incompetence. As one summary of a study in the *Journal of Experimental Psychology* stated: "Kids perform better in school if they know failure, and trying again is part of the learning process." In other words, by reframing our children's perspective on failure as being constructive we can help them achieve better learning and cognitive outcomes.

The failure of my wife's doctors in Boston to reverse her deteriorating health forced us to take a divergent path in the medical community in order to successfully resolve her medical condition. After seven years of trying every known Western medical approach to her sickness, we tried a naturopathic doctor who treated her in ways that were never attempted at the hospitals in Boston. The short story is that the doctors in Boston had recommended we move back to her home area for her to pass away, and the naturopathic doctor had her in complete recovery within two years. The failure of one medical community opened our eyes to health approaches in another medical community, which saved my wife's life.

Alexander Graham Bell—scientist, innovator, and inventor of the telephone—said it best about failure and opportunity: "When one door closes, another door opens; but we so often look so long and regretfully upon the closed door, that we do not see the ones which open for us." Strive to see all the open doors around you at all times—be a divergent thinker—but do it especially when you feel as though you have failed. How you frame your experiences will either limit or expand the number of connections available to you that can potentially help overcome a myriad of difficulties.

Language Matters

The way you word or frame a question can increase or decrease your ability to connect to capabilities. A 2015 study, for instance, investigated how well people could figure out others' relationships from their interactions. When men were told that the exercise was a test of their "social skills," they did "somewhat worse than women." However, when they were told it was a test for "complex information processing," men did "better." Although the study was part of a larger work on "stereotype threat" (we tend to conform to stereotypes when we are reminded of them), my purpose in mentioning the research is to show how you can turn a cultural liability into an asset by simply being mindful of the words you use. Language matters. By simply choosing different words to explain a problem or ask for assistance or tailoring your language to a specific audience, you increase the likelihood of a positive response.

How you ask for help or assistance can change the level of response as well as quality of help you get. When our family, for example, recently added a new puppy to our household, my wife and I initially struggled to get our sons to help when it wasn't "convenient" for them. When we simply asked, they tended not to help, especially if they had something else to do. When we forced them to help, their quality of "play" with the puppy was nothing but pure reluctance. However, when we asked what their opinion would be of kids who spend more time playing video games than with their puppy each day, they stood in silence for a moment and then ran to our newest four-legged family member and apologized to him. The boys have been more helpful than ever with Kalev, and getting them to that level of care was all about the language my wife and I used.

Learning a foreign language opens you up to a world of perspectives and different ways of thinking that help you connect to answers that can only be found by being exposed to other cultures and languages. Try to use the framework of another language to see a problem from a different angle. For example, different cultures have different concepts of time that could influence your ability to address a problem. One of the first things I learned in both my Chinese and Estonian language classes was how they exclude the future tense for words to the point where you feel that the future is innately part of the present. In English we separate the present from not only the future, but also the past. How we speak about the future has been shown in recent studies to affect our spending and saving habits; speakers of languages with the future tense save less than cultures that exclude it.

Although many educators and policymakers of the past century believed that learning a second language would "interfere" with intellectual development, researchers are now showing that it strengthens social and cognitive skills. Recent studies have demonstrated that simply being exposed to another language improves your ability to stay focused and solve problems as well as to empathetically understand another's perspective. "Multilingual exposure, it seems," according to Katherine Kinzler, of Cornell University, "facilitates the basic skills of interpersonal understanding." Research by Albert Costa, of the University of Pompeu Fabra in Spain, found that "the key difference between bilinguals and monolinguals may be more basic: a heightened ability to monitor the environment."

Having a heightened awareness of your environment and a clear understanding of the context you may find yourself in at any given moment improves your ability to successfully handle surprising or unexpected events and situations, which we all inevitably face. Being surrounded by different languages gives you more freedom to choose how to handle life's unexpected challenges. The more you surround yourself with people who speak different languages, the greater your ability to connect to ideas and perspectives that can help you achieve success. When you connect with others, a byproduct is that you are also strengthening your ability to connect to capabilities.

Shifting and combining perspectives help to connect you to capabilities that you may have overlooked or would never have considered if you remained a one-dimensional thinker. Strive to walk a divergent path in life, and you will find that you have access to capabilities that a convergent thinker will never know. Alexander Graham Bell, who was a model of divergent thinking, said: "The only difference between success and failure is the ability to take action." Acting to solve is what we turn our attention to next.

6

Act to Solve

When I first met twelve-year-old J. T. Lewis, he constantly looked down and seemed to be falling deeper into despair. He had just lost his six-year-old brother in a mass school shooting. His mom was trying every therapy known to the traditional and nontraditional medical communities to help him find his way through the trauma, but it was J.T. who found his own path forward and up. What did he do? He reached out to a community of geno-cide orphans halfway around the world for insights into dealing with the traumatic loss of a loved one and found that they had problems he thought he could help with.

J.T. started a foundation, Newtown Helps Rwanda, at the ripe old age of thirteen to help the orphans address some of their problems as he was trying to work through his loss. Among other projects, J.T.'s foundation has raised money to send a genocide orphan to four years of college and provide for eight siblings under her care, helped build a self-sustaining fish pond for a former child soldier in Uganda, and provided the initial large donation toward buying a seizure-alert dog for twins with Dravet syndrome. With every new project J.T. tackles, a piece of the despairing young boy I first met melts away to reveal a confident young man with a sense of purpose.

J.T. could have attended to his own grief. Instead, he reached out to others and took action to alleviate their pain. If anyone had an excuse to withdraw from the world and take care of himself, it was J.T. Yet he found reasons to help others, and in so doing he was able to alleviate his own pain. When you act to help others, you solve some of your own problems.

You don't have to go to extraordinary measures to be a compassionate achiever; many times all that is required is the ability to act. As one Park Slope, Brooklyn, resident who recently helped a homeless man on her block get back on his feet said, "It wasn't that hard to do—you just had to be willing to do it. It turns out that people who mean well aren't actually willing to do much."

The most infamous case of the tragedy of indifference and inaction is the 1964 murder of Kitty Genovese outside her apartment building in Queens, New York. In what is now called by researchers the "bystander effect" or the "Genovese syndrome," approximately a dozen of her neighbors saw or heard her being attacked for thirty minutes but did nothing to help—they weren't "willing to do much." Although the incident was more complex and nuanced than simplifying it to the bystander effect, the point is that many people believe that it is better to not become "involved" with others. This step of compassion, acting to solve, is based on the understanding that helping others is a win-win interaction; a byproduct of helping others, as J.T. discovered, is that it also benefits you. When you ignore or refuse to help others, you bypass an opportunity to strengthen yourself.

Many of us find it easier not to take action because we believe that the "path of least resistance" or the "principle of least effort" is the most cost-effective approach to daily life with regard to our time, money, and resources. It's one of the reasons most Americans don't vote in midterm elections (only 42 percent of eligible voters cast a ballot) and only slightly more than half of us vote in presidential elections. Many Americans believe that it isn't worth the time and effort to change their daily routine for one day to vote. We are so routine oriented that only 13 percent of us change our doctors in any given year even though "70 percent of Americans aren't satisfied with their doctor-patient relationship." Many of us could make ourselves stronger and healthier if we became more physically active, but nearly 80 percent of American adults don't meet the requirement for the minimally recommended amount of exercise each week. One study "linked physical inactivity to more than 5 million deaths worldwide per year, more than those caused by smoking." We tend to follow the "path of least resistance" and don't act to solve, even though the path is physically killing and politically dividing us. There is plenty of evidence to support Henry David Thoreau's words: "The path of least resistance leads to crooked rivers and crooked men."

But, let me assure you, if you can listen, understand, and connect, then you can act to solve a wide range of problems. You can take action to help others, which paradoxically helps you. Indeed, researchers have found that helping others benefits you in mental and physical ways no matter how weak or strong you are. As Daniel Wegner and Kurt Gray highlight in their book, *The Mind Club*, when people who are considered "helpless" and "vulnerable" help others, they are "transform[ed] into agents with increased self-confidence and personal power." Another study has shown that taking action to help others helps you to live longer, because it reduces the effects of stress on your body. The researchers found, in other words, that helping others when you are in a stressful situation adds years, not stress, to your life.

Taking action, even when it's challenging, painful, or just *hard*, is Step 4 of becoming a compassionate achiever. Taking action, as we discussed in the beginning of the book, is what centrally differentiates compassion from empathy, which does not require you to act in any way to address a problem. In this step, you'll learn skills and ways of thinking that will help you to gain confidence in your ability to act and create positive change, even if there are obstacles blocking your path, such as fear. You will learn how to build your reservoirs of resilience and sense of responsibility as well as understand when and how to act by following the principle of "nondoing":

Skill 1: Overcoming fear

Skill 2: Developing responsibility and resilience

Skill 3: Practicing the act of nondoing

Over the course of the first three steps, you've developed a complex understanding of the problem or situation and have connected to resources to help you address it. With the three skills covered in Step 4, you'll be able to make change happen.

SKILL 1

The Courage to Try: Overcoming Fear

If you want to lift yourself up, lift up someone else.
—BOOKER T. WASHINGTON

There is a price to pay for allowing fear to stop us from taking action that helps others. The costs are paid in societal and individual decline. Researchers such as Robert Putnam, in political science, and Paul Zak, in economics, have shown that when people in a community help one another, they build bonds of trust that strengthen their neighborhoods, towns, and cities. The health of civil society strengthens as the number of people who help each other increases. When you help another, it also physically and psychologically strengthens you. The social interaction of helping another provides individual benefits to you. The price we pay by not taking action to help others is the diminishment of ourselves and the deterioration of our communities. "Fear has never been a good adviser," according to Chancellor Angela Merkel, "neither in our personal lives nor in our society." Fear is a major cause of inaction, and there are several ways to overcome it.

By overcoming doubt, ignorance, and pessimism, you will not only overcome fear, but also tap into your inner reserves of courage and self-confidence, enabling you to act to help others. Striving to build a healthy sense of self-confidence to minimize self-doubt, continuously educating yourself to erase ignorance, and learning to become a realistic optimist are important ways to overcome your fear of taking action.

Working with others—cooperation—is another way of overcoming the fear to act. As we've discussed throughout this book, making connections is essential in every step of being a compassionate achiever. It should come as no surprise that connections play a primary role in overcoming the fear of taking action. With every step you take toward connecting with others and building courage, you distance yourself from fear's paralyzing effect.

Building Your Courage

You can try to hold back fear, but it will simply build up over time. You can even try to avoid fear, but it will still be lurking around you, which means that you will probably be unwilling to engage life in new ways. We need to go to the sources of fear to weaken its paralyzing effect on action. The three main sources of fear are doubt, ignorance, and pessimism.

Boosting Your Self-Confidence

Insecurity, or self-doubt, is one source of fear. Self-confidence makes taking action, especially when immediate action is needed, much easier. Boost your self-confidence in the following ways:

- *Speak to yourself as you would speak to one of your own best friends.* We're often much kinder to our friends than we are to ourselves. Take time out to think about the "good ole days" (as you would with any longtime best friend) when you achieved something that made you feel useful, appreciative, and unconquerable. A best friend builds you up by reminding you of the times you excelled and bolsters your self-confidence with stories and other evidence showing your worth, value, and abilities. In order to lift myself up when someone doubts me, I take myself back to the "glory days" of high-school sports when I got my first start in soccer and scored two goals within thirty seconds. When I need to feel appreciated, I think of helping my wife deliver our three sons through water births, where my hands were the first to touch them. And in instances when I need to help myself overcome a specific fear, I purposely recall the feeling I had as soon as I overcame my fear of heights by conquering the "slide for life" obstacle at Ft. Leonard Wood. The obstacle is not a slide in any traditional sense of the word. You climb a fifty-foot tower and, as you ascend, the rungs get farther apart; I had to jump to reach the last two. Once you climb to the top (with no safety harness or net), you need to jump to a rope to "slide" yourself down horizontally hand over hand. We all have memories of doing things we didn't think we could do; remind yourself of those times.

- *Find a power mantra.* When I'm facing a daunting task, I repeat the phrase "I can do anything, I can do anything" over and over again. It helps me to see a daunting task as a challenging opportunity. I've noticed that my sons now say it to themselves before activities they are afraid to do, such as getting a vaccine at the doctor's office or right before a play performance to overcome stage fright.

- *Use self-talk with your first name, not a personal pronoun ("I" or "me").* According to new research, I would significantly improve the effect of my power mantra if I slightly changed it to "Chris can do anything,

Chris can do anything." Ethan Kross, director of the Emotion and Self-Control Laboratory at the University of Michigan, has found that using your first name in self-talk "minimizes social anxiety" and "empowers [people], so what others see as a threat, they see as a challenge." Kross explains that the positive results of using your first name are due to the perception that you are "distancing" yourself from the problem you are facing.

- *Meditate.* After exercising each morning, I reserve ten minutes to meditate. I use guided meditations that derive from Buddhism, and my go-to guide is Rick Hanson. I meditate either inside or outside depending on the weather, and I always begin with gratitude for the people who enrich my life. I focus loving thoughts on my family, then friends, and finally acquaintances, concentrating on an image of each face in my mind's eye. I conclude the meditation by thinking of how I helped or was kind to another person the previous day. This helps me to see that I am worthy of compassion. Since I was kind and generous to others, I must not be half bad and deserve a little compassion myself. I then thank my brain (which sounds funny to say, but I do it because focusing on your brain, as research in neuroplasticity shows, can help to strengthen it), heart, and soul for the person I am becoming. I found that I am very much like J.T. in this respect: focusing on others first, especially in meditation, helps me to appreciate my own value and renew my sense of purpose.

Educating Yourself

Ignorance breeds fear through misunderstanding and misperception. Striving to continuously educate yourself is the central way to erase ignorance. Other than endlessly attending school, here are three ways to do so:

- *Triangulate perspectives.* There are more than two ways to understand every issue. Many of us become stymied in a situation or issue because we normally hear only two sides of a problem, and we think our choice of action is either "this" or "that." However, more often than not, there are choices we haven't considered. I learned about triangulation in the military: we took action once we had three different ways of confirming the location of a person we were seeking. Once you have at least three perspectives on the problem you're facing (you've educated yourself with more information than most people), take action with confidence, knowing that you are heading in a thoughtful direction toward addressing the problem.

- *Learn how others emotionally and cognitively understand an issue.* Neuro-scientists have clearly shown that emotion and cognition are interwoven, especially when we learn. Understanding people's emotional perspective on an issue is just as important as understanding how they intellectually comprehend it. Emotions, as we discussed earlier, are the basis for cognition and affect what and how we learn. Strive to learn how people feel about a topic and not just what they think about it. Connecting with someone on both the emotional and the intellectual levels builds a sense of camaraderie that fosters action.

- *Always question.* Many of us view questioning as a tactic to slow or defer action. When I think about the role of questions, however, I can't help but see the word "quest." I see questions as helping to guide me toward acting in an educated way. If you don't ask questions, how do you find answers and better questions? When you start asking questions, you also need to start recognizing that the "quest is on" to address an issue. Questions don't only have to take place before you act; they can help guide you while acting.

Becoming a Realistic Optimist

Researchers, beginning with Albert Bandura in psychology, have found that the best predictor of your success is whether you believe you will succeed. This is what the field of positive psychology is founded upon. Sophia Chou, of Taiwan National University, has found in her research, however, that there are two basic types of optimists: realists and idealists. "Realistic optimists" are those who are hopeful that they will succeed, but know that they have to pay attention and work through any potential obstacles to their success. "Idealistic optimists" are Pollyannas who think that good things will always happen and are blind to any potential problems and difficulties. Success is something you make happen if you're a realistic optimist and, in contrast, success is something that happens to you if you're an idealistic optimist. Realistic optimists take action to attain positive results, and idealists wait for the action to provide them with positive results. Chou, Oettingen, and other researchers all show that the realists are much more successful than the idealists. There are several ways to become a realistic optimist:

- *Surround yourself with positive, upbeat, confident people and separate yourself from negative people.* Your internal life tends to sync with your external life. "Social relationships—both quantity and quality—affect," according to a study in the *Journal of Health and Social Behavior,* your "mental health, health behavior, physical health, and mortality risk." When you are surrounded by people who see you in a positive light, you are more likely to see yourself and your accomplishments in a positive light as well. And optimism is contagious.

- *Listen to or sing along with songs that make you feel hopeful and powerful.* I regularly listen to songs that make me feel hopeful and strong, such as Louis Armstrong's "What a Wonderful World" and The Script's "Superheroes." While some people may "eat an apple a day to keep the doctor away," I enlist an earworm to help me keep pessimism at bay.

- *See action as an opportunity rather than a burden.* Reframe any problem that you may confront and action that you may have to take as an opportunity to build success rather than as a burden you are forced to carry. When given lemons, take action by making lemonade.

I consider positivity skills my seatbelt in life. They give me the confidence to travel anywhere, even into the thorniest thicket of challenges, and protect me from negative self-talk when things go sideways. Inevitably, at some point, we will all experience failure: the project that falls apart, the fund-raiser that doesn't reach your goals, the perfect solution that turns into a perfect storm of trouble. Your effectiveness as a compassionate achiever depends not on avoiding failure, but how you handle it when you do experience it.

Handling Failure

Don't let the fear of failure prevent you from taking action. The tools to build your self-confidence mentioned above will bolster your ability to face failure, but it also helps to learn how to handle failure. There are several ways to keep trying even if one of your greatest fears comes true:

- *Be a "realistic optimist" when viewing failure.* Being a realistic optimist not only builds courage, but also helps you to see other solutions that might be better than the one you tried. As Chou says of realistic optimists: "Every time they face an issue or a challenge or a problem, they won't say, 'I have no choice and this is the only thing I can do.' They will be creative, they will have a plan A, plan B, and plan C." Look for options B, C, and D (as a realistic optimist, I added another choice), choose one, and take action.

- *Separate failure from your identity.* Your failures are signposts that help guide you to who you become, but they do not define who you are. Imagine if Abraham Lincoln let his many failures, which included eight lost elections and two failed business attempts, define who he was. He learned from his failures to eventually become not just president of the United States, but one of the greatest presidents (if not the greatest) this country has ever had.

- *Do not deny failure; acknowledge it.* See failure as a part of learning and not as an aspect of defeat. If you want to learn from your failure, you have to acknowledge that it happened. You need to "talk about failures without apologizing," as sociologist Brené Brown recommends. Pretending a failure or set of failures didn't occur is like sweeping dirt under the rug. You're going to eventually trip over it again.

- *Fall forward.* When you fall, do you fall down or fall forward in the direction you want to go? In the game of football, a runner with the ball looks to gain an extra yard even when being taken down. That extra yard can make all the difference in whether the team keeps the ball and scores a touchdown or has to kick it away to the other side. When you fall, which we all do, fall forward, and you just might land on a second chance (or a new set of downs) for achieving your goal.

- *Plug into your support network to move ahead.* Your friends and mentors usually have ideas and perspectives that can help you see ways forward through a failure. When Michael Jordan didn't make his high-school basketball team, his mom didn't let him sulk. She told him to get out on the court and practice in order "to prove to the coach that he had made a mistake." Our mentors have the ability to help us see our failures in ways that are motivating and comforting—but only if we connect with them. Mentors can lighten the load of a failure that is weighing you down, but only if you share it with them.

Failures are inevitable, and being prepared to work through and learn from them can keep you motivated to find paths that eventually lead to success (we'll go deeper into this subject in the next section when we discuss resilience). You'll increase the likelihood of finding those paths if you handle failure as something that is constructive rather than destructive. From learning to become a realistic optimist to simply sitting down and talking with your mentors, you can turn failure from an immobilizing into a motivating experience.

You Don't Have to Go It Alone: Working with Others

When I think about being alone, I think of the film *It's a Wonderful Life*. Jimmy Stewart plays a small-town banker named George Bailey who finds himself in desperate need of $8,000 to keep his struggling Building & Loan open. (That was a lot of money in 1945.) George thinks he needs to solve his money issue all on his own, and over the course of the movie, as he fails to find a solution, he falls deeper and deeper into despair and hopelessness. But when his friends find out that he needs help, they rally together and raise the money for him. George had forgotten how many people cared about him and that collectively they could accomplish a great deal—more than any of them could on their own.

When confronting a problem that seems impossible to handle, an overwhelming sense of fear can sometimes lead to a state of inaction, or worse—in George's case, he was contemplating suicide. And this is where one of the lessons George learned is helpful to us: you don't have to solve every problem—or even any problem—all on your own.

Cooperating, working with others toward a common end or resolution to a problem, is another way to overcome the fear of taking action. Cooperating with others strengthens your resolve to act, because you know there is a web of people who will support and catch you if you fail and fall.

We have seen this over and over again in communities that have recently experienced floods, our own and also those in other parts of the world. Through video footage from the news and social media, we have seen strangers rescuing strangers (both human and animal) from devastating floodwaters. People cooperatively formed human chains to reach a stranded person or dog in waters that would sweep an individual away. As each new person joins the chain to help, two or three more run to be part of it. It's as if you're watching dominoes in reverse; as one person stands up to help, so does another, then another and then another, over and over again. By cooperating with each other, they emboldened each other.

If you've been part of some type of team, from high-school sports to military service, then you know how being in a cooperative environment can motivate you. It's as if being part of a team generates its own kinetic energy for acting. Cooperation fosters action.

Cooperation can be spontaneous and flexible or formally organized. One of the most amazing spontaneous acts of cooperation that my family and I witnessed was when three women in the city of Tartu, Estonia, came to the rescue of another woman whom they did not know. As we were walking along one of the city's main streets in the middle of the afternoon, a young woman came running out of a side street about fifty yards ahead of us screaming "Get away" in Russian to a man chasing after her. Before another gentleman and I were able to help the woman out, three Estonian women immediately turned around and locked arms with the woman to protect her from the man coming at her. The man was so stunned that he stopped about five yards away. One of the women said, "There is a policeman up ahead, and we are walking her to him." The three Estonian women consoled the other woman as they walked safely to the policeman. When I think of cooperation, I think of that incident. Alone they would have had a difficult time being able to stop the man, but together they were emboldened in their resolve to stand up to him and take the woman to safety.

Cooperating with others helps you to stand up to problems that may be too big or difficult to solve on your own. The two basic forms of cooperation are *collaboration* and *coordination*.

Collaboration

Collaboration involves jointly planning and deeply comanaging a course of action. It's not a casual undertaking, but one that requires a commitment of time and resources from each individual participating. Collaboration requires a high level of interdependent action as well as continual communication and constant monitoring among the participants to plan and execute an agreed-upon strategy.

Collaborating is most necessary when dealing with an active issue or problem, such as a person (a bully on the playground, a disparaging boss in the office, a brutal dictator of a country) or a situation (a drought-ravaged community, a dangerous refugee camp). Correcting the individual or helping the situation requires a strong unified response. It took the collaborative effort of the Allied powers to stop Adolf Hitler. It took the collaborative efforts of several academic departments to stop an arrogant administrator from accumulating power that would have been detrimental to the entire institution. It took the courage of one of my boys and his friends to stop a bully. The story of the Underground Railroad in helping enslaved people to freedom was all about collaboration. From the Humane Society, which protects animals against cruelty, to the American Red Cross, which helps people overcome disasters, collaboration has been an important method for effective problem solving. One of the most inspirational stories of addressing a current horrifying problem that demands collaboration is Love146.

Love146, based in New Haven, Connecticut, has one goal: the complete abolition of child trafficking and exploitation around the world. The organization was founded by a "couple of musician friends" who wanted to do something as "regular people" to stop one of the "most severe human rights abuses imaginable." The name comes from a young girl the founders of the group saw when they voluntarily took part in an undercover government operation to close down a brothel involved in the sexual exploitation of children. The young girl had no name, just a number: 146.

In a 2016 interview about Love146's efforts, president and cofounder Rob Morris said that their expertise on the issue at the founding of the organization was next to nothing; it was based only on what they had "heard about child trafficking." Morris says, "My expertise is knowing what I don't know," and that is why he "brings in" or collaborates with specialists from all angles and areas of the problem. One of Love146's core values in stopping child trafficking is collaboration: "We collaborate. We don't reinvent the wheel. Instead, we ask, 'How can we be helpful?' As specialists, we are more effective when we collaborate with other specialists. We are stronger together."

From playgrounds to battlegrounds, collaboration is one of the most effective ways of addressing problems. Another way is through coordination.

Coordination

If collaboration is used to counter an active problem or situation, coordination is about prevention. Coordination is the synchronization of individual actions so that they complement each other in achieving your goal. Instead of deeply comanaging interdependencies as you would in collaboration, you synchronize individual actions so that they create constructive interrelationships. Coordination is about maintaining low levels of interdependence with intermittent communication simply to ensure that everyone is doing their part to avert apathy.

In international politics, coordination is used to address "dilemmas of common aversion," such as preventing pollution. The most widely used example of successful coordination in international environmental politics is the Montreal Protocol, which was established to protect against depletion of the ozone layer. It is the only environmental treaty that has been universally ratified by all countries, and it has been used to eliminate the use of almost one hundred environmentally dangerous gases throughout the world. Signed in 1987, with enforcement starting in 1989, the Montreal Protocol is the reason why ozone-depleting compounds have decreased steadily since 1994, helping the ozone layer to become healthier each year. Each country is responsible for enforcing the protocol and accumulating its own data, thereby creating a coordinated system of environmental protection: the world's countries have successfully synchronized their policies to reconstruct the ozone layer to the benefit of all.

An example of coordination on the regional and national levels has been Flights for Life, which was founded in 1984 to transport blood to secluded rural areas in Arizona to prevent unnecessary deaths. The all-volunteer pilots operate 24 hours, 365 days per year and now fly missions in New Mexico. They coordinate their flights for public hospitals and private individuals. The organization has grown from 4 pilots "who wanted to do more with their airplanes than poke holes in the sky" to nearly 250 aviators who, according to their mission statement, will "assist other volunteer flight organizations in fulfilling similar missions where and when needed, within the United States." Flights for Life is a coordinated life-saving effort to keep the blood flowing in people and places around the country.

Examples abound on the local level and include everything from "neighborhood watches," which seek to prevent and reduce crime, to local volunteer fire departments, which respond not only to fires but also to life-threatening situations such as car accidents, shootings, and drug overdoses. More Americans died of drug overdoses (forty-seven thousand) in 2014 than were killed in car accidents (thirty thousand). With drug addiction on the rise in many communities, the idea that you can simply move away or isolate yourself from it is not a realistic choice. In response, many parents of addicts have decided to take action by cooperating with one another in different ways. The organization Shatterproof takes a coordinated path to curb drug addiction by holding "events to combat stigma and lobbies for legislation to fight addiction." The small and informal network of moms of drug addicts known as Soul Sisters also uses coordination, offering on-demand help to each other via the Web and text messages. Nar-Anon takes a more collaborative approach by providing a highly structured twelve-step program.

Often coordination leads to collaboration. For example, the Women's Center in Fairfield County, Connecticut, recently brought together male leaders from a wide array of organizations within the community (police chiefs, politicians, entrepreneurs, and heads of nonprofits) to create a loose-knit group called "Men Against Domestic and Sexual Violence." Although it is currently a group of men meeting for breakfast about what they can do to prevent and respond to instances of domestic and sexual violence when they occur, the group's name has it already poised to become an organization oriented toward collaboration. The Women's Center facilitated cooperation by creating a negative space, and that simple step is the key for successfully working together.

Fostering Cooperation Through a Negative Space

Pagan Kennedy's book *Inventology* introduced me to the idea of "negative space." Kennedy's book about the process of invention defines a negative space as a "free space where sharing is the norm," or in legal speak a "zone in which people create without seeking a patent for their ideas." Being able to create negative space for people to communicate with each other in a more productive and positive manner is an excellent skill for a compassionate achiever to develop. Establishing a negative space where you and others can safely share ideas encourages cooperation. There are numerous ways to develop negative space between people where pessimism and distrust are reduced and optimism and trust are increased. Here are a few ways:

- *Grant all ideas a fair hearing.* All ideas offered should be considered in an equal manner. If people believe you are giving their ideas short shrift, they are less likely to share ideas in the future.

- *Give credit.* Whoever came up with an idea should be given credit for being its source. When credit is not given where it is due, people are likely to keep their ideas to themselves, and soon all sources of ideas will dry up.

- *Get humble and vulnerable.* Remember that solving the problem is not about you. It's about everyone else: those participating in addressing the problem and those being helped. Admit when you don't know something and own the mistakes you make. No one wants to work with a "know-it-all" or someone who blames others for mistakes.

- *Ask more open than closed questions.* Asking open questions provides a chance for everyone to voice their ideas to the group in a manner in which everyone feels included. They all know that the question is "open-ended." When you ask a lot of closed questions, the one or two word responses can make people feel as though they are being interrogated and limited rather than respected and liberated to speak.

- *Go ABCD.* Go Above and Beyond the Call of Duty to help others in the space. Don't wait for others to ask for your help if they seem confused and stalled. Offer ideas that support others' points of view even if they contrast with yours. If you need to sacrifice your ideas for someone else's so that you all, as a team, develop the most effective solution, sacrifice them (you'll have earned the Purple Heart of negative space).

A well-constructed and well-executed negative space can encourage a wide array of positive ideas that can help you address all types of problems. When you create negative space, you stoke the embers of cooperation and innovation.

Taking action means taking on all fears you may have about solving a problem. From becoming a realistic optimist to developing negative space, there are many paths you can follow to clear any fears that may be inhibiting you from acting. In short, you don't have any excuse not to act. If you think about it, you have to actually find an excuse not to help others. Are you someone who makes excuses or someone who takes action? The next section is focused on helping you strengthen your resilience and sense of responsibility, so that action is your standard reaction.

SKILL 2

Testing Your Mettle:
Strengthening Responsibility and Resilience

But the line dividing good and evil cuts
through the heart of every human being.
—ALEKSANDR SOLZHENITSYN

Your mettle, your ability to persevere in the face of adversity, will be tested by callousness, indifference, and fear. Yet, just as steel is made stronger by fire, your capacity to take action can be made stronger by difficult, challenging times. In order to strengthen metal, it has to be heated. In the processes of tempering and annealing, metal is heated above its recrystallization temperature, generally until it glows. When glowing, the metal's atoms become latticed or woven together to such an extent that the metal, after it is slowly cooled, becomes stronger.

Two traits will help strengthen your mettle: a strong sense of responsibility toward the individual or group you are trying to help and a high level of resilience.

Responsibility

When you feel responsibility toward people, your sense of obligation will strengthen your resolve to help them, even when the going gets tough. Especially so, in fact. When you value responsibility, nothing less than a successful outcome is acceptable. When you honor responsibility, complex conundrums are seen as opportunities to find simple solutions. You know that puzzles are made for one reason: to be solved. Although others may summarily dismiss an escalating problem as impossible to solve, you see it as a chance to summit a mountain believed to be unconquerable. Even if your first attempts fall short, a strong sense of responsibility will haul you back on your feet to try again. A sense of responsibility makes you realize that, although trying is good, it is not good enough.

Research from the medical and educational communities supports the idea that a sense of responsibility is not only important for accomplishing a goal; it strengthens your persistence as well. As one study examining the persistence of working through a painful task, which was published in the *Journal of Behavior Therapy and Experimental Psychiatry,* concluded: a "sense of responsibility . . . increase[s] task persistence." Another study about learning communities found that "students in these programs reported an increased sense of responsibility to participate in the learning experience, and an awareness of their responsibility for both their learning and the learning of others." Being responsible is about being effective in finding solutions that resolve not only your own difficulties, but also those of others.

The founders of Love146 purposely set up the organization to harness the sense of responsibility that most of us (psychopaths excluded) feel toward helping others. Rob Morris, president and cofounder, said in a recent interview: "The name Love146 is our daily reminder that this is not about an issue or a cause, but this is about individual people, and we fight differently for individuals than we do for an issue or a cause." The number, you will remember, was the only "name" a young victim of sexual exploitation had. Love146's approach of focusing on the individual is supported by the research of Scott and Paul Slovic. The Slovics have shown that we are more likely to act when one person needs our help, but "less prone to take appropriate action as the number of lives at stake increases" or the problem seems too amorphous, what the Slovics call "compassion fade."

A person whose sense of responsibility was so strong that he avoided "compassion fade" and never gave up on helping others is Abdul Sattar Edhi, someone I consider a model of compassionate achievement. Edhi, a prominent Pakistani philanthropist and humanitarian who died in July 2016, created the Edhi Foundation over sixty years ago to aid the poor and destitute of Pakistan. The foundation has "rescued over 20,000 abandoned infants, rehabilitated over 50,000 orphans and trained over 40,000 nurses." Edhi was committed to helping all of humanity regardless of religion, caste, or sect and faced religious and political harassment and persecution as a result. Yet his resolve never wavered. He was fond of saying, "My religion is humanitarianism, which is the basis of every religion in the world." Edhi believed that all human beings are sacred and that their sacredness is not determined by any ethnic or class designation.

Because life is sacred, it results in responsibility. Every life is sacred, and so every life is responsible to every other. I define the sacred as that which is unassailable, inviolable, intrinsically important, and "entitled to the highest respect or reverence." The fields of philosophy and theology are home to important literature and debates about sacredness (see the works of and debates between Ronald Dworkin and Michael Perry), but I consider sacredness a quality beyond any religion or subjective interpretation. *Webster's New Universal Unabridged Dictionary* lists six definitions of "sacred," only two of which reference religion; the other four have absolutely nothing to do with it.

Life is sacred no matter whose life it is, for no person is more or less unassailable or inviolable than any other based on ethnicity, class, position or rank, or held beliefs. Sacredness is also beyond the concept of dignity. Sacredness and dignity are not synonymous, because the latter is based on the idea that there is a spectrum of worth or value; the former does not assign any relative value: every life is intrinsically important on an equal level when seen through the concept of sacredness.

This is one reason why I believe that there should be a Universal Declaration of Sacredness or, at the very least, that the current Universal Declaration of Human Rights should replace "dignity" with "sacredness" in the first sentence of its preamble. Humankind has experienced killings on the local level and fought wars on the international level over religious and other perspectives that placed the dignity of one set of believers over that of another set of followers. If every life is sacred, then every life is both inviolable and responsible for every other life. Let me be clear: everyone is sacred, and we all have a responsibility to each other.

The principle of being responsible for each other is one of the basic virtues that our military purposefully teaches its soldiers, and it is something that many veterans struggle with when reentering civilian life. Being responsible for each other becomes habit in the service, but one of the first depressing things they notice when reentering civilian life is how many people don't feel and act that way. Military personnel are taught that the unit is only as strong as its weakest link and to leave no one behind. It's been argued to me, at times, that we should simply "eliminate" the weakest link, and then it would be gone. Putting aside the ethical and moral issues of such an argument (never mind that it completely ignores the concept of sacredness), the logical problem is that there will always be someone who is the weak link relative to everyone else. If you follow the idea of eliminating the weak link, then you will have to "eliminate" everyone eventually. You wouldn't have to worry about the strength of your unit, because you wouldn't have a unit. In each platoon I served with, we looked out for and after each other even if we didn't personally like each other. The same should hold for our local communities and broader society: if we want healthy communities and a strong society, we need to strengthen our sense of responsibility for each other.

John Donne's poetic words "No man is an island" get to the heart of the matter. Researchers from the fields of astrophysics, biology, and quantum physics have provided modern evidence for the truth of Donne's seventeenth-century words. In their thought-provoking book *Living with the Stars*, which weaves together findings in astrophysics, genetics, and pathology, the husband and wife team of Karel and Iris Schrijver conclude: "The story of our bodies is one of impermanence as much as one of connections. . . . [We are] intertwined and interdependent in so many ways that we are continually surprised to see the consequences of our actions ripple through the world around us." The scientific evidence of our interconnectedness is overwhelming and also supported by sociological studies that focus on healthy and weak communities.

People who believe and act as though they are an island weaken the communities in which they live. Robert Putnam's *Bowling Alone* is one of the most widely read books showing how the less interconnected a society is, the weaker it becomes, and his *Making Democracy Work* provides an in-depth case study of how and why interconnections are so important to the vitality of a community. The importance, in a phrase, is "social capital." Interconnected communities generate social capital, which he defines as "features of social organization such as networks, norms and social trust that facilitate coordination and cooperation for mutual benefit." The deeper and wider the interconnections are, the greater the sense of responsibility people have for each other and the stronger their communities become. Social capital has been found to produce many benefits and advantages ranging from providing efficient and effective "material goods and services" to fostering physically and emotionally healthy lifestyles.

One way to think of the difference between highly interconnected and rich social-capital communities and those on the opposite end of the spectrum is to consider the difference between sidewalk and fenced communities. In general, the more fences there are to wall off others, the weaker a community becomes, and, in contrast, the more sidewalks there are to connect with others, the stronger a community becomes. Researchers at places such as the University of Kansas and the University of New Hampshire have found that "higher levels of social capital are found in areas that are perceived to be more walkable, as measured by the number of places people can walk to in their community." In other words, because sidewalks increase walkability, they help people to interact with one another, thereby fostering an increase in social capital, which strengthens the community. Fences close and sidewalks open the flow of interaction between people. Fences don't develop social capital, and they certainly don't improve any sense of community. A community's level of social capital and overall strength are dependent, however, upon the sense of responsibility that each person develops toward others.

Developing Responsibility

Responsibility is a habit that can be developed and broadened to help you take action and initiative toward helping others. Responsibility is a value that can be cultivated on the personal as well as the group level. It's about building an individual and communal sense of obligation to act and follow through on tasks. Some ways of developing responsibility include:

- *Learning and practicing empathy:* Develop negative space where people feel free to express what they think and how they feel. Understanding what people are thinking about an issue is called cognitive empathy and understanding how they feel about it is called affective empathy. When others see you trying to empathize with their situation and perspective, they are more likely to act with you. Simon Baron-Cohen, author of *Zero Degrees of Empathy,* demonstrates that people without empathy have "an inability to get close to other people." Empathy is a connection to others that helps you to act in a way in which everyone feels included.

- *Reducing feelings of competitiveness:* Try to eliminate any competitiveness and aggressiveness you may have toward another when addressing a problem together. An important aspect of developing a sense of responsibility is to generate an awareness of how you may be able to help others and how they may be able to help you take action. If you approach an issue with others from a competitive and aggressive angle, such as "I'm in charge" or "I know more, so follow me," they will likely disconnect from you and any action you propose. Any sense of obligation to take action is diminished the more you approach responsibility as a zero-sum game.

- *Stepping up:* Reducing competitiveness doesn't mean you shouldn't be the first to step up and do something, especially when no one else is saying or doing anything. If no one is saying or doing anything, suggest an idea or take action. When something needs to be done, do you look around for someone else to do it or do you take care of it? Practice being the one who steps up and proposes ideas as well as takes action.

- *Looking forward, not backward:* "Fault is backward looking," according to John Coleman in the *Harvard Business Review,* "and responsibility is forward looking." Don't worry about why you or someone you're trying to help may be in a particular situation; just focus on what needs to be done to address the problem. Any responsibility you have is in front of you and not behind you.

- *Accepting consequences:* When you make mistakes, assume accountability. We all make mistakes and owning them is a way of not ever having to pay for them again. When others see you assuming accountability, they increase their trust in you and trust is the bedrock of broader, coordinated action.

Moving from individual responsibility to a shared sense of responsibility is what makes a community not only civically and physically healthier, but also more innovative.

Sharing Responsibility

The benefits of broadening a sense of responsibility to include other people and groups in addressing a problem are—besides the obvious ones of having others carry some of the load and being able to pick you up if you should fall— that it fosters effective, efficient, and innovative solutions to problems. Recent innovations in delivering health care to people in Maryland and researching cancer treatment in Texas demonstrate the power of sharing responsibility in taking action to alleviate serious problems.

Maryland hospitals provide an example of how sharing responsibility for the health of their constituents through a network of institutions has effectively and innovatively improved care and health across the board. No one hospital could have had as significant an impact as the group has had by sharing the responsibility to keep their communities healthy. The state changed the incentive structure of how hospitals receive payment, so that they now share responsibility with each other and their patients in preventing health crises. The hospitals in Maryland used to, like most hospitals still do across the United States, get paid for the services they provided to patients *after* they walked through their medical doors. The hospitals got paid for services rendered: the more services provided, the more money they could charge. In other words, the more sick people a hospital admitted, the more potential earnings it could reap.

Maryland, however, has flipped the incentive structure so that hospitals seek to do more prevention than treatment of illnesses (don't worry, you still receive high-quality treatment for illnesses if you need it throughout Maryland). Instead, hospitals in Maryland now receive a fixed amount of money annually for patient care regardless of how many tests and procedures they do, and if there is extra money left over at the end of the year, the hospitals get to keep it. Every hospital in Maryland is part of this health-care experiment with first-year results of $100 million in cost savings and slower rates of hospital readmissions than the national average. By sharing responsibility for prioritizing preventative care on a community level, Maryland hospitals have positively impacted both their bottom line and their patients' health.

We've all been impacted directly or indirectly by what cancer can do to a person's health. I lost my mother-in-law to cancer only a few years ago. Cancer researchers around the world are a prime example of how a sense of responsibility can lead to tireless action in attempting to solve a problem. Among other projects, researchers in the field have set up systems such as the Global Alliance for Genomic Health, which seeks to share data and knowledge in an effort to coordinate treatments and possible cures. I will focus on one team of researchers in Texas to highlight the impact of how a sense of responsibility impels action.

A research team at the Houston Methodist Institute of Academic Medicine, led by Mauro Ferrari (and called the "Ferrari Lab"), has developed an innovative approach to stopping metastatic cancer using nanotechnology. Ferrari, who has been trying to develop a cure for cancer for over twenty years, was asked what keeps him going after decades of frustrating work. He simply replied, "It's an ethical responsibility." Like most—if not all—cancer researchers, Ferrari sees his research as more than a job; it has become his mission. Despite numerous disappointments over the years, his and his team's sense of responsibility toward saving lives has helped them to keep focus firmly on trying and trying again to find a cure. It's not pursuit of personal glory that drives Ferrari and his team; it's their commitment to help those with cancer. Their persistence yielded positive results in 2016. The Ferrari Lab developed a solution that completely cured half of the mice with metastatic tumors in their lungs from triple negative breast cancer and extended the lives of the ones that eventually died by four to five human years.

The case of the Ferrari Lab also highlights another benefit of developing a sense of responsibility: it strengthens resilience.

Resilience

Resilience is essential in acting to solve a problem, because you may fail to find a solution to it the first couple of times you try—and trying is not good enough. I cannot imagine doctors and researchers battling cancer doing so without resilience. Resilience is defined by the American Psychological Association as "the process of adapting well in the face of adversity, trauma, tragedy, threats, or even significant sources of stress." Resilience is not the avoidance of emotional, cognitive, and physical problems or difficulties but the ability to confront them in a constructive way. In fact, the more you have endured difficulties, the greater your reservoir of resilience becomes. And it's a reservoir, according to researchers, that we can use as a "fuel" to "drive" our actions. In recent studies of Olympic athletes, psychologists have found "that the experience of overcoming major emotional challenges can sometimes instill extra resilience in young athletes and fuel their exceptional drive." Resilience is a virtue that deepens and strengthens the more you use it.

Resilience is more than recovering or "bouncing back." When you are being resilient, according to Eric Greitens in *Resilience,* "Your objective is to use what hits you to change your trajectory in a positive direction. . . . Resilience is often endurance with direction." When you're resilient, you find ways and paths to overcome your problem, but sometimes you can't return to the person you were before the adversity.

For example, many people consider Scarlett Lewis, a friend of mine and a mother who lost her six-year-old son in the Sandy Hook tragedy, resilient, but she'll be the first to tell you that "you can never 'bounce back' to the person and life you had before losing a child." Scarlett is a model of how to "adapt well in the face of adversity," but her life has taken a new direction, as she's found positive ways to go beyond the tragedy and accomplish goals that will try to help other parents avoid what she had to endure. Through her nonprofit organization called the Jesse Lewis Choose Love Movement, Scarlett promotes and implements social and emotional learning (SEL) curriculum in schools throughout the United States, because she believes that if the shooter had had SEL and had developed the ability to understand and manage emotions and feel empathy, he would not have killed her son and the other children. There is no doubt that Scarlett has changed her trajectory in a hopeful and constructive direction.

Resilience is more hope than optimism. "Hope is the belief that the future will be better than the present," according to psychologists, "and that you have some power to make it so. It differs from optimism, which is the belief that things will work out no matter what you do." There is "strategy" and "agency" in hope, but optimism is mostly based on serendipity and acquiescence. The difference can be explained by using the common adage about how optimists and pessimists see a partially filled glass of water. You've heard it before: while pessimists see the glass as half empty, optimists see the glass as half full. People who are hopeful, in contrast, see a glass that is refillable. Resilience is finding your own agency in times of difficulty and urgency.

Famous examples of resilient people abound. J. K. Rowling's life was in disarray before the success of her Harry Potter book series. Rowling was nearly penniless, on government welfare, a single mom who typed out each version of *Harry Potter and the Philosopher's Stone* to send to publishers, because she couldn't afford photocopying. After the book was rejected dozens of times, one publisher gave it a second look because his eight-year-old daughter couldn't stop reading it. Rowling was unequivocally persistent in finding a way to get her book published and continue her love of writing. Her resilience kept pushing her to act on her hope of a writing career that is now a storybook tale of its own.

Similarly, Stephen King's first book, *Carrie*, was rejected over thirty times before it was published. While King was going through the rejection process, his wife and fellow writer, Tabby, worked a second shift at Dunkin' Donuts; they could barely afford to live in their doublewide trailer. King became so frustrated with trying to write *Carrie* that he threw several pages of it in the trash and was ready to give up on it. The next day Tabby took the pages out of the trash and told him, "You've got something here. I really think you do." King finished *Carrie* nine months later. Tabby's belief in her husband became the source of his resilience, which propelled him to finish the novel. It's not just Olympic athletes and famous writers who can develop resilience. We all have the ability.

Developing Resilience

Many of the skills you've been developing over the course of this book will help you to develop resilience. Prioritizing positivity and reframing failure are abilities that highly resilient people share. Responsibility helps build resilience, because it provides meaning and purpose to your actions. With meaning and purpose, you increase the likelihood that you will continue to pursue your goal, no matter how difficult it becomes. Taking responsibility for your own actions also increases your levels of resilience. By accepting the consequences of the choices you make, you recognize that you are in control of whether you thrive and flourish or break and wither in the face of hardship, failure, and difficulty. Here are some other ways to develop resilience:

- *Mobilize support.* Surround yourself with people who believe in you, are honest with you, and have more experience than you. Every Tuesday I meet with three mentors for lunch at our local diner for what I affectionately call the Wise Men Lunch. My mentors are more experienced teachers and authors who help keep me accountable, inspire me by simply being who they are, and, perhaps most important, help me get through and rise above difficult times. The experiences, ideas, and lessons they share with me, when taken as a whole, are like having an extra guide or playbook for addressing life's problems. Their support makes me feel as though I have an extra advantage in overcoming professional and personal issues.

- *Laugh more.* I laugh more than anything else throughout the Wise Men lunches (I try to rationalize that I don't need to do sit-ups because of all the laughing). One of the most important things that they have taught me is to be able to laugh at myself. When you can laugh about a problem you're in, as Steven and Sybil Wolin outline in their book *The Resilient Self,* it becomes difficult to remain a "victim" of your circumstance. In *The Survivor of Personality,* Al Siebert shows that when people choose to look at an overwhelming situation with humor, it empowers them to overcome it. Siebert explains: "Laughing reduces tension to more moderate levels"; "the person who toys with the situation creates an inner feeling of 'This is my plaything; I am bigger than it. . . . I won't let it scare me.'"

   Viktor Frankl, who survived a concentration camp, experienced first-hand the power of humor to help us "rise above any situation, even if only for a few seconds." Medical research from the University of Maryland and Loma Linda University confirms this, showing how laughter changes the body in ways that help it become resilient (i.e., dilating blood vessels and releasing beta-endorphins). If you want to increase your resilience, laugh more. And Sophie Scott, the deputy director of the University College London's Institute of Cognitive Neuroscience, recommends spending more time with your friends: you are thirty times more likely to laugh with people you know than with those you don't know.

- *Be adaptable.* When I'm down because something hasn't worked out the way I had hoped, I immediately look around for the opportunity that I hadn't considered because I was focused on something else. Resilience is not avoiding getting knocked off course; it's about looking for new directions and paths to follow on your way up from being knocked down.

- *Hammer one nail at a time.* When building a house, carpenters will tell you that they achieve it one nail at a time. When climbing a steep mountain, rock climbers will tell you they summit one spike (or piton) at a time. When you have a large problem or complex situation, focus on one task at a time, and you will increase not only your prospect of overcoming the issue, but also your reservoir of resilience. Judy Willis, a neurologist who works on education issues, has found that "dividing big assignments or jobs into small tasks will give [students] the confidence to get started and the resilience to persevere." In short, establish realistic goals each day and recognize that some goals are unattainable unless you accomplish smaller ones. Focus on hammering home the small accomplishments that move you closer to achieving your ultimate goal.

- *Take the hill and keep going.* My cross-country coach taught us that when we reached the top of a long hill—when you and everyone else who is running want to take a deep breath and slow down—we should go faster and even sprint if we could. Although I thought I was going to suffocate the first time I did it, it not only became easier to do every time I did it, but also made me run faster on other parts of the course. I remembered thinking that if I could run faster at the top of hill, I could run even faster during the flat parts of the trail. I've taken that perspective and applied it to the rest of my life. When you feel as though you can't go on, know that you can go faster and farther than you thought.

- *Find the intrinsic value in what you do.* Focus on what intrinsically motivates you to accomplish your goals and overcome obstacles. When you follow an intrinsic purpose in anything you do in life, you achieve your goals more effectively than if you followed any extrinsic motivations. I mentioned the 2014 study of more than eleven thousand West Point cadets earlier, but it's worth repeating the authors' conclusion: "Helping people focus on the meaning and impact of their work, rather than on, say, the financial returns it will bring, may be the best way to improve not only the quality of their work but also—counterintuitive though it may seem—their financial success."

  Prioritizing intrinsic values and having a sense of purpose has also been found to be an important factor in helping people overcome trauma.

In a 2008 study of trauma victims, one of the researchers said, "We found that the most important psychosocial factor associated with resilience or recovered status was a sense of higher purpose in life." Laurie Ahern, the president of Disability Rights International, uses the "wish" she had as an abused child to be "rescued" as her motivation to help children with disabilities around the world. Discover your sense of purpose and follow your intrinsic motivations, and you will deepen your reservoir of resilience.

Building a sense of responsibility and strengthening your resilience help you to not only take action, but also sustain it. Honoring responsibility and practicing resilience help you live a life, no matter its length, filled with intrinsic meaning and practical effectiveness. It's a life where intentions are necessary but never satisfactory because results, solutions, and achievements are what ultimately matter. Seneca, a first-century Roman philosopher, statesman, and dramatist, tells us of his nighttime practice of reviewing his actions each day, beginning with questions: "What evils have you cured yourself of today? What vices have you fought? In what sense are you better? . . . When the torch has been taken away and my wife [is asleep], I examine my entire day and measure what I have done and said. I hide nothing from myself." Seneca's advice is basically to take the time to self-reflect. The importance of taking the time to reflect is what we turn our focus to next.

SKILL 3

Just Sit There: The Power of Nondoing

The way to do is to be.

—LAO TZU

How do you help a large group of people stand up for themselves and feel empowered? You create the space for them to sit. Leymah Gbowee, the Nobel Peace Prize–winning leader of the women's peace movement in Liberia that ended the Second Liberian Civil War, knows firsthand that creating a space for girls with "no hope or seemingly no hope" is just as important as direct action. Providing girls in rural communities with the space to sit together allowed them the opportunity to interact, communicate, and reflect in powerful new ways that yielded many possible solutions to the problems they were facing and sparked the desire and determination to realize them. According to Gbowee, "When these girls sit, you unlock intelligence, you unlock passion, you unlock commitment, you unlock focus, you unlock great leaders." Tremendous change is the result. This is the power of nondoing.

Nondoing functions like an internal mirror, helping you to see who you are and can become, what you have done, and what you may do next. Because some people have yet to acknowledge the presence of their internal mirror or have not taken the time to look at it, they don't understand how strong they really are or can be. It's crucial for you to be able to access your own internal mirror and to help others do so as well, so that they can, in Gbowee's words, "unlock all of the great things that they hold within themselves." When people become "unlocked," they are free from their own limitations to act.

Consider, for a moment, how physical mirrors are used around the world for accomplishing various tasks, and you'll see the potential that our internal mirrors have for finding and solving problems. Mirrors are used not only for people to look at themselves but also to generate power (solar energy is generated this way) as well as shine and direct light in the middle of darkness (i.e., flashlights, searchlights, floodlights, and spotlights). Mirrors are also used to measure distance between two points: Apollo 11 left a mirror on the moon so that we could measure its distance from earth. In addition, they are used to expose blind spots (i.e., curved mirrors on vehicles), communicate (i.e., used to flash sunlight when hiking), and increase clarity (i.e., they are used in high-end televisions to improve pixels). Our internal mirrors have the potential to help us do many of the same things: unlock internal strength such as the will to act (generate power), foster resilience in our darkest times, take measure of our character, expose personal weaknesses, improve our intra- and interpersonal communication skills, and help us see ourselves and the world more clearly.

Contrary to what the term "nondoing" might imply, you are not being idle. The act of nondoing is *not* the same as doing nothing. It is an intentional act and requires as much effort, discipline, and practice as any other. Actually, being introspective is one of the highest forms of action.

Think of what happens when you look into the mirror in your bathroom. Although you may be still when looking into it, are you really doing nothing? Aren't you learning something about who you are on the outside? And when you see something you don't like, such as your hair, don't you take action to change it?

Taking the time to sit, as Gbowee advises, is an act of nondoing that enables you to gain a better sense of your strengths and weaknesses, so that you can improve and strengthen your overall character. Your internal mirror shows what you are like, and only you can see what is reflected. Are not taking measure and trying to improve ourselves some of the highest forms of action we can undertake? Reflecting will also help you acquire a clear-eyed perspective on any situation you may find yourself in. Sometimes the best course of action is simply to be, so that you are prepared to take action.

Practicing Nondoing

When I think of nondoing, I think of another of Seneca's often recited passages: "Luck is what happens when preparation meets opportunity." The luck that Seneca is talking about is not the type of luck that just happens to you. The same is true of nondoing; it doesn't just occur spontaneously or effortlessly. The most effective practitioners of nondoing know that there is a lot of work that transpires before luck happens or the act of nondoing occurs.

- *Prepare to see with clarity.* Astronomy is one of my favorite hobbies, and I've been asked many times, "How do you just sit there and watch the sky?" As a very amateur astronomer, I get excited about the "chase," the process of trying to find a celestial object in the night sky through my lens. From acquiring weather reports, to researching the alignment of stars and planets on a given night, to calibrating the settings of my telescope, I enjoy the work that goes into being able to "just sit there." The difference between the act of nondoing and doing nothing is that the people who do the work of perfectly aligning their telescope to see specific constellations and planets will most likely acquire greater understanding and appreciation of the night sky than those who did nothing to prepare themselves to sit there. Who do you think will find more awe in the experience, and who do you think will find more frustration? You can probably guess which of the two will have more focus and resilience when confronted with mosquitoes. The act of nondoing includes prepping yourself so that you can just be in the moment and with the universe.

• *Move past doing nothing.* One of my sons got off the school bus and immediately began tearing up. He said, "Dad, a mean kid called me a wimp at recess, and his friends laughed." As we walked home from the bus stop, he told me the entire wimp story and then asked what he should do when something like that happens. He explained that he'd done nothing and was afraid that the kid would do it again.

My son is the farthest thing from a boxer, but he has a warrior's spirit. He is a kid who brought a piece of chalk to school so that he could draw a "compassion circle" on the blacktop at recess, so that anyone who needed a hug to feel better could get one. He will stand up for what he believes is right and use his dry sense of humor and love of anything bookish to make his stand, or circle, as the case may be. Since he had been studying outer space in school and at home over the last few weeks, I asked him to think about (or reflect on) our discussion on dark matter a few days before. His eyes lit up, and he said "Oh yeah . . . WIMP!"

WIMP, in cosmology, stands for a "weakly interacting massive particle," and many theorists believe that it is the glue that keeps the universe together. After we talked about the science, he said, "I have an idea for when that kid calls me a wimp again. I'll just say thank you for calling me a weakly interacting massive particle and for thinking of me as the glue that keeps our universe together." The short story is that the kid from recess did call him a wimp again that same week, and my son said his thanks. It was a different scene getting off the bus that day when my son said, "The mean kid didn't know what to do and just walked away!" I guess you can call my son's WIMP response an updated or cosmological version of the "I am rubber and you are glue" saying.

My son needed a little help to move past his initial reaction to do nothing in response to the bully, but once I encouraged him, he was enthusiastic about the act of nondoing. By taking the time to reflect, he found an answer to his own question. Nondoing can provide you with new and constructive methods of interacting with all types of people.

• *Stay seated.* Have you ever just wanted to get up from a discussion or click off the television or radio when a person you are listening to is saying something that is the polar opposite of what you believe? It's as though you and the other person are magnetic poles repelling each other. The act of nondoing requires that you stay with the discussion or program.

Listening to someone you disagree with provides an opportunity to expose and therefore learn from your own blind spots on a subject. If you listen with compassion instead of contempt to your critics, you increase wisdom rather than wrath. When you listen, you have the opportunity to learn something new.

When I initially presented some of my ideas about compassion's power in success and achievement, it was my critics who pointed out that Darwinism made my argument weak: it was, in their way of thinking, the "Jenga piece" in my "faulty tower of compassion." I quickly acquired as many of Charles Darwin's works as possible and carefully read through them searching for the Jenga pieces that could take down my argument. Instead, I found that most of Charles Darwin's work, especially *The Descent of Man* (chapters 2, 4, and 5), not only supports the general argument of this book; it doesn't support the idea of what most call Darwinism. Darwin's research shows that "survival of the kindest" is more correct for explaining which species climb the evolutionary ladder efficiently and effectively. If I hadn't taken the time to listen to my strongest critics, I would most likely not have discovered some of the strongest ideas supporting the connection between compassion and success. Those who oppose your ideas can make you stronger, just as magnetic opposites create a much stronger bond and whole than poles that are alike. Critics can be some of your best teachers, if you're willing to let go of defensiveness and embrace nondoing.

• *Use your emotions.* Great musicians know that playing music exceptionally well is about more than being technically proficient. It's essential to emotionally connect with the music. Good music goes beyond technical ability. When you only focus on the technical aspects of playing, the music sounds very robotic and mechanical. When you let go of technique and rely on your preparation and practice, you allow yourself to be with the music instead of "working at it." You need to be able to play the music the way you feel it, so everyone listening can feel it too. Playing jazz made me a better musician, because it helped me learn how to go with the music that was happening in the moment; it helped free me from my fear of not being perfect in a performance, which ironically made me a better performer.

Charlie "Yardbird" Parker, one of the most influential jazz musicians of all time, talked about overcoming the fear of just being with the sound: "Don't be afraid, just play the music." A musician at almost any level knows that playing your instrument with others definitely creates a whole greater than the sum of its parts. And the same principle applies here as well: not focusing on doing the technical side of playing an instrument creates a fuller experience with the music, because it allows the sounds to blend. Great performances consist of harmony in both people and sound. Musicians become musical artists when they allow themselves to overcome their technical fears and embrace the emotion of their music.

Emotions are equally important when practicing nondoing. Your rational mind has a role to play in reflection, but so do your emotions. Uncorking your emotions and recognizing how you feel, whether it is anger, frustration, or hopefulness, will provide you with valuable insight into the situation and why and how you should act. Don't wallow in your emotions or become stuck in them. Reflecting in a steady state of anger is never going to lead to a constructive solution. But acknowledging what you're feeling and using that knowledge to direct your examination of an obstacle or exploration of possible solutions will help you to "play the music" of nondoing better.

- *Wander.* To wander is to bring light into an unknown place. In today's society, where focus and efficiency are priorities, there is much that we overlook or bypass on the way to accomplishing whatever goal is foremost on our personal and professional lists. We've created many unknown places both in our communities and in our own minds. They are places discovered only by those of us who wander.

  Wandering, according to Keri Smith in her wildly entertaining book *The Wander Society,* is "the act of unplanned, aimless walking/exploring/ ambling with a complete openness to the unknown. Wandering is not about a specific place or destination . . . or movement as a means to an end. Instead, it's about letting the soul and mind roam." You can be a "sitting wanderer": although your body is serenely still (doing nothing), your mind is passionately roaming (the act of nondoing). "The stationary wanderer," in Smith's words, "can observe, be present, pay attention, and be open to the unknown—all while remaining still."

The neuroscience and practical benefits of wandering are well documented and commonly experienced, as anyone who has come up with an idea in the shower can attest to. Neuroscientists have found that mind wandering is generated in the brain's dorsolateral prefrontal cortex (dlPFC), which is "the last brain region that you would expect to get involved with something as frivolous as mind wandering," according to Robert Sapolsky, "because it's a relatively recently evolved brain region, central to executive functions like long-term planning, working memory, and decision making." One reason, Sapolsky and others suggest, for why mind wandering is generated from that area is that it is important for working through multiple scenarios and solutions to a problem. As Scott Barry Kaufman and Carolyn Gregoire demonstrate in *Wired to Create*, "Idle though it may seem, the act of mind wandering is often anything but mindless."

Because wandering is about losing yourself so that you can find direction or discover answers, it—like all forms of nondoing—emphasizes effectiveness over efficiency. Wandering is an indirect route toward being effective, and there are many ways to jump-start it, from meditating to hiking. I cleared a meandering trail through my back woods, which my family calls the Pondering Path, for the purpose of clearing my mind so it can wander. When I lived in Boston, I always found a paved pondering path to help me find lost thoughts and ideas. I would wander the city at night, absorbing its energy in the hope of shedding light on a solution to a problem. The idea of being lost, when you practice nondoing, becomes less disorienting and more exciting, because you see it as a passport to wander into new worlds of wonder. As Henry David Thoreau said, "The only people who ever get anyplace interesting are the people who get lost." Wandering is purposely getting lost so that you accidently find what you were looking for.

- *Be patient.* Many of us tend to be impatient when something doesn't happen right away. We become frustrated and annoyed, ultimately sabotaging our efforts. The people who are the most effective at nondoing have learned that answers don't always reveal themselves immediately, and understanding often isn't instantaneous. They have learned to wait.

The Hardest Part: Holding Back

My definition of nondoing focuses on it as an act of reflection, but there are many interpretations. For example, the act of nondoing, *wu-wei* in Chinese, is a central concept of Taoism: "The Tao does nothing, yet leaves nothing undone." It involves knowing when to act and when it is better not to act. Think of trying to grow a plant from a seed. You plant a seed, fertilize and water it, and see that, once it sprouts, it has plenty of light. But if you do too much watering or fertilizing or alter its light cycle, it dies. To grow a healthy plant, you need to know when to leave it alone.

Some of the most difficult times in life are when we have to hold ourselves back from doing something. To help my sons build resilience, my employees improve leadership skills, and my students develop inquisitiveness and risk taking, I know it is best for me to hold back in certain situations and do nothing. But it's hard! Probably *the* hardest part of helping others (Tom Petty was right on so many levels). It is especially hard when it means letting one of my children struggle through a difficult situation in order to help him in the long run.

Although I tried to prepare one of my sons for some problems he might face at school for a medical issue he was overcoming, I knew that if I tried to talk to his classes before he went back to school I could possibly make his transition worse. Some of his peers had already started making fun of the way he was breathing when they heard him around town. I wanted to "set the table" at school to shield him from ridicule by telling his classmates what was going on, but I also recognized that there was something bigger at stake than the immediate problem with his peers, and that was the opportunity to build self-confidence, responsibility, and resilience himself. I held myself back, and my son took it upon himself to handle the situation. He asked his teachers if he could explain his medical condition to his classmates and used a couple of Darth Vader jokes to explain his unique breathing sounds (the ridicule disappeared). Holding back may, at times, make you feel as though you are not doing your job (for example, being a good father in this instance), but many more times than not it helps others grow in ways that make you feel proud and lucky to be with them.

You can structure work and learning environments to help you be better able to hold yourself back, so that others can move forward in their thinking and career. At work, I see myself as the bow that gets pulled back and my employees as the arrows that are launched forward. When it comes to hitting your targets at work, it's all about the quality of arrows in your quiver. The key for structuring work so that, as you pull back on doing things, your employees can move forward in their careers is to hire people who are "intrinsically motivated giants." David Ogilvy, former CEO of Ogilvy & Mather, warned, "If each of us hires people who are smaller than we are, we shall become a company of dwarfs. But if each of us hires people who are bigger than we are, we shall become a company of giants."

When I think of Ogilvy's idea, I think of the importance of surrounding yourself with people who are not only highly skilled but motivated by ideas and values that cannot be exhausted: intrinsic values. Intrinsically motivated people, for example, do their job or pursue their education for its own sake and not for money or other reward. It becomes easier to hold yourself back when you have intrinsically motivated giants walking around the office. Once you get the giants walking, get out of the way.

Achieving success sometimes demands that you just sit: sit and reflect upon your actions, feelings, and thoughts. The act of nondoing can be the step you need to take in order to come up with creative and innovative solutions to problems. It's a way to turn the arguments of your greatest critics into some of the most important ideas that guide your thoughts and actions. It's a state of being that helps you to more fully understand who you are (for example, a wimp, or a weakly interacting massive particle), so you can find innovative solutions hidden within you to problems and issues all around you. Nondoing is the key that "unlocks" the limitations you place on yourself to act. Free yourself by embracing nondoing.

PART THREE

THE RIPPLE EFFECT

7

Conquest of the Common Virtue

Give light, and the darkness will disappear of itself.
—DESIDERIUS ERASMUS

One compassionate achiever is all it takes to start spreading the ripples of success through a community. It begins with you and how you interact with people on a daily basis. All of your personal interactions are like small stones of compassion dropped into a pond, creating ripples that reach far beyond you.

Approach each day with a compassionate mindset and take actions to reinforce your commitment. Start the day with a simple ten-minute meditation. Sign the Charter for Compassion so that your thoughts become the words you live by. Volunteer at a food pantry or charitable organization.

As you make compassionate actions a priority in your life, compassion will become a habit. Helping others at work, taking the time to listen, and remembering to say thank you will become effortless.

Compassion is contagious. Your acts of compassion will make others more likely to act with compassion. In *Hive Mind*, Garrett Jones shows how compassion spreads among neighbors, an idea he calls the "imitation channel." According to Jones, "If you have cooperative, patient, well-informed neighbors, that probably makes you a bit more cooperative, patient, and well-informed." It's up to you to start whatever imitation channel you want in your community. Why not create a hive of compassion?

Local Interactions

Compassion should be our compass when navigating local political and civic interactions. One of the reasons I became involved in helping communities become towns and cities of compassion through the Charter for Compassion

was that I've seen too many people disrespect each other and their differences at town meetings and other functions, to the detriment of their community. One step in changing the tone and tenor of town dialogue so that it
is more constructive is to help your town begin the process of becoming a
town of compassion.

We are fortunate in my town, Brookfield, Connecticut, to be home to
citizens who have started several compassion-focused civic and nonprofit
organizations. These include the Compassion Group, which meets the first
Monday of every month to discuss a wide range of compassion ideas, from
metaphysics to self-help, and Brookfield Cares, which focuses on addressing
mental health and addiction issues. These groups and many more bring local
citizens together in an effort to address community concerns and are laying
the groundwork for Brookfield to become a town of compassion.

Introducing young people to compassion initiatives is like watching children ride a bicycle for the first time without crashing. They are excited to
take off, but also seem to recognize something deeper: that the balance and
speed to ride was within them the entire time.

My university, Western Connecticut State University (WCSU), has not
only a Creativity and Compassion Club, where students have addressed homelessness and abuse issues, but a book club, begun by the students, for the purpose of discussing compassionate action within the broader academic and
wider civic communities. What was supposed to be an experiment in developing leadership qualities in WCSU students has turned into a regional and
national model program called the Leadership, Compassion and Creativity
Certificate (LCCC) program. The first three purposes of LCCC are to:

**Establish a community of learners working together to better not
only themselves, but also one another;**

**Encourage leadership as a process through which people work
together to create a positive impact; and**

**Gain the skills to serve others in this community and the global
world, specifically increasing students' civic engagement.**

The LCCC participants recognize the importance of respect and civility in
every interaction because they understand how it strengthens their organizations and communities. They are tomorrow's leaders (as opposed to bosses)
in business, education, and politics while already being today's compassionate achievers in their local communities.

National Interactions

A country led by compassionate achievers would collaborate, coordinate, and cooperate its way to political, economic, and civic success. Every country, just like every person and organization, has its weaknesses and strengths, but by walking with compassion, a country can avoid repeating historic mistakes while simultaneously strengthening its current society.

There have been too many times in American history, for example, where leaders have taken the do-nothing attitude of allowing legality to perpetuate social injustice, of overlooking suffering simply because the actions that caused the suffering were considered legal. The argument they make is that because the action is legal, they have no obligation to address the suffering that is caused by the action. Legal actions, of which slavery is one of the most egregious examples, have caused suffering in every country. Although slavery was legal in the United States, it was morally and ethically wrong; justice loses out to law in such cases. Compassionate achievers, in contrast, make their countries stronger by continuously attempting to align justice and the law, thereby also helping their country to avoid hypocrisy, especially when it comes to human rights.

From the human right to clean water to the rights of the LGBT (lesbian, gay, bisexual, and transgender) community, legal policies are still perpetuating injustice. Compassionate achievers are the people striving to make clean water a basic human right (even though people die in seven days without water, it is not considered a human right in most developed countries, including the United States), and they are the citizens and organizations standing up to governments that have legalized LGBT discrimination. Compassionate achievers eternally embrace justice even when the law deserts or forsakes it.

Compassionate achievers live the meaning of English diplomat James Bryce's patriotism: "Patriotism consists not in waving a flag, but in striving that our country shall be righteous as well as strong. . . . Our country is not the only thing to which we owe our allegiance. It is also owed to justice and to humanity." Compassion turns our daily pledge of allegiance, "with liberty and justice for all," into actions that benefit all people and strengthen our country.

Global Interactions

Physicists have long proven that we are all interconnected. The policies and actions of the world's 193 countries, however, have yet to catch up to the science of interdependence. We seem to acknowledge our interconnected-ness in fits and starts with international treaties such as the United Nations Declaration of Human Rights and the Mine Ban Treaty, but we have not concluded a legally binding document that enforces clean water as a human right. Although there are many global problems that can seem overwhelm-ing, such as climate change and immigration, taking one compassionate step on the local level can begin to affect change on the international level. Leo Tolstoy points the paradoxical way toward constructively affecting the global community: "Everyone thinks of changing the world, but no one thinks of changing himself." Becoming a compassionate achiever is the first step toward creating a compassionate world.

One act, even one push of a button, can make a positive difference in a world where the scale and number of problems can become overwhelming. In one of the most important books about the effect of data on emotions, meaning, and action, *Numbers and Nerves*, Scott and Paul Slovic explain how we become "psychophysically numb" or "fall prey to *compassion fade*, actually becoming less concerned and less prone to take appropriate action as the number of lives at stake increases" (emphasis in original). They bor-row the poet Zbigniew Herbert's phrase "the arithmetic of compassion" to demonstrate the ways that numerically or quantitatively large problems can overwhelm "our human-scale sensory apparatus and cognitive processes." Immigration provides a case in point for both numbness and compassion fade.

As immigration issues have become more intense over the last few years around the world, some have become not only numb, but hardened to the plight of today's immigrants. Politicians call for creating special immigrant IDs, modeling World War II internment camps, and building "big and beau-tiful" walls. A picture snapped by one photographer, however, generated a wave of civic compassion throughout the Western world. The image was of three-year-old Alan (Aylan) Kurdi's lifeless body, which washed ashore on the Turkish coast in September 2015. His drowning was part of the Syrian refugee crisis, and the picture partially reversed compassion fade about immigrants and refugees in a significant way.

Not only did the picture of his death make the refugee/immigrant issue an important part of the 2015 Canadian federal election (half a world away, where his father unsuccessfully applied for Canadian refugee status just three months before the drowning), but it also caused thousands of citizens located on the European front lines of the crisis to rise up and help refugees despite their government's law prohibiting such help. Risking jail time for simply being a good Samaritan by driving refugees from Hungary to safety in Austria, one volunteer, Hans Breuer, explained that his mission was personal and worth the risk: "My father was a refugee seventy years ago. Half of his family was killed by the Nazis. Today the Nazis are the Islamic State, and the Jews are the Syrians running away. . . . It's the same situation. A lot of what we see here reminds us of those years."

When the laws of some countries abandoned justice for the Syrian refugees, Breuer and thousands of others quite literally drove up to give it to them and to take them to safety. As the Slovics highlight in their explanation of ways to overcome compassion fade in *Numbers and Nerves*, "Stories and images have the power to help us understand large, complex problems that we cannot comprehend through quantitative information alone." The picture of little Alan Kurdi made more people around the world understand the importance of addressing the complex problem of immigration than any statistics could.

Although some may minimize and even criticize as naive the thought that what you do on the personal and local levels can have a global effect, many of the people we consider heroes believed otherwise. Mother Teresa echoed what many compassionate achievers have voiced: "I alone cannot change the world, but I can cast a stone across the waters to create many ripples." If we are willing to walk life's roads as compassionate achievers, we all can make real-world ripples that bring out the best of humanity.

Tree Rings

I knew of the World Wide Web, but I definitely did not know of the "Wood Wide Web" until I read Peter Wohlleben's work. Wohlleben, a career forest ranger and author of *The Hidden Life of Trees*, eloquently explains the interconnectedness of trees, including how they are able to communicate and share nutrients. Trees, similar to us, are social beings, and their level of interdependence or network strength determines their individual vitality. The less connected a trees is, the weaker that individual tree becomes. As some naturalists argue, "creating too much space between trees can disconnect them from their networks, stymieing some of their inborn resilience mechanisms." We need to pay mind to the spaces and walls that disconnect for they are the gaps that weaken us as individuals and as communities.

Robert Frost wrote the line "Good fences make good neighbors" in the poem *"Mending Wall"* not as a symbol of division and disconnect, but of unity and togetherness. Frost's stone wall separates his apple trees from his neighbor's pine trees; the two neighbors come together each year to repair the wall, which is in fact not really needed. It's a story about reconnecting and improving ties with your neighbor. The only walls that should be built, if we take Frost at his word, are walls that help mend connections between people. Fences or walls are only good if they make people better connected and more understanding of each other; this is very different from the mistaken idea that a good neighbor is one you don't see and interact with because of a "big and beautiful" wall.

Every person has a story to tell, but so does every tree. The stories of trees, including Frost's apple and pine, can be read very clearly through their rings. Dendrochronology, the study of reading tree rings, can reveal very specific details: how old a tree is, whether it experienced fire or pest damage, and what the specific weather conditions were during precise periods in its life. A year filled with rain, for example, produces a wide ring, but drought creates a narrow band.

When I read that disconnections caused some of the trees' "inborn resilience mechanisms" to fail, resulting in their downfall, I couldn't help but think of Will Durant's quote about how "a great civilization is destroyed from within." Compassion is the "inborn resilience" of every person, and that resilience is the root source of communal strength. A lack of compassion results in societal weakness or, in Durant's terms, destruction of civilization from within.

When your time is at its end, what will your life's tree rings say about you? Will they say that your life was filled with compassion or will they simply show nothing but self-absorption? Choosing compassion is to follow the natural instinct that helped humanity survive and thrive.

The Modern Spartacus

To do more for the world than the world
does for you—that is success.
—HENRY FORD

"I am Spartacus" is one of the most unforgettable and powerful lines in all of cinema history. Those three simple words represent hope, resilience, and struggle in overcoming all odds to achieve success. The phrase epitomizes loyalty in every sense of the word, even in and perhaps especially in dire circumstances. Spartacus's name has echoed throughout history since the first century BC, when he, as a slave gladiator, organized and led a slave army that defeated waves of Roman imperial legions in nine successive battles over two years. Spartacus was defeated in the tenth battle, when he was betrayed by pirates and his army became trapped and cornered. This battle made his name known around the world and throughout time not for what he did, but for what his men did for him. When the Roman leader who had surrounded the slave army asked for the identity of Spartacus in exchange for their lives, not one of his soldiers gave Spartacus away. In the movie version's ending, when Spartacus stands up, willing to give himself up to spare his men, all six thousand rise up and proudly exclaim, "I am Spartacus." In the film as in real life, they are crucified for remaining loyal to their leader and the cause of freedom.

The Romans had experienced two other slave rebellions before the one led by Spartacus and easily handled them. This rebellion was different. The Roman Republic quickly lost control of the situation and even the fortified walls surrounding their cities, for which they were famous, couldn't protect them. Spartacus overcame many Roman walls, from the wall of oppression that forced him to be a gladiator to becoming the first military commander to breach the supposed impregnable Roman tactical fortifications in Rhegium,

Italy. There wasn't a Roman wall—psychological, physical, or even historical—that Spartacus seemingly couldn't overcome and it shook the mightiest republic in the world to its very core.

LUCA's Followers

Where the followers of Spartacus overcame all types of Roman walls through violence, compassionate achievers who follow LUCA—

Listening to learn

Understanding to know

Connecting to capabilities

Acting to solve

—overcome all types of walls in life through kindness. And if walls are constructed, compassionate achievers abide by Robert Frost's advice and use them to mend ties, not to divide people. The followers of LUCA understand not only Frost's words about the meaning of a wall, but also Darwin's research into how evolutionary success is achieved: through compassion in words and actions.

LUCA's followers see Darwin's "evolutionary logic," for instance, in the idea of what it truly means to be an alpha male. As Carl Safina points out, the "alpha male stereotype" of a man "who is snarling and aggressive . . . comes from a *misunderstanding* of the real thing" (emphasis mine). The idea of an alpha male originated from the study of wolves, but the researchers who study them describe the animals as compassionate achievers rather than aggressive competitors. Rick McIntyre, a twenty-year veteran researcher of Yellowstone wolves, says:

> The main characteristic of an alpha male wolf is a quiet confidence, quiet self-assurance. You know what you need to do; you know what's best for your pack. You lead by example. You're very comfortable with that. You have a calming effect. Think of an emotionally secure man, or a great champion. Whatever he needed to prove is already proven. . . . Imagine two wolf packs, or two human tribes. Which is more likely to survive and reproduce? The one whose members are more cooperative, more sharing, less violent with one another; or the group whose members are beating each other up and competing with one another?

An alpha male is not what we incorrectly stereotype him to be: a merciless leader of the pack whose power is based on bravado and brawn. Rather, he is a role model of building strength through kindness.

Real alpha males and females (matriarchs make most of the decisions in wolf packs) are compassionate achievers. They are people who have untangled the misconceptions about attaining power, strength, and influence to reveal paths for achieving success that follow virtue. Compassionate achievers challenge the notion that you have to look out for number one in order to be number one.

The Doubters: Misunderstanding "One," "Won," and "Own"

The idea of being number one, for most people, means having won something that makes you stand alone on top of whatever proverbial mountain you climbed. Being number one, I think we all can agree, definitely means that you are a winner, but must it also mean that you stand alone? I don't think it does, and neither does the field of mathematics, where the number one obviously comes from. One is connected to everything else in math, and that idea is reflected in the other name given to it: unity. Mathematicians call it unity because of its multiplicative identity. In our overindividualistic society we see one as independent (similar to seeing walls as divisions), but in mathematics the number one unites. Although it is independent of any other numeral, it composes them all (i.e., $1 \times 4 = 4$ and $1 \times 8 = 8$). In math, it means to make whole or to make one out of many. We see this idea every day without noticing it; simply flip over a dollar bill and read the inscription on the banner the eagle is holding. It says *E pluribus unum*, "Out of many, one."

Those who use "I need to look out for number one" as an excuse for not helping someone else simply don't understand basic mathematics. Compassionate achievers not only understand the true meaning of the number one, but live it every day by finding ways to make one out of many through cooperation, coordination, and collaboration. LUCA's followers understand that the societal math of compassion subtracts separation as it multiplies connections, the sum of which is a united community.

The notion "to each his own," especially Socrates's version of it as "when everyone minds his own business," has also been used as an argument for not caring about the problems of the people around you. The subscribers of "to each his own" believe that they are not interconnected to the people around them. They seemingly believe and act as though any problems or issues that the people around them are dealing with have no effect upon their "business." I heard about a professor who wrote in the signature block of his e-mails, "Your problems are not my problems, so please don't bring them to me or my class." I wonder how welcome students felt in his courses and during his office hours. Do you think he built a strong learning community among his students? Do you think he had high enrollment and mostly positive reviews for his classes? "To each his own" thinking had an effect on him, but he certainly didn't see it that way.

Basic biology and quantum physics show that we are all interconnected and that we are only as strong as our weakest link, even within our own bodies. As Greg Graffin, author of *Population Wars*, says in summarizing how our bodies consist of several different types of organisms, such as microbial cells, which "outnumber human cells 10 to 1": "We are not simply individuals who have won some evolutionary competition; we are systems of cooperating species." The natural world consists of a web of interconnections that make life an "all for one and one for all" rather than a "to each his own" type of existence. Compassionate achievers not only build an interpersonal web of relations, but continually find ways to make it stronger, so that they and the people around them thrive and not just survive.

The critics and doubters of compassionate achievers misunderstand the fundamentals of math and basic science. One—as an individual or a number—is not separate from anything. Our societal perspective warps our perceptions when we think about looking out for number one. If we *actually* looked out for number one, we would have compassion for one another, because we would intrinsically search for understanding and meaning in our interactions: we would be looking out for our multiple identities in what we do and who we become.

Some argue that to get ahead in life and to win at work, "it pays to be a jerk." The strongest argument for the work-jerk approach to success is in research that shows that the connection between being a narcissistic CEO and success is "U-shaped": jerks end up at the "extremes of the success spectrum" according to Donald Hambrick of Penn State University. Steve Jobs is often used as an example in that he was both fired and hired as the CEO of Apple. In short, jerks sometimes succeed and sometimes don't. That's not too surprising.

However, Tomas Chamorro-Premuzic shows in the *Harvard Business Review* that even when jerks attain individual success, "their success comes at a price, and that price is paid by the organization" through employee theft, absenteeism, and turnover. Christine Porath, of Georgetown University, illustrates that there are additional costs of "jerk" success to an organization and its members. Porath shows that incivility at work causes an organization to underperform because of a decrease in employee cognitive functions and an increase in health problems that range from cardiovascular disease to obesity.

The costs eventually catch up to work jerks. Any success that is attained is usually short-lived and nonsustainable. From Bernie Madoff to Enron, people and organizations that are solely motivated by and pursue their own interests at the cost of others' find their success fleeting for two main reasons: support and sabotage. Because work jerks usually bully their way to the top, they find themselves without any support or assistance when they fail (and we all inevitably fail at some point). They don't have access to any assistance because they burned most, if not all, bridges of possible support getting to where they are. Would you help those who knock people down in an effort to build themselves up?

Work jerks also eventually cause their own fall or limit their own success. Porath shows that "sooner or later, uncivil people sabotage their success—or at least their potential." Because of the way they think and act, they elicit either a "payback" or "box-in" mentality from the people they took down or those who had witnessed it. People either seek revenge (intentional or unconscious) for what a work jerk did to them (payback) or limit their potential for achieving success by denying them various types of workplace opportunities (box-in). As Walter Isaacson writes in his biography of Steve Jobs: "Nasty was not necessary. It hindered him more than it helped him." In other words, Jobs could have been more successful if he had been less arrogant and more compassionate. In an *Atlantic* article summarizing several studies about the effectiveness of jerks in the workplace, Jerry Useem concludes: "Being a jerk will fail most people most of the time."

Compassionate achievers, in contrast, succeed most of the time. Where the success of Spartacus's followers ended after only two years, people following LUCA will overcome walls and maintain success throughout life, because they are building a network of support and assistance. Nelson Mandela's words, mentioned earlier, are apt here: "I never lose. I either win or learn." Compassionate achievers never lose, because they continually find ways to "either win or learn." LUCA means "bringer of light" in several languages, and those who follow LUCA illuminate solutions to problems. The following people are light bringers because of their ideas and actions.

Compassionate Achievers

Martin Couney

What would you do if you knew of a new machine that could save thousands of premature babies from dying, but nobody in the medical establishment believed you or would even give it a try? How about opening a "baby hatchery" on Coney Island's boardwalk, in between two sideshows called the Congo Village and the Tyrolean Yodelers, to get the technology noticed and the preemies saved? That is exactly what Martin Couney—the doctor who introduced incubators to the United States—did in 1903.

- Listen to learn: Couney learned about the incubator from his mentor, Pierre Budin, in Paris. Budin asked Couney to manage a display of six premature babies in incubators at the 1896 Berlin World's Fair. Couney, in short, learned about the possibility of saving preemies through an incubator by supervising a World's Fair exhibit. Couney listened and learned from his mentor when most of the medical community in Europe and the United States thought the entire idea was quackery. Couney was open to learning something that challenged traditional thought as it nurtured new life. He was definitely a life-saving knownaut!

- Understand to know: Couney understood that most medical professionals at the time thought the technology was a farce, but he knew that if he brought the idea to the American public's awareness, it would increase the likelihood that it would eventually gain acceptance. Couney's hope was that he could "give up his carnival display when there were decent medical alternatives." That is exactly what he did in 1943, when his idea started to become part of mainstream medicine.

- Connect to capabilities: Because the American medical establishment believed that the "baby hatchery" technology was ineffective, Couney could not access financial and technological resources. He sought the capabilities he needed from Europe and the American public. With respect to Europe, he imported its incubators. In order to pay for the equipment, facility, medical personnel, and staff, he charged twenty-five cents per person to see the preemies. He even used a very young Cary Grant to say, "Don't pass the babies by," to coax the Coney Island visitors to enter the exhibit. He never charged the parents of the preemies a dime for anything, and his operation was possibly the first real crowdfunded medical enterprise in the United States.

- Act to solve: As Couney acquired the necessary resources to operate his clinic/exhibit, he hired a wide array of personnel from wet nurses to cooks, all of whom he held to high professional standards. By the time they finished their work together, they had saved approximately six thousand five hundred children. There wasn't a hospital in the United States treating preemies when Couney started, but by the time he closed his doors, hospitals had created the beginnings of what we now call neonatal wards. Couney saved thousands of lives in his lifetime, and his idea has continued to save lives ever since. In short, his solution to a problem that caused suffering to countless people has created an endless ripple of life and hope throughout time.

John Riordan

When the lives of our families are threatened, all of us—compassionate achievers or not—would do something to save them. In the spring of 1975, John Riordan's entire family was threatened overseas, and although his bosses back home initially tried to help, they eventually told him to abandon them for the sake of his own safety. You might think his bosses heartless, but you also need to understand who was included in Riordan's idea of family: all of his workers and their immediate family members.

- Listen to learn: Riordan was the Saigon, Vietnam, branch manager of First National City Bank (now Citibank) in 1975 when he received corporate orders from New York to shut down the bank and evacuate all personnel, because his city was about to fall to the North Vietnamese. The central problem for Riordan's branch workers was that only Americans and their family members could be evacuated. Riordan heard his superiors' advice to escape with his own life, but he also listened to the pleas for help from his subordinates. He quickly learned about the workers' dire circumstances and tried to understand how to address the situation.

- Understand to know: Almost everyone he asked for assistance said that they didn't know of a way to help his workers. He clearly understood, however, that if he did nothing, his subordinates would be tortured or killed because they worked with him and for his American company.

- Connect to capabilities: Riordan first organized his workers and their families in two villas and then connected with an operative with the Central Intelligence Agency (CIA). The CIA operative explained that the only way the Vietnamese workers and their families would be allowed to leave the country would be via American military cargo planes. But to get on any of them you needed to be a family member of an American citizen. The self-described rule follower would have to break several international and American rules in order to save his coworkers.

- **Act to solve:** Riordan solved the problem of American-only travel by making his workers and their families his own sons and daughters. Claiming all 106 of them as his family on travel paperwork to the United States, Riordan had to make multiple trips to the airport. No one questioned him, and they all made it to safety just days before Saigon fell to the North Vietnamese. As a compassionate achiever, Riordan broke the law so that he could serve justice.

The Compassionate One: "I Am LUCA"

Where the phrase "I am Spartacus" epitomizes loyalty, I hope that "I am LUCA" comes to symbolize compassion. Those who subscribe to LUCA not only survive, but also thrive in what they seek to achieve. Although both phrases represent protecting and helping people, only LUCA weaves individuals together to increase the strength of everyone: to make one out of many and many into one. When you choose to walk life's paths as a compassionate achiever, your level of strength and success become greater than the sum of your personal achievements, because the success of others becomes yours too. Becoming a compassionate achiever starts with a very simple statement that acknowledges a part of who you are: "I am LUCA."

Acknowledgments

A book focused on compassion is really a book about strength. There have been many people who have strengthened not only this book but also me through their listening, understanding, capabilities, and actions. I hope that you, the reader, are fortunate to have a network of friends and colleagues that are as brilliant and compassionate as those that I now have a chance to thank.

Emily Cole Prescott is my research assistant, first reader of drafts, footnote organizer, questioner, journal tracker, and indispensable Evernote partner. When it comes to research, her levels of tenacity and meticulousness are second to none. I haven't worked with a more organized person than Emily. When you work with Emily you really get two amazing people in one because her husband, Ryan, jumps in to help and quickly becomes a steady source of knowledge, encouragement, and laughter. Thank you Emily and Ryan.

Julia Pastore, Eva Avery, Lisa Zuniga, and Ann Moru of HarperCollins/ HarperOne are artists: they are sculptors of words. Julia has been my mentor in the publishing process since our first phone call. Her guidance, questions, ideas, and editorial perspective have shown me how to maintain a healthy balance between seeing the forest and the trees. Ann refined my responses to Julia's constructive criticisms in ways that made arguments stronger and ideas clearer. I thought I knew *The Chicago Manual of Style* before writing this book but Ann has taken me to new levels of understanding. I've learned so much from the HarperCollins/HarperOne editorial team and all I can say is *Aitäh* ("thanks" in Estonian). (Ann, I believe that I just used sections 7.49–50 of *The Chicago Manual of Style*.)

Marilyn Allen, my literary agent, has believed in me from the moment I came to her seeking advice. Thank you Marilyn for a kitchen-table talk that has changed my life for the better and thank you Ron Jaffe for introducing me to her.

Jessica Lin, assistant director of the Center for Compassion, Creativity and Innovation (CCCI) as well as the Kathwari Honors Program, has assumed many of my administrative responsibilities for both organizations since February 2016 and that has allowed me to focus on teaching, researching, and writing. Without her capable and thoughtful leadership and organizational skills, this book would probably still be in pre-production. Thank you Jess.

I've been fortunate to meet regularly with very successful people in a wide range of occupations and they have had a profound impact on me. Every Tuesday I meet with three amazing teachers and authors at the Holiday Diner for a meal I call The Wise Men Lunch. The Wise Men are Herb Janick, Ed Hagan, and John Malone. Thank you guys for your sage advice and nonstop humor, all of which "recharge my batteries." Another group of successful people who provide support, connections, and knowledge in strengthening CCCI and me have been Ray Boa, Mario DeVivo, Carl Dunham, Scott Nadal, Augie Ribeiro, Paul Steinmetz, and Dane Unger. They are members of CCCI's Advisory Council and also have risen to the top of their respective fields, which range from construction to medicine. Their business, legal, political, and personal guidance is reflected throughout this book. Dane has become an especially close friend and big brother; our heart-to-heart talks have been a form of meditation for me. Dane also connected me with my publishing attorney, Alan J. Kaufman, who is the best in the business. Thank you, gentlemen, for being role models of compassionate achievers not only in your respective professions but also in our local community.

I've learned so much from all of my students but several have been especially important to this book because of how closely I've worked with them. Our conversations have been highlighted in parts of the book and they have been my "lead dolphins" in the Kathwari Honors Program: Alexis Koukos, Kimberly Lockwood, Jessie Plouffe, and Rachel Rossier. They are the reason I am hopeful about the future. Also deserving special thanks are my two sections of Honors400 in Spring 2016; some of our in-class discussions led me to rewrite portions of the book. I hold my tall, cold glass of chocolate milk high in honor of you all.

There are several organizations and their leaders who have been especially helpful in combining my research with civic engagement. Marilyn Turkovich, executive director of The Charter for Compassion, has connected me with numerous communities and universities to assist them with becoming colleges and cities of compassion. Marilyn's hospitality, warm heart, and sharp mind make every visit with her seem like an intellectual "coming home." Brookfield CARES and Men Against Domestic & Sexual Violence (a subgroup of The Women's Center of Greater Danbury) have been models of compassionate achievement right in my own backyard and I feel privileged to play small roles in both organizations. Donna and Ben Rosen have hosted an annual local event in western Connecticut called KentPresents that has allowed me to interact with leaders from around the world on issues and problems facing humanity; thank you Donna and Ben for your generosity and hospitality. The number of staff, administrators, and students at Western Connecticut State University (WCSU) who have supported my work and that of CCCI is so high that it is impossible to individually thank all of them here (I have a lot of thank-you hugs to give out). A special thank you goes to former WCSU Provost Jane Gates and President James Schmotter for supporting and promoting compassionate initiatives on campus. Thank you also President John Clark for continuing to structure university life in ways that promote the weaving of research with civic engagement. The Jesse Lewis Choose Love Movement has offered me ways to not only research compassion in education but also construct and implement curriculum across the country. Thank you Scarlett Lewis for including me in your effort to make our classrooms more compassionate places.

A family that sets the standard for "choosing love" every day, the Lewis family, is my model of resilience. Scarlett, J.T., and Maureen Lewis as well as Bob Comfort have been sources of inspiration, laughter, and warmth over the past four years. Thank you Jesse Lewis for introducing us through your courage and compassion.

My father-in-law (Gary Culhane) and brother-in-law (Blair Culhane) have been my go-to guys when life's practical and mechanical difficulties arise. They helped me to focus on the book and not on water heaters and broken-down cars. Thank you Dad and Blair for being the masters of my mechanical universe.

The Norman clan, especially Mom (Barb) and Trish Norman, have been pure rays of love. They have been family to me since I was seven and the way "our" three boys light up when they're around makes me feel loved six times over. Thank you Mom Norman and Tee-Tee.

I began this book with a story of my wife and there isn't a better way to end it than by thanking her and our three sons. When I think of everything that is hopeful and loving in life, I think of Elly. I started with a story about Elly because I started to recognize what a compassionate achiever does by watching her. From giving me time to write at home to giving all she has to our three sons, she continues to amaze me by how she always finds more ways to give to everyone who comes to her in trouble and need. She is my light that shines in dark and bright times. Thank you Elly for being my inspiration and thank you for our three lil dudes. Cade, Quinn, and Cole: thank you for your hugs, love, and trust. I am blessed to be your dad. You might not understand this now but you are my strength. I hope that our weekend morning diner breakfast talks never end and I hope that whatever you do in life, you do as compassionate achievers.

Notes

Introduction: Compassionate People Finish on Top—Together

2: *"two different phenomena"*: Kai Kupferschmidt, "Concentrating on Kindness," *Science* 341 (20 September 2013): 1336–39.

2: *Research focused on a dopamine-processing gene:* Bruce J. Ellis and W. Thomas Boyce, "Biological Sensitivity to Context," *Current Directions in Psychological Science* 17/3 (2008): 183–87; Johnathan D. Rockoff, "Nature vs. Nurture: New Science Stirs Debate," *Wall Street Journal,* 16 September 2013, http://www.wsj.com/news/articles/SB1000142 4127887323527004579079132234671374.

4: *A child is bullied every seven minutes:* National Center for Education Statistics, "Student Reports of Bullying and Cyber-Bullying: Results from the 2011 School Crime Supplement to the National Crime Victimization Survey," prepared by Synergy Enterprises, Inc., http://nces.ed.gov/pubs2013/2013329.pdf. "Learn How to Prevent Bullying in Schools," Bullying Prevention Institute, accessed October 9, 2016, http://www .bullyingpreventioninstitute.org/Outreach.aspx.

4: *Some companies consider "nice":* Rachel Feintzeig, "'Nice' Is a Four-Letter Word at Companies Practicing Radical Candor," *Wall Street Journal,* 30 December 2015, http://www .wsj.com/articles/nice-is-a-four-letter-word-at-companies-practicing-radical-candor -1451498192.

4: *"incivility in America has risen to crisis levels":* Weber Shandwick, Powell Tate, and KRC Research, "Civility in America 2013," May 2013, https://www.webershandwick .com/uploads/news/files/Civility_in_America_2013_Exec_Summary.pdf.

4: *Stress from work alone is estimated:* Statistic Brain Institute, "Stress Statistics," July 2016, http://www.statisticbrain.com/stress-statistics/.

4: *Extra costs to businesses:* Shandwick, Tate, and KRC Research, *"Civility in America 2013."*

5: *"Almost 80 percent":* Rick Weissbound et al., "The Children We Mean to Raise: The Real Messages Adults Are Sending About Values," *Making Caring Common Project* (Cambridge, MA: The President and Fellows of Harvard College, 2014), http://sites .gse.harvard.edu/sites/default/files/making-caring-common/files/mcc_report_the _children_we_mean_to_raise_0.pdf.

1. The Connection Between Compassion and Success

9: *"Enhanced interrogation techniques": Interview with* Sir Richard Dearlove, at the Kent-Presents festival, Kent, Connecticut, 19 August 2016.

10: *Richard Dawkins famously argued:* Richard Dawkins, *The Selfish Gene,* 30th anniversary ed. (New York: Oxford Univ. Press, 2006), 19.

10: *"I perhaps attributed too much":* Charles Darwin, *The Descent of Man and Selection in Relation to Sex,* 2nd ed. (1874), chap. 2, p. 214; chap. 5, p. 452.

10: *"Those communities which":* Darwin, *The Descent of Man,* chap. 4, p. 371.

11: *"today would be termed empathy":* Paul Ekman, "Darwin's Compassionate View of Human Nature," *Journal of the American Medical Association* 303/6 (10 February 2010): 557–58; Line Goguen-Hughes, "Survival of the Kindest," *Mindful: Taking Time for What Matters,* December 23, 2010, http://www.mindful.org/in-body-and-mind-psychology/survival-of-the-kindest.

11: *He outlines in chapter 4:* Darwin, *Descent of Man,* chap. 4, pp. 425–26.

11: *"the almost ever-present instinct":* Darwin, *Descent of Man,* chap. 4, p. 393.

11: *selfishness may have been an advantage:* Edward O. Wilson, *The Meaning of Human Existence* (New York: Liveright, 2014), 176–78.

11: *"groups that work together altruistically":* Edward O. Wilson, *The Social Conquest of Earth* (New York: Liveright, 2012), 166; Clive Cookson, "The Buzz Word," review of *The Social Conquest of Earth,* by Edward O. Wilson, *Financial Times,* 5–6 May 2012.

12: *"our ability to function as team players":* David Sloan Wilson and Edward O. Wilson, "Evolution: Survival of the Selfless," *New Scientist* 196/2628 (3 November 2007): 42–46.

12: *Elsewhere, the Wilsons show:* David Sloan Wilson and Edward O. Wilson, "Evolution 'for the Good of the Group,'" *American Scientist* 96/5 (September/October 2008): 380–89.

12: *"Within groups selfish individuals beat":* Wilson, *Meaning of Human Existence,* 33.

12: *Biologists from Michigan State University:* Christoph Adami and Arnd Hintze, "Evolutionary Instability of Zero-Determinant Strategies Demonstrates That Winning Is Not Everything," *Nature Communications* 4/2193 (1 August 2013): Letters 1–7; Anna Dreber et al., "Winners Don't Punish," *Nature* 452 (20 March 2008): 348–51.

12: *James Q. Wilson:* Arthur C. Brooks, "Social Science with a Soul," *Wall Street Journal,* 3 March 2012; Brooks's summary is clearly supported in James Q. Wilson, *The Moral Sense* (New York: Free Press, 1993), vii, xiv, 225, 250–51.

13: *Wilson showed that:* Wilson, *Moral Sense,* 23.

13: *"the roots of primate social behavior":* Steve Kemper, "No Alpha Males Allowed," *Smithsonian,* September 2013, 41.

13: *the case of the "little American monkey":* Darwin, *Descent of Man,* chap. 4.

13: *"the condition of multiple generations":* Wilson, *Social Conquest,* 133.

13: *Ants . . . created cooperative and "symbiotic relationships":* Wilson, *Social Conquest,* 120.

13: *"cooperativeness, empathy, and patterns of networking":* Wilson, *Social Conquest,* 290.

13: *"the final reserve of altruism":* Wilson, *Social Conquest,* 251.

14: *the early reptilian brain:* The evolutionary model of the brain, called the triune brain, was first proposed by physician and neuroscientist Paul D. MacLean in *The Triune Brain in Evolution* (New York: Plenum, 1990).

14: *"Selflessness is the default option":* Victoria Sayo Turner, "It Takes Effort to Be Selfish," *Scientific American,* April 2016, http://www.scientificamerican.com/article/it-takes-effort-to-be-selfish/.

14: *"our primary drive"*: Leonardo Christov-Moore et al., "Increasing Generosity by Disrupting Prefrontal Cortex," *Social Neuroscience*, March 2016, doi: 10.1080/17470919 .2016.1154105.

14: *Oxytocin activates the neurotransmitters*: See Shawn Achor, *The Happiness Advantage* (New York: Crown, 2010), esp. 43–45; Paul J. Zak, *The Moral Molecule: The Source of Love and Prosperity* (New York: Dutton, 2012), esp. 63–66.

15: *"Oxytocin . . . orchestrates the kind of generous"*: Zak, *The Moral Molecule*, xii.

15: *charity is "neurologically similar"*: William T. Harbaugh, Ulrich Mayr, and Daniel R. Burghart, "Neural Responses to Taxation and Voluntary Giving Reveal Motives for Charitable Donations," *Science* 316 (15 June 2007): 1622–25; Elizabeth Svoboda, "Hard-Wired for Giving," *Wall Street Journal*, 31 August–1 September 2013, C1–2.

15: *"the vagus nerve innervates"*: Dacher Keltner, *Born to Be Good: The Science of a Meaningful Life* (New York: Norton, 2009), 229.

15: *the centerpiece of Porges's research*: Stephen W. Porges, "The Polyvagal Perspective," *Biological Psychology* 74/2 (February 2007): 116–43.

16: *When we have a lower heart rate*: Stephen W. Porges, "Social Engagement and Attachment: A Phylogenetic Perspective," *Roots of Mental Illness in Children, Annals of New York Academy of Sciences*, http://condor.depaul.edu/dallbrit/extra/psy588/porges NYAS.pdf.

16: *"As the vagus nerve fires"*: Keltner, *Born to Be Good*, 230.

16: *Other researchers in psychology*: Nancy Eisenberg et al., "The Relations of Children's Dispositional Prosocial Behavior to Emotionality, Regulation, and Social Functioning," *Child Development* 67 (1996): 974–92.

16: *Studies in areas from political economics to psychology*: Mariano Grondona, "A Cultural Typology of Economic Development," in Lawrence E. Harrison and Samuel P. Huntington, eds., *Culture Matters: How Values Shape Human Progress* (New York: Basic Books, 2000): 44–55; Amy Wrzesniewski et al., "Multiple Types of Motives Don't Multiply the Motivation of West Point Cadets," *Proceedings of the National Academy of Sciences of the USA* 111/30 (29 July 2014): 10990–95.

16: *"goal-achieving mentality"*: Caitlin Esch, "Money Triggers Social Insensitivity . . . and Hard Work," *Marketplace*, NPR, 3 December 2015.

17: *"less interpersonally attuned"*: Kathleen D. Vohs, "Money Priming Can Change People's Thoughts, Feelings, Motivations, and Behaviors: An Update on 10 Years of Experiments," *Journal of Experimental Psychology: General* 144/4 (August 2015): 86–93.

17: *"Only intrinsic values are inexhaustible"*: Grondona, "A Cultural Typology," 45.

17: *meaningfulness comes from being a "giver"*: Roy F. Baumeister et al., "Some Key Differences Between a Happy Life and a Meaningful Life," *Journal of Positive Psychology* 8/6 (2013): 505–16.

17: *"Helping people focus on the meaning"*: Amy Wrzesniewski and Barry Schwartz, "The Secret of Effective Motivation," *New York Times*, 4 July 2014, http://www.nytimes.com /2014/07/06/opinion/sunday/the-secret-of-effective-motivation.html; Wrzesniewski et al., "Multiple Types of Motives."

17: *They also found that cadets*: Wrzesniewski et al., "Multiple Types of Motives."

17: *"greater self-esteem"*: Rachel L. Piferi and Kathleen A. Lawler, "Social Support and Ambulatory Blood Pressure: An Examination of Both Receiving and Giving," *International Journal of Psychophysiology* 62/2 (November 2006): 328–36.

18: *"activism cure"*: Meredith Maran, "The Activism Cure," in Dacher Keltner, Jason Marsh, and Jeremy Adam Smith, eds., *The Compassionate Instinct* (New York: Norton, 2010), 195–202.

18: *"a clear, positive correlation":* Sigal G. Barsade and Olivia A. O'Neill, "What's Love Got to Do with It? A Longitudinal Study of the Culture of Companionate Love and Employee and Client Outcomes in the Long-Term Care Setting," *Administrative Science Quarterly* 59/4 (December 2014): 551–98; Alena Hall, "Compassionate Work Culture Can Really Benefit the Bottom Line, Too," *Huffington Post*, http://www.huffingtonpost .com/2015/04/29/compassion-at-work_n_7057382.html?utm_hp_ref=healthy-living (April 29, 2015).

18: *"report 1.7 times higher job satisfaction":* Jessica Amortegui, "Why Finding Meaning at Work Is More Important Than Feeling Happy," *Fast Company*, http://www.fast company.com/3032126/how-to-find-meaning-during-your-pursuit-of-happiness-at -work (June 26, 2014).

18: *larger improvements with respect to academic . . . measurements:* Joseph A. Durlak, Roger P. Weissberg, Kriston B. Schellinger, Allison B. Dymnicki, and Rebecca D. Taylor, "The Impact of Enhancing Students' Social and Emotional Learning: A Meta-Analysis of School-Based Universal Interventions," *Child Development* 82, no. 1 (January/February 2011): 405–432.

18: *an $11 return on every $1 spent:* Clive Belfield et al., "The Economic Value of Social and Emotional Learning" (New York: Center for Benefit-Cost Studies in Education, Teachers College, Columbia University, 2015).

19: *Because compassion activates oxytocin:* Zak, *The Moral Molecule;* Jeremy Adam Smith and Pamela Paxton, "America's Trust Fall," in Keltner, Marsh, and Smith, *Compassionate Instinct*, 203–12.

19: *"The old adage":* Lydia Dishman, "Is Competition Killing Your Productivity?" *Fast Company*, 11 November 2013, http://www.fastcompany.com/3021287/dialed /is-competition-killing-your-productivity.

19: *"Eighty-three percent of participants":* David Gelles, "The Mind Business," *Financial Times*, 24 August 2012, http://www.ft.com/cms/s/2/d9cb7940-ebea-11e1–985a -00144feab49a.html.

20: *saved $2,000 in yearly health-care costs:* Gelles, "Mind Business."

20: *"as much as half of the difference":* James Heskett, *The Culture Cycle: How to Shape the Unseen Force That Transforms Performance* (Upper Saddle River, NJ: FT Press, 2012), 15.

20: *"high levels of productivity":* Heskett, *The Culture Cycle*, 23.

20: *"intrinsic need satisfaction":* Paul P. Baard, Edward L. Deci, and Richard M. Ryan, "Intrinsic Need Satisfaction: A Motivational Basis of Performance and Well-Being in Two Work Settings," *Journal of Applied Social Psychology* 34/10 (2004): 2064.

20: *"a clear, positive correlation":* Barsade and O'Neill, "What's Love Got to Do with It?"; Alena Hall, "Compassionate Work Culture Can Really Benefit the Bottom Line, Too," *Huffington Post*, http://www.huffingtonpost.com/2015/04/29/compassion-at -work_n_7057382.html?utm_hp_ref=healthy-living (April 29, 2015).

20: *"Top executives are attracted":* Melissa Korn and Anita Hofschneider, "How to Get Ahead as a Middle Manager: Try These Tips," *Wall Street Journal*, 7 August 2013, http://www.wsj.com/articles/SB10001424127887323838204578654404251084008.

21: *compassion and empathy started to decline:* Sara H. Konrath, Edward H. O'Brien, and Courtney Hsing, "Changes in Dispositional Empathy in American College Students over Time: A Meta-Analysis," *Personality and Social Psychology Review* 15/2 (2011): 180–98; David Desteno, "The Kindness Cure," *Atlantic*, 21 July 2015, http:// www.theatlantic.com/health/archive/2015/07/mindfulness-meditation-empathy -compassion/398867/.

21: *"Eighty-one percent of 18- to 25-year-olds"*: Konrath, O'Brien, and Hsing, "Changes in Dispositional Empathy," 187.

22: *Zak discusses successful ways:* Zak, *The Moral Molecule*, 48–49.

22: *"how people might rely on touch"*: Dacher Keltner, "The Compassionate Instinct," in Keltner, Marsh, and Smith, eds. *Compassionate Instinct*, 12.

22: *The role of practicing meditation:* Kupferschmidt, "Concentrating on Kindness," 1338; Kate Pickert, "The Mindful Revolution: The Science of Finding Focus in a Stressed-Out, Multitasking Culture," *Time*, 3 February 2014, 40–46.

22: *"increased the number of people who helped"*: David DeSteno, "Compassion Made Easy," *New York Times*, 14 July 2012, http://www.nytimes.com/2012/07/15/opinion/sunday /the-science-of-compassion.html?_r=0.

22: *"Our fundamental question was"*: "Brain Can Be Trained in Compassion, Study Shows," *Association for Psychological Science*, 22 May 2013, http://www.psychologicalscience .org/index.php/news/releases/compassion-training.html; Helen Weng et al., "Compassion Training Alters Altruism and Neural Responses to Suffering," *Psychological Science* 24/7 (21 May 2013): 1171–80.

2. LUCA: The Four-Step Program for Cultivating Compassion

25: *Wesley Autrey was waiting:* Cara Buckley, "Man Is Rescued by Stranger on Subway Tracks," *New York Times*, 3 January 2007, http://www.nytimes.com/2007/01/03/nyregion /03life.html.

3. Listen to Learn

29: *A study in the journal Animal Behaviour:* Natalie Angier, "The Owl Comes Into Its Own," *New York Times*, 25 February 2013, http://www.nytimes.com/2013/02/26/science/long -cloaked-in-mystery-owls-start-coming-into-full-view.html; Alexandre Roulin, Arnaud Da Silva, Charlene A. Ruppli, "Dominant Nestlings Displaying Female-Like Melanin Coloration Behave Altruistically in the Barn," *Animal Behaviour* 84 (23 September 2012): 1229–36, http://dx.doi.org/10.1016/j.anbehav.2012.08.033.

29: *"An owl . . . can hear a mouse"*: San Diego Zoo, "San Diego Zoo Animals," http://animals .sandiegozoo.org/animals/owl.

29: *scientists have found that the neurons:* Kate Wong, "Owl Hearing Relies on Advanced Math," *Scientific American*, 13 April 2001, http://www.scientificamerican.com/article .cfm?id=owl-hearing-relies-on-adv.

30: *"It doesn't take a Ph.D. or M.D."*: Mark Lukach and Kate Slovin, "Exquisite Listening: America's First Suicide Prevention Hotline Celebrates 50 Years," *The Daily Good*, 21 July 2012, https://www.good.is/articles/exquisite-listening-america-s-first -suicide-prevention-hotline-celebrates-50-years.

30: *"Listen first, and listen well"*: University of Wisconsin School of Medicine and Public Health, "Listening Plays Role in Suicide Prevention," news release, 15 April 2009, http://www.med.wisc.edu/news-events/listening-plays-role-in-suicide-prevention/837.

30: *With a 24 percent jump in the U.S. suicide rate:* Andrea Petersen, "As Suicide Rates Rise, Scientists Find New Warning Signs," *Wall Street Journal*, 7 June 2016, http://www.wsj .com/articles/as-suicide-rates-rise-scientists-find-new-warning-signs-1465235288; Sally C. Curtin, Margaret Warner, and Holly Hedegaard, "Increase in Suicide in the United States, 1999–2014," U.S. Department of Health and Human Services NCHS Data Brief 241, April 2016, http://www.cdc.gov/nchs/data/databriefs/db241.pdf.

30: *because more Americans commit suicide:* Melonie Heron, "Deaths: Leading Causes for 2014," U.S. Department of Health and Human Services Centers for Disease Control and Prevention National Center for Health Statistics, National Vital Statistics Reports 65, no. 5, 30 June 2016, http://www.cdc.gov/nchs/data/nvsr/nvsr65/nvsr65_05.pdf.

30: *one American takes his or her own life:* Lukach and Slovin, "Exquisite Listening."

30: *twenty veterans per day:* Leo Shane III and Patricia Kime, "New VA Study Finds 20 Veterans Commit Suicide Each Day," *Military Times,* 7 July 2016, http://www.military times.com/story/veterans/2016/07/07/va-suicide-20-daily-research/86788332/.

30: *"people need to listen, without judgment":* Janet I. Tu, "Listening—The Common Ground Amid Conflict," *Seattle Times,* 3 August 2007, http://www.seattletimes.com/seattle -news/listening-8212-the-common-ground-amid-conflict/. You can find out more about the Compassionate Listening Project by visiting the project's website: http://www .compassionatelistening.org.

31: *"genuine listening" is "required":* Mila Hakanen and Aki Soudunsaari, "Building Trust in High-Performing Teams," *Technology Innovation Management Review* (June 2012): 38–41, http://timreview.ca/article/567.

31: *"Listening is not a reaction":* Maria Popova, "Telling Is Listening: Ursula K. Le Guin on the Magic of Real Human Conversation," review of *The Wave in the Mind,* by Ursula K. Le Guin, *BrainPickings,* 21 October 2015, https://www.brainpickings.org/2015/10/21 /telling-is-listening-ursula-k-le-guin-communication/.

31: *"successful human relationship . . . involves entrainment":* Popova, "Telling Is Listening"; Ursula Le Guin, *The Wave in the Mind* (Boston: Shambhala, 2004), 195–96.

31: *"revealed a surprising tendency":* Uri Hasson et al., "Intersubject Synchronization of Cortical Activity During Natural Vision," *Science* 303, 1634 (12 March 2004): 1634.

31: *"the simple act of tapping one's hands":* David DeSteno, "Compassion Made Easy," *New York Times,* 14 July 2012, http://www.nytimes.com/2012/07/15/opinion/sunday/the-science -of-compassion.html?_r=0.

31: *"parts of our brains are in synchrony":* "My Neurons, My Self," presented at the World Science Festival, video, 5 June 2016, http://livestream.com/WorldScienceFestival/events /5415988/videos/125252689.

32: *"It is the province of knowledge":* "Oliver Wendell Holmes," *BrainyQuote,* accessed 7 August 2016, http://www.brainyquote.com/quotes/quotes/o/oliverwend385593.html.

32: *"If there is any secret to success":* "Henry Ford," *BrainyQuote,* accessed 7 August 2016, http://www.brainyquote.com/quotes/quotes/h/henryford400461.html.

32: *In a 2015 study:* Samantha Cole, "New Research Shows We're All Bad Listeners Who Think We Work Too Much," *Fast Company,* 26 February 2015, http://www.fastcompany .com/3042863/the-future-of-work/new-research-shows-were-all-bad-listeners-who -think-we-work-too-much.

32: *The catch is that 98 percent:* "Accenture Research Finds Listening More Difficult in Today's Digital Workplace," *Accenture,* news release, 26 February 2015, https: //newsroom.accenture.com/industries/global-media-industry-analyst-relations /accenture-research-finds-listening-more-difficult-in-todays-digital-workplace.htm; "#ListenLearnLead:GlobalResearch2015,"*Accenture,*2015,https://www.accenture.com /us-en/_acnmedia/Accenture/Conversion-Assets/Microsites/Documents13 /Accenture-IWD-2015-Research-Listen-Learn-Lead.pdf.

32: *Previous research showed:* Catherine Lampton, "Heard of the Listening Gap?" *NCRP eJournal,* 9 June 2016, http://www.ejournalncrp.org/heard-of-the-listening-gap/.

32: Education Digest *reported:* Rebecca Brent and Patricia Anderson, "Teaching Kids How to Listen," *Education Digest* 59/5 (January 1994), http://0-eds.b.ebscohost.com.www

.consuls.org/eds/detail/detail?sid=0b330627–01d3–4a56–8ad7-dd4dc07506f0%40 sessionmgr104&vid=0&hid=112&bdata=JnNpdGU9ZWRzLWxpdmU%3d#AN =9312297844&db=aph.

32: *"the most vital skill for accomplishing tasks"*: Lampton, "Heard of the Listening Gap?"

32: *most schools and businesses don't teach*: Lampton, "Heard of the Listening Gap?"

32: *"Well, that's the news from Lake Wobegon"*: "Listening Information," website of "A Prairie Home Companion with Chris Thile," American Public Media, http://prairiehome .org/listen/.

37: *one study on how hearing improved in mice*: Abby Olena, "Not Seeing Is Hearing?: Hearing Improves in Mice Deprived of Visual Stimulus for a Week, According to a Study," *The Scientist Magazine*, 7 February 2014, http://www.the-scientist.com/?articles .view/articleNo/39117/title/Not-Seeing-Is-Hearing-/; Emily Petrus et al., "Crossmodal Induction of Thalamocortical Potentiation Leads to Enhanced Information Processing in the Auditory Cortex," *Neuron* 81 (5 February 2014): 664–73, doi: http://dx.doi.org /10.1016/j.neuron.2013.11.023.

37: *"One friend, one person"*: "E. H. Mayo," *GoodReads*, accessed 7 August 2016, http:// www.goodreads.com/author/quotes/15308599.E_H_Mayo.

41: *Judge a man by his questions*: "Voltaire," *BrainyQuote*. accessed 7 August 2016, http:// www.brainyquote.com/quotes/quotes/v/voltaire100338.html.

41: *"A great photograph is one that"*: "Ansel Adams," *AZQuotes*, accessed 7 August 2016, http://www.azquotes.com/author/74-Ansel_Adams.

41: *"but if you try sometimes"*: Rolling Stones, "You Can't Always Get What You Want," *Let It Bleed*, released 28 November 1969, 2013 Abkco Music & Records.

42: *"A photograph is usually looked at"*: "Ansel Adams."

43: *"an answerer's level of informativeness"*: Robert X. D. Hawkins et al., "Why Do You Ask? Good Questions Provoke Informative Answers," Stanford University Computation and Cognition Lab, paper presented at the Proceedings of the Thirty-Seventh Annual Conference of the Cognitive Science Society, 22–25 July 2015, https://mind modeling.org/cogsci2015/papers/0158/paper0158.pdf.

43: *"A good photograph"*: "Ansel Adams."

48: *the more synchronized two brains are*: Uri Hasson, "Defend Your Research: I Can Make Your Brain Look Like Mine," *Harvard Business Review*, December 2010, https://hbr .org/2010/12/defend-your-research-i-can-make-your-brain-look-like-mine; Greg J. Stephens, Lauren J. Silbert, and Uri Hasson, "Speaker-Listener Neural Coupling Underlies Successful Communication," *Proceedings of the National Academy of Sciences of the USA* 107/32 (10 August 2010): 14428, doi: 10.1073/pnas.1008662107.

48: *"Successful communication…requires"*: Stephens, Silbert, and Hasson, "Speaker-Listener Neural Coupling."

48: *"You don't take a photograph"*: "Ansel Adams."

48: *Although the funnel model*: London Deanery, "Skillful Questioning and Active Listening," accessed 30 September 2015, http://www.faculty.londondeanery.ac.uk/e-learning /appraisal/skilful-questioning-and-active-listening.

49: *Studies have shown*: Matthieu Ricard, *Altruism: The Power of Compassion to Change Yourself and the World* (New York: Little, Brown and Company, 2015): 71.

49: *"To photograph truthfully and effectively"*: "Ansel Adams."

49: *"Two people can see the same input"*: John Medina, *Brain Rules*, ed. Tracy Cutchlow, 2nd ed. (Seattle: Pear Press, 2014), 169.

52: *"In human intercourse the tragedy begins"*: "Henry David Thoreau," *BrainyQuote*, accessed 7 August 2016, http://www.brainyquote.com/quotes/quotes/h/henrydavid 139220.html.

52: *most people break silence:* Melissa Dahl, "The Body Odd: Four Seconds Is All It Takes for Silence to Get Awkward," *NBC News*, 27 January 2011, http://bodyodd.nbcnews .com/_news/2011/01/27/5879375-four-seconds-is-all-it-takes-for-silence-to-get -awkward?lite; Namkje Koudenburg, Tom Postmes, and Ernestine H. Gordijn, "Disrupting the Flow: How Brief Silences in Group Conversations Affect Social Needs," *Journal of Experimental Social Psychology* 47/2 (March 2011): 512–15, doi:10.1016/j .jesp.2010.12.006.

52: *Basil Rathbone:* For more about Basil Rathbone's film career, see "Basil Rathbone," *IMDb.com*, accessed 6 August 2016, http://www.imdb.com/name/nm0001651/.

53: *"the curious incident of the dog in the nighttime"*: Sir Arthur Conan Doyle, "Silver Blaze," accessed 5 November 2016, http://www.eastoftheweb.com/short-stories/ubooks/silvblaz .shtml, especially section 21.

53: *"sound yields to silence"*: Thich Nhat Hanh, *Silence: The Power of Quiet in a World Full of Noise* (San Francisco: HarperOne, 2015), 176.

53: *"space between notes"*: Hanh, *Silence*, 176.

53: *Silences or pauses:* Daniel A. Gross, "This Is Your Brain on Silence," *Nautilus* 016, 21 August 2014, http://nautil.us/issue/16/nothingness/this-is-your-brain-on-silence.

53: *Although the "Mozart effect"*: Lynn Waterhouse, "Multiple Intelligences, the Mozart Effect, and Emotional Intelligence: A Critical Review," *Educational Psychologist* 41/4 (2006): 207–25.

53: *there is a musical effect:* "The Most Powerful Effect in Music—The Grand Pause," *Music of Yesterday*, accessed 18 August 2015, http://musicofyesterday.com/historical -music-theory/most-powerful-effect-music-grand-pause/.

53: *"The music is not in the notes"*: "Wolfgang Amadeus Mozart," *GoodReads*, accessed 7 August 2016, https://www.goodreads.com/author/quotes/22051.Wolfgang_Amadeus _Mozart. A similar quote is also attributed to Claude Debussy; "Claude Debussy," *BrainyQuote*, accessed 7 August 2016, http://www.brainyquote.com/quotes/quotes/c /claudedebu204265.html.

53: *"peak brain activity occurred during"*: Mitzi Baker, "Music Moves Brain to Pay Attention, Stanford Study Finds," *Stanford Medicine News Center*, 1 August 2007, https:// med.stanford.edu/news/all-news/2007/07/music-moves-brain-to-pay-attention -stanford-study-finds.html; Devarajan Sridharan et al., "Neural Dynamics of Event Segmentation in Music: Converging Evidence for Dissociable Ventral and Dorsal Networks," *Neuron* 55 (2 August 2007): 521–32, doi: 10.1016/j.neuron.2007.07.003.

54: *Our neural wiring of attention clicks on:* Matt Juul, "Why the Music of 'Jaws' Is Still Terrifying," *Boston*, 16 June 2015, http://www.boston.com/culture/entertainment/2015 /06/16/why-the-music-of-jaws-is-still-terrifying.

54: *"catalyzes our powers of perception"*: George Prochnik, *In Pursuit of Silence* (New York: Anchor, 2010), 293.

54: *"There is the dumb silence of slumber or apathy"*: Paul Goodman, *Speaking and Language: Defence of Poetry* (New York: Vintage Books, 1971), 15.

55: *"occur when a person"*: Paul Ekman, "Micro Expressions," accessed October 8, 2016, http://www.paulekman.com/micro-expressions/. Jacob Fagliano, "The Importance of Recognizing Microexpressions in the Workplace," *HR & Talent Management*, 29 March 2014, http://www.hrtalentmanagement.com/2014/03/29/the-importance

-of-recognizing-microexpressions-in-the-workplace/. There is also an online quiz that measures your ability to read microexpressions. I highly recommend that you explore this quiz to start learning about how to not only read other people's expressions, but also realize how yours may be perceived by others.

56: *upwards of forty-three facial muscles:* Jerry Adler, "Face to Face," *Smithsonian,* December 2015, 46–51.

56: *engineers in the field of affective computing:* Tony Schwartz, "Humanity as a Competitive Advantage," *New York Times,* 18 September 2015, http://www.nytimes.com /2015/09/19/business/dealbook/humanity-as-a-competitive-advantage.html?mab Reward=CTM&action=click&pgtype=Homepage&region=CColumn&module =Recommendation&src=rechp&WT.nav=RecEngine&_r=0.

56: *Although there are many people:* Rosamond Hutt, "Bill Gates on Reddit: I Agree with Elon Musk and Stephen Hawking About Artificial Intelligence," *World Economic Forum,* 10 March 2016, https://www.weforum.org/agenda/2016/03/bill-gates-on-reddit-i-agree -with-elon-musk-and-stephen-hawking-about-ai/.

57: *The game was made famous:* Adam Mazer, William Rotko, and Billy Ray, *Breach,* directed by Billy Ray, Universal Studios Home Entertainment, 12 June 2007, DVD.

58: *"how the changing expressions":* Gavin Francis, *Adventures in Human Being* (New York: Basic Books, 2015), 47.

59: *"we cannot easily distinguish":* Christopher Chabris and Daniel Simons, *The Invisible Gorilla* (New York: Broadway Paperbacks, 2009), 46.

59: *An "expectation calculation":* Lauren L. Emberson, John E. Richards, and Richard N. Aslin, "Top-Down Modulation in the Infant Brain: Learning-Induced Expectations Rapidly Affect the Sensory Cortex at 6 Months," *Proceedings of the National Academy of Sciences of the USA* 112/31 (4 August 2015): 9585–90, www.pnas.org/cgi/doi/10 .1073/pnas.1510343112.

60: *"with positive affect broadening":* Taylor W. Schmitz, Eve De Rosa, and Adam K. Anderson, "Opposing Influences of Affective State Valence on Visual Cortical Encoding," *Journal of Neuroscience* 29/22 (3 June 2009): 7199–207.

60: *"and the more likable":* Robert Sapolsky, "Pretty Smart? Why We Equate Beauty with Truth," *Wall Street Journal,* 18–19 January 2014, C2.

60: *"we do not see with our eyes":* Medina, *Brain Rules,* 223.

60: *One of the key findings of a meta-analysis:* Amber Bloomfield et al., "What Makes Listening Difficult?: Factors Affecting Second Language Listening Comprehension," University of Maryland Center for Advanced Study of Language, April 2010.

60: *"the likelihood that any information":* Elizabeth A. Kensinger, Rachel J. Garoff-Eaton, and Daniel L. Shacter, "Effects of Emotion on Memory Specificity: Memory Trade-Offs Elicited by Negative Visually Arousing Stimuli," *Journal of Memory and Language* 56 (2007): 575–91.

61: *Our mental defaults are so strong:* Nicholas Rule, "Snap Judgment Science: Intuitive Decisions About Other People," *Observer* 27/5 (May/June 2014), http://www.psychological science.org/index.php/publications/observer/2014/may-june-14/snap-judgment-science .html.

62: *"We can learn a lot":* Maria Popova, "How to Listen Between the Lines: Anna Deavere Smith on the Art of Listening in a Culture of Speaking," *BrainPickings,* accessed 25 November 2015, https://www.brainpickings.org/2015/01/29/anna-deavere-smith-talk -to-me/?mc_cid=9300b7fb0a&mc_eid=ff5704bce9.

4. Understand to Know

67: *"The evil that is in the world":* Albert Camus, *The Plague,* trans. Stuart Gilbert (New York: Vintage, 1991), 131.

67: *South Korea understood the difference:* Rory Sutherland, "Perspective Is Everything," *TED Talk,* December 2011, http://www.ted.com/talks/lang/en/rory_sutherland_perspective _is_everything.html.

69: *To understand the things that are:* "Hypatia," *BrainyQuote,* accessed 17 August 2016, http://www.brainyquote.com/quotes/quotes/h/hypatia414120.html.

70: *longtime fans of Dr. Seuss books:* Dr. Seuss, *Oh, the Places You'll Go!* (New York: Random House, 1990).

70: *Carol Dweck calls this way:* Carol Dweck, *Mindset: The New Psychology of Success* (New York: Ballantine, 2006), 7.

71: *"The opposite of every truth":* Hermann Hesse, "Govinda" (chap. 12), *Siddhartha,* Literature Network, accessed 24 June 2016, http://www.online-literature.com/hesse /siddhartha/12/.

71: *"I never lose":* Jim Schleckser, "Nelson Mandela's Secret to Winning," *Inc.,* 21 June 2016, http://www.inc.com/jim-schleckser/nelson-mandela-s-secret-to-winning.html.

71: *These folks have what:* Dweck, *Mindset,* 6.

75: *"If you stand for nothing":* "Malcolm X," *BrainyQuote,* accessed 21 August, 2016, http:// www.brainyquote.com/quotes/quotes/m/malcolmx379121.html. The original quote is: "A man who stands for nothing will fall for anything."

78: *"Thinking about our own thinking":* Dietrich Dörner, *The Logic of Failure: Recognizing and Avoiding Error in Complex Situations,* trans. Rita and Robert Kimber (New York: Metropolitan, 1996), 195.

79: *"There is plenty of time to sleep":* Benjamin Franklin, "The Way to Wealth," *The Autobiography of Benjamin Franklin,* ed. Frank Woodworth Pine (1916; Project Gutenberg, 2006), https://www.gutenberg.org/files/20203/20203-h/20203-h.htm.

79: *Researchers have found:* http://www.npr.org/sections/health-shots/2013/10/18/23621 1811/brains-sweep-themselves-clean-of-toxins-during-sleep; https://www.nih.gov/news -events/news-releases/brain-may-flush-out-toxins-during-sleep.

79: *The above scenarios were based:* Kimberly Yam, "Police Deliver Groceries to Struggling Grandma Caught Shoplifting to Feed Family of 6," *Huffington Post,* 12 December 2014, http://www.huffingtonpost.com/2014/12/12/officer-buys-eggs-for-gma-caught -stealing_n_6310630.html.

81: *scientists at the Max Planck Institute:* Florian Rosado, "How Does Your Brain Combine the Five Senses?" *Relia Wire,* 7 June 2016, http://reliawire.com/brain-five-senses /?utm_content=buffercdc8c&utm_medium=social&utm_source=twitter.com &utm_campaign=buffer; Cesare V. Parise and Marc O. Ernst, "Correlation Detection as a General Mechanism for Multisensory Integration," *Nature Communications* 7/11543 (6 June 2016), doi:10.1038/ncomms11543, http://www.nature.com/ncomms /2016/160606/ncomms11543/pdf/ncomms11543.pdf.

81: *people's emotions can be detected:* James Hamblin, "Emotions Seem to Be Detectable in Air," *Atlantic,* 23 May 2016, http://www.theatlantic.com/science/archive/2016/05 /the-gas-of-emotion/482922/; Jonathan Williams et al., "Cinema Audiences Reproducibly Vary the Chemical Composition of Air During Films, by Broadcasting Scene Specific Emissions on Breath," *Nature: Scientific Reports* 6 (2016), doi: 10.1038/srep25464, http://www.nature.com/articles/srep25464.

82: *"I would rather feel compassion"*: "Thomas Aquinas," *AZQuotes*, accessed 11 August 2016, http://www.azquotes.com/quote/409360.

82: *The other is that monkeys*: S. Grant, "The Difference Between Chimps and Bonobos," *KnowledgeNuts*, 18 August 2013, http://knowledgenuts.com/2013/08/18/the-difference -between-chimps-and-bonobos/.

82: *Elie Wiesel, Nobel Peace laureate*: Brenda Cronin and Rory Jones, "Elie Wiesel, Holocaust Survivor and Nobel Laureate, Dies at 87," *Wall Street Journal*, 2 July 2016, http://www .wsj.com/articles/nobel-laureate-holocaust-survivor-elie-wiesel-dies-at-87–1467492558.

83: *"the capacity for recognizing"*: Daniel Goleman, *Working with Emotional Intelligence* (New York: Bantam, 1998), 317.

83: *This general consensus is grounded*: Paul Ekman, "What Scientists Who Study Emotion Agree About," *Paul Ekman Group*, 12 April 2016, https://www.paulekman.com /uncategorized/scientists-study-emotion-agree/. This article had been originally published in *Perspectives on Psychological Science*.

86: *From studies on people who lost*: Taylor W. Schmitz, Eve De Rosa, and Adam K. Anderson, "Opposing Influences of Affective State Valence on Visual Cortical Encoding," *Journal of Neuroscience* 29/22 (June 2009): 7199–207, doi: 10.1523/JNEURO SCI.5387–08.2009, http://www.jneurosci.org/content/29/22/7199.short.

86: *The work of neuroscientist Antonio Damasio*: Antonio Damasio, *Descartes' Error: Emotion, Reason, and the Human Brain* (New York: Penguin, 2005).

87: *"The reasoning system evolved"*: Damasio, *Descartes' Error*, xi–xiii.

87: *My reverence for Commander Spock*: Damasio, *Descartes' Error*, 53.

87: *"reduction in emotion may constitute"*: Damasio, *Descartes' Error*, 53.

87: *"sometimes a feeling is all"*: "Top Ten Best Captain Kirk Quotes," *Top 10 Best*, accessed 21 August 2016, http://www.top10-best.com/c/top_10_best_captain_kirk_quotes.html.

88: *"a new view of intelligence"*: Mary Helen Immordino-Yang, *Emotions, Learning, and the Brain: Exploring the Educational Implications of Affective Neuroscience* (New York: Norton, 2016), 27–28.

88: *the five areas Goleman identifies*: Goleman, *Working with Emotional Intelligence*, 317.

89: *"Self-awareness is the keystone"*: Goleman, *Emotional Intelligence*, 10th anniversary reissue edition (New York: Bantam, 2006), 43.

89: *"Emotional self-control . . . underlies accomplishment"*: Goleman, *Emotional Intelligence*, 43.

90: *"predict whether a relationship"*: Erika Beras, "This Algorithm Can Predict Relationship Trouble," *Scientific American*, transcript, 5 July 2016, http://www.scientificamerican .com/podcast/episode/this-algorithm-can-predict-relationship-trouble/.

90: *emotional intelligence has a "dark side"*: Adam Grant, "The Dark Side of Emotional Intelligence," *Atlantic*, 2 January 2014, http://www.theatlantic.com/health/archive/2014/01 /the-dark-side-of-emotional-intelligence/282720/.

90: *"In suggesting that emotional intelligence"*: Grant, "Dark Side."

90: *Having strong overall emotional intelligence*: Grant, "Dark Side."

90: *"handling emotions in relationships well"*: Goleman, *Working with Emotional Intelligence*, 318.

90: *Other social competencies that Goleman includes*: Goleman, *Working with Emotional Intelligence*, 318.

91: *"to mobilize and inspire others"*: Goleman, *Emotional Intelligence*, 112–13.

91: *"bespeaks an* emergence *of a crucial emotional aptitude"*: Goleman, *Emotional Intelligence*, 112.

91: *Emotionally manipulating*: Grant, "The Dark Side."

91: *Goleman focuses on empathy*: Goleman, *Emotional Intelligence*, 43.

91: *"five basic emotional and social competencies"*: Goleman, *Working with Emotional Intelligence*, 318.

92: *when we think compassionately*: Kai Kupferschmidt, "Concentrating on Kindness," *Science* 341 (20 September 2013): 1337.

92: *"empathy can also provoke a distress"*: Matthieu Ricard, *Altruism: The Power of Compassion to Change Yourself and the World* (New York: Little, Brown and Company, 2015): 55.

92: *This has been commonly*: Ricard, *Altruism*; 57; Jamil Zaki, "How to Avoid Empathy Burnout," *Nautilus*, 7 April 2016, http://nautil.us/issue/35/boundaries/how-to-avoid -empathy-burnout. This article provides information on how to avoid empathy burnout. Also see Adam Waytz, "The Limits of Empathy," *Harvard Business Review*, January– February 2016, https://hbr.org/2016/01/the-limits-of-empathy?utm_campaign=HBR &utm_source=linkedin&utm_medium=social.

93: *My go-to song is "Superheroes"*: The Script, *No Sound Without Silence*, Sony Music Entertainment, released 12 September 2014, iTunes.

94: *"Emotions . . . are not add-ons"*: Immordino-Yang, *Emotions, Learning, and the Brain*, 21.

94: *a moment without emotion*: When people have emotional blindness, or the inability to identify and describe emotions in themselves, the condition is called alexithymia. For more about this condition, see David Robson, "What Is It Like to Have Never Felt an Emotion?" *BBC Future*, 19 August 2015, http://www.bbc.com/future /story/20150818-what-is-it-like-to-have-never-felt-an-emotion.

95: *"The main part of intellectual education"*: "Oliver Wendell Holmes Jr.," *BrainyQuote*, accessed 21 August 2016, http://www.brainyquote.com/quotes/quotes/o/oliverwend 138605.html.

95: *Understanding comes from "warming"*: William B. Wood, "Teaching Concepts Versus Facts in Developmental Biology," *CBE–Life Sciences Education* 7 (Spring 2008): 10–16.

95: *Trees in a forest are deeply interconnected*: Sally McGrane, "German Forest Ranger Finds That Trees Have Social Networks, Too," *New York Times*, 29 January 2016, http://www.nytimes.com/2016/01/30/world/europe/german-forest-ranger-finds-that -trees-have-social-networks-too.html. A print version of this article was published in the *New York Times* with the title "Where We See Tangled Trees, He Sees Social Networks" on 30 January 2016.

95: *"they can count, learn and remember"*: McGrane, "German Forest Ranger Finds."

95: *"Take away a neuron's connections"*: Olaf Sporns, "Network Neuroscience," in *The Future of the Brain: Essays by the World's Leading Neuroscientists*, ed. Gary Marcus and Jeremy Freeman (Princeton, NJ: Princeton Univ. Press, 2015), 92.

96: *"All learning is understanding relationships"*: Rita Pierson, "Every Kid Needs a Champion," *TED Talk*, May 2013, http://www.ted.com/talks/rita_pierson_every_kid_needs_a _champion/transcript?language=en.

96: *"leads to better retention"*: Matthew D. Lieberman, *Social: Why Our Brains Are Wired to Connect* (New York: Crown, 2013), 288.

96: *"Social motivations—the need to avoid"*: Lieberman, *Social*, 281.

96: *ever-increasing levels of artificial intelligence*: Artificial intelligence is defined as the science of making "intelligent machines" that "perceive their environment" and learn knowledge, so that they "can take action to maximize their chances of success" (created by combining definitions from John McCarthy, "What Is Artificial Intelligence?" last modified November 12, 2007, accessed October 8, 2016, http://www-formal.stanford.edu/jmc /whatisai/node1.html, and Stuart J. Russell and Peter Norvig, *Artificial Intelligence: A Modern Approach*, 2nd ed. [Upper Saddle River, New Jersey: Prentice Hall, 2003]).

97: *"summoning the demon"*: Samuel Gibbs, "Elon Musk: Artificial Intelligence Is Our Biggest Existential Threat," *Guardian*, 27 October 2014, http://www.theguardian.com /technology/2014/oct/27/elon-musk-artificial-intelligence-ai-biggest-existential-threat.

97: *"I agree with Elon Musk"*: Rosamond Hutt, "Bill Gates on Reddit: I Agree with Elon Musk and Stephen Hawking About Artificial Intelligence," *World Economic Forum*, 10 March 2016, https://www.weforum.org/agenda/2016/03/bill-gates-on-reddit-i-agree-with-elon -musk-and-stephen-hawking-about-ai/.

97: *"The development of full artificial intelligence"*: Rory Cellan-Jones, "Stephen Hawking Warns Artificial Intelligence Could End Mankind," *BBC News*, 2 December 2014, http://www.bbc.com/news/technology-30290540.

97: *"More than Moore strategy"*: M. Mitchell Waldrop, "More Than Moore," *Nature* 530 (11 February 2016): 144–47.

97: *"Watson knows a lot of things"*: Michael Strevens, "What Is the Difference Between Knowledge and Understanding?" *Big Questions Online*, 19 May 2014, https://www.big questionsonline.com/2014/05/19/what-difference-between-knowledge-understanding/.

100: *Rod MacKinnon, had severe muscle cramps*: Matthew Futterman, "A New Way to Prevent Muscle Cramps," *Wall Street Journal*, 11 July 2016, http://www.wsj.com/articles /a-new-way-to-prevent-muscle-cramps-1468256588.

100: *"it's your neurons"*: Futterman, "A New Way."

100: *"There exist pairs of games"*: Jorge Hidalgo Aguilera, "Novel Mechanisms for Phase Transitions and Self-Organization in Living Systems" (Ph.D. diss., Universidad de Granada, 2014), 69.

101: *However, in winter the combination*: Discussion with Honors 400 Students, Western Connecticut State University, Fall 2016 Semester.

101: *"some forgetting . . . often essential"*: Peter C. Brown, Henry L. Roediger III, and Mark A. McDaniel, *Make It Stick: The Science of Successful Learning* (Cambridge, MA: Belknap, 2014), 4, 77.

101: *Utah is successfully addressing homelessness*: Terrence McCoy, "The Surprisingly Simple Way Utah Solved Chronic Homelessness and Saved Millions," *Washington Post*, 17 April 2015, https://www.washingtonpost.com/news/inspired-life/wp/2015/04/17/the -surprisingly-simple-way-utah-solved-chronic-homelessness-and-saved-millions/.

101: *Many state politicians*: McCoy, "The Surprisingly Simple Way."

102: *They call their program Housing First*: Kelly McEvers, "Utah Reduced Chronic Homelessness by 91 Percent; Here's How," *NPR*, 10 December 2015, http://www .npr.org/2015/12/10/459100751/utah-reduced-chronic-homelessness-by-91-percent -heres-how.

102: *"$8,000 per homeless person"*: McEvers, "Utah Reduced Chronic Homelessness."

102: *"approaching a functional zero"*: McCoy, "The Surprisingly Simple Way."

102: *Utah's approach is also being used*: Jesse Ferreras, "Medicine Hat Homelessness Could Reach Its End This Year," *Huffington Post Alberta*, 14 May 2015, http://www.huffington post.ca/2015/05/14/medicine-hat-homelessness-end-2015_n_7280232.html.

103: *"Give me six hours to chop down"*: "Abraham Lincoln," *BrainyQuote*, accessed 21 August 2016, http://www.brainyquote.com/quotes/quotes/a/abrahamlin109275.html.

103: *The irony is that international test scores*: National Center for Education Statistics, "Program for International Student Assessment," accessed 23 July 2016, https://nces.ed.gov/surveys/pisa/.

103: *"I believe in standardizing automobiles"*: "Albert Einstein," *AZQuotes*, accessed 22 August 2016, http://www.azquotes.com/quote/844415.

103: *the problem with standardized testing*: Brown, Roediger, and McDaniel, *Make It Stick;* Benedict Carey, *How We Learn: The Surprising Truth About When, Where, and Why It Happens* (New York: Random House, 2014).

103: *The most effective way of making information*: Henry L. Roediger III, "How Tests Make Us Smarter," *New York Times* Sunday Review, 18 July 2014, http://www.nytimes.com/2014/07/20/opinion/sunday/how-tests-make-us-smarter.html?_r=0.

104: *The reason is that an emotion creates*: John Medina, *Brain Rules*, ed. Tracy Cutchlow, 2nd ed. (Seattle: Pear Press, 2014), 112.

104: *"reason about the thoughts, motives"*: Nicholas Epley, *Mindwise: Why We Misunderstand What Others Think, Believe, Feel, and Want* (New York: Knopf, 2014), xiii.

104: *"inhabit the largest social groups"*: Epley, *Mindwise*, xvi.

106: *Each walk gave her an entirely new perspective*: Alexandra Horowitz, *On Looking: A Walker's Guide to the Art of Observation* (New York: Scribner, 2014).

106: *Johansson's book, The Medici Effect*: Frans Johansson, *The Medici Effect: What Elephants and Epidemics Can Teach Us About Innovation* (Boston: Harvard Business School, 2006), 3.

107: *"By stepping into the intersection"*: Johansson, *Medici Effect*, 20.

108: *Businesses such as LiquidSpace*: Rachel Butt, "There Are 2,000 Empty Restaurants During the Day in New York—And This Startup Is Trying to Do Something About It," *Business Insider*, 10 June 2016, http://www.businessinsider.com/spacious-wants-to-turn-restaurants-into-coworking-spaces-2016-6; Liquidspace, "Office Smarter," accessed 23 July 2016, https://liquidspace.com.

108: *Kaltschnee has created the Danbury Hackerspace*: You can find out more about the Danbury Hackerspace at https://danburyhackerspace.com.

108: *If you live the Medici Effect*: Johansson, *Medici Effect*, 20.

108: *"The creation of a thousand forests"*: "Ralph Waldo Emerson," *BrainyQuote*, accessed 21 August 2016, http://www.brainyquote.com/quotes/quotes/r/ralphwaldo151956.html.

5. Connect to Capabilities

109: *If you like to solve puzzles*: Tessa Berenson, "The Escape Room—A Rubik's Cube That Locks the Door Behind You," *Time*, 31 August 2015.

109: *People who are good at connecting*: Malcolm Gladwell, *The Tipping Point: How Little Things Can Make a Big Difference* (New York: Back Bay, 1996), 34.

110: *"know lots of people"*: Gladwell, *Tipping Point*, 38.

110: *"value and pleasure in a casual meeting"*: Gladwell, *Tipping Point*, 46.

110: *"They manage to occupy"*: Gladwell, *Tipping Point*, 48.

110: *"By having a foot in so many"*: Gladwell, *Tipping Point*, 51.

110: *"are masters of the weak tie"*: Gladwell, *Tipping Point*, 54.

110: *"Connectors" are a "special few"*: Gladwell, *Tipping Point*, 37–38.

110: *"a handful of people"*: Gladwell, *Tipping Point*, 41.

111: *"Some people feel the rain"*: "Roger Miller," accessed October 1, 2016, http://quote investigator.com/2012/09/21/get-wet/.

111: *"Everything in this world"*: "Nikos Kazantzakis," *BrainyQuote*, accessed 23 August 2016, http://www.brainyquote.com/quotes/quotes/n/nikoskazan176145.html.

112: *After only five days*: Moises Velasquez-Manoff, "When the Body Attacks the Mind: A Psychological Theory of Mental Illness," *Atlantic*, July/August 2016, http://www.theatlantic .com/magazine/archive/2016/07/when-the-body-attacks-the-mind/485564/.

112: *"an infusion of antibodies"*: Velasquez-Manoff, "When the Body Attacks the Mind."

112: *"If I was not my son's mother"*: Velasquez-Manoff, "When the Body Attacks the Mind."

115: *the school aide in Ohio*: Suzanne Stratford, "School Aide Being Called Hero After Rescuing Student from Dog Attack," *Fox 8 Cleveland*, 2 December 2015, http://fox8.com/2015 /12/02/school-aide-being-called-hero-after-rescuing-student-from-dog-attack/.

115: *the "nursing home hero"*: Bryan Mims, "Nursing Home 'Hero' Says He Was Just Doing His Job," *WRAL*, 9 April 2009, http://www.wral.com/news/local/story/4926061/.

115: *the law enforcement personnel*: Eliott C. McLaughlin and Christina Zdanowicz, "San Bernardino Detective Who Promised to 'Take a Bullet' Says He's No Hero," *CNN*, 9 December 2015, http://www.cnn.com/2015/12/09/us/brave-officer-jorge-lozano evacuates -san-bernardino-building/index.html.

115: *"I know now that man is capable"*: Albert Camus, *The Plague*, trans. Stuart Gilbert (New York: Vintage, 1991), 163.

115: *"I don't know what it means"*: Camus, *Plague*, 163.

116: *Recent national surveys on civility*: *Civility in America 2013: Executive Summary*, Weber Shandwick, KRC Research, Powell Tate, 2013, accessed 26 February 2016, http://www.webershandwick.com/uploads/news/files/Civility_in_America_2013_Exec _Summary.pdf.

116: *"crisis levels, up from 65 percent"*: "Nearly All Likely Voters Say Candidates' Civility Will Affect Their Vote; New Poll Finds 93 percent Say Behavior Will Matter," press release, 28 January 2016, http://www.webershandwick.com/news/article /nearly-all-likely-voters-say-candidates-civility-will-affect-their-vote.

116: *We see different races*: Jane Elliott, interview by Del Walters, *Al Jazeera America News Daily*, Al Jazeera, 27 June 2015, http://america.aljazeera.com/watch/shows/live -news/2015/6/a-deeper-look the-psychology-of-racism-part-2.html. Elliott's full quote is: "There are not four or five different races, there's only one race on the face of the earth, and we're all members of that race: the human race."

116: *"Atticus told me to delete the adjectives"*: Harper Lee, *To Kill a Mockingbird* (New York: Warner, 1982), 59.

117: *"A person's name . . . is the greatest connection"*: Joyce E. A. Russell, "Career Coach: The Power of Using a Name," *Washington Post*, 12 January 2014, https://www .washingtonpost.com/business/capitalbusiness/career-coach-the-power-of-using-a -name/2014/01/10/8ca03da0-787e-11e3-8963-b4b654bcc9b2_story.html.

118: *"As employees were involved"*: Amy Rees Anderson, "Can Compassion Contribute to Success?" *Forbes: Entrepreneurs*, 6 December 2015, http://www.forbes.com/sites /amyanderson/2015/12/06/can-compassion-contribute-to-success/#2db5b86b2feb.

118: *"But I would also submit to you"*: Anderson, "Can Compassion Contribute to Success?"

119: *A pedagogical method called*: Matthew D. Lieberman, *Social: Why Our Brains Are Wired to Connect* (New York: Crown, 2013), 289.

119: *learned "material in order to teach it"*: Lieberman, *Social*, 289.

119: *"predictor of professional success"*: Jennifer Breheny Wallace, "The Secret of Popularity," *Wall Street Journal*, 22 July 2016, http://www.wsj.com/articles/the-secret-of-popularity-1469196965.

119: *"there is a collective I.Q."*: Charles Duhigg, "What Google Learned from Its Quest to Build the Perfect Team," *New York Times Magazine*, 25 February 2016, http://www.nytimes.com/2016/02/28/magazine/what-google-learned-from-its-quest-to-build-the-perfect-team.html; Anita Williams Woolley et al., "Evidence for a Collective Intelligence Factor in the Performance of Human Groups," *Science* 330/686 (2010), doi:10.1126/science.

119: *"as long as everyone got a chance"*: Duhigg, "What Google Learned."

119: *The other answer that the researchers*: Duhigg, "What Google Learned."

119: *"describes a team climate"*: Amy Edmondson, "Psychological Safety and Learning Behavior in Work Teams," *Administrative Science Quarterly* 44/2 (June 1999): 350–83.

120: *Being grateful has been shown*: Susan Pinker, "When Does Gratitude Bring Better Health?" *Wall Street Journal*, 17 December 2015, http://www.wsj.com/articles/when-does-gratitude-bring-better-health-1450384249.

120: *One of the most effective ways*: "Gratitude," *Greater Good: The Science of a Meaningful Life*, University of California Berkeley, accessed 25 July 2016, http://greatergood.berkeley.edu/topic/gratitude/definition.

120: *"a relationship-strengthening emotion"*: "What Is Gratitude?" *Greater Good: The Science of a Meaningful Life*, University of California Berkeley, accessed 25 July 2016, http://greatergood.berkeley.edu/topic/gratitude/definition; Robert A. Emmons and Michael E. McCullough, "Counting Blessings Versus Burdens: An Experimental Investigation of Gratitude and Subjective Well-Being in Daily Life," *Journal of Personality and Social Psychology* 84/2 (2003): 377–89, http://greatergood.berkeley.edu/pdfs/GratitudePDFs/6Emmons-BlessingsBurdens.pdf.

121: *For example, studies and surveys*: Kylie Croot, "Thanking Your Way to the Top: Why Practicing Gratitude at Work Makes You Better at Your Job," *Redii*, 13 November 2015, https://www.redii.com/blog/thanking-your-way-to-the-top-heres-why-gratitude-at-work-makes-you-better-at-your-job/.

121: *"Whether the feeling or the behavior"*: Susan Pinker, "When Does Gratitude Bring Better Health?" *Wall Street Journal*, 17 December 2015, http://www.wsj.com/articles/when-does-gratitude-bring-better-health-1450384249.

121: *"expressing gratitude to colleagues"*: Janice Kaplan, "Gratitude Survey," reported for the John Templeton Foundation, June–October 2012, accessed 29 February 2016, in Emiliana R. Simon-Thomas and Jeremy Adam Smith, "How Grateful Are Americans?" 10 January 2013, http://greatergood.berkeley.edu/article/item/how_grateful_are_americans.

121: *"little sparks of gratitude"*: "Dale Carnegie," *AZQuotes*, accessed 23 August 2016, http://www.azquotes.com/quote/855825.

122: *"Executives who withhold gratitude"*: Kaplan, "Gratitude Survey," 14.

122: *Expectations have also been proven to cause*: Siri Carpenter, "Sights Unseen," *American Psychological Association* 32/4 (April 2001): 54, http://www.apa.org/monitor/apr01/blindness.aspx.

122: *In a famous study known as the "invisible gorilla"*: Daniel J. Simons and Christopher F. Chabris, "Gorillas in Our Midst: Sustained Inattentional Blindness for Dynamic Events," *Perception* 28 (1999): 1059–74.

122: *Go to the note*: https://www.youtube.com/watch?v=vJG698U2Mvo; Daniel Simons, "The Monkey Business Illusion," YouTube, 28 April 2010, https://www.youtube.com /watch?v=IGQmdoK_ZfY.

122: *The problem was that at least half*: Simons and Chabris, "Gorillas in Our Midst."

123: *In two famous studies about expectations*: Robert Rosenthal and Lenore Jacobson, *Pygmalion in the Classroom* (New York: Holt, Rinehart and Winston, Inc., 1968); Elisha Babad, Jacinto Inbar, and Robert Rosenthal, "Pygmalion, Galatea, and the Golem: Investigations of Biased and Unbiased Teachers," *Journal of Educational Psychology* 74, no. 4 (August 1982): 459–74.

123: *"when we expect certain behaviors"*: "The Pygmalion Effect," Center for Teaching Excellence, Duquesne University, accessed 29 February 2016, http://www.duq.edu /about/centers-and-institutes/center-for-teaching-excellence/teaching-and-learning /pygmalion.

124: *Discovering and acknowledging "the hidden potential"*: "Nikos Kazantzakis."

125: *"There are two ways of spreading light"*: "Edith Wharton," *BrainyQuote*, accessed 22 August 2016, http://www.brainyquote.com/quotes/quotes/e/edithwhart100511.html.

125: *"Although this might be for black girls"*: Zolan Kanno-Youngs, "An 11-Year-Old's Drive Is #1000blackgirlbooks," *Wall Street Journal*, 26 February 2016, http://www.wsj.com /articles/an-11-year-olds-drive-is-1000blackgirlbooks-1456535514. You can also listen to an interview with Marley Dias, "Where's Color in Kid's Lit? Ask the Girl with 1,000 Books (And Counting)," *NPR Morning Edition*, interview recording, 26 February 2016, http://www.npr.org/programs/morning-edition/2016/02/26/468216058 /morning-edition-for-february-26–2016.

126: *Websites such as InnoCentive*: Pagan Kennedy, *Inventology: How We Dream Up Things That Change the World* (New York: Houghton Mifflin Harcourt, 2016), 159.

126: *"increasing civil society's influence"*: InnoCentive, https://www.innocentive.com, accessed 24 August 2016.

126: *"outsiders, rather than those within a field"*: Kennedy, *Inventology*, 160.

126: *The idea of crowdsourcing*: U.S. Department of Health and Human Services, *About Donation and Transplantation*, "The Need Is Real: Data," http://www.organdonor.gov /about/data.html, last viewed on 24 August 2016.

126: *Although we all know organ donation*: USDHHS, *About Donation and Transplantation*.

126: *"a better measure of local damages"*: Robert Lee Hotz, "Twitter Storms Can Help Gauge Damage of Real Storms and Disasters, Study Says," *Wall Street Journal*, 11 March 2016, http://www.wsj.com/articles/twitter-storms-can-help-gauge-damage-of-real-storms -and-disasters-study-says-1457722801.

126: *"Twitter reactions can be so swift"*: Hotz, "Twitter Storms Can Help Gauge"; Yury Kryvasheyeu et al., "Rapid Assessment of Disaster Damage Using Social Media Activity," *Science Advances* 2 (11 March 2016), doi: 10.1126/sciadv.1500779.

127: *Nearly two-thirds of Americans*: Pew Research Center, "U.S. Smartphone Use in 2015," 1 April 2015, http://www.pewinternet.org/files/2015/03/PI_Smartphones_0401151 .pdf.

127: *over three-quarters use social media*: Pew Research Center, "Social Media Usage: 2005–2015," 8 October 2015, http://www.pewinternet.org/files/2015/10/PI_2015–10 –08_Social-Networking-Usage-2005–2015_FINAL.pdf.

129: *One in four teens admit:* Lisa M. Jones, Kimberly J. Mitchell, and David Finkelhor, "Online Harassment in Context: Trends from Three Youth Internet Safety Surveys (2000, 2005, 2010)," *Psychology of Violence* 3/1 (2013): 53–69; "Cyberbullying Facts," Cyberbullying Research Center, http://cyberbullying.org/facts, accessed 26 July 2016.

129: *"The Compassion Team . . . is devoted":* Penelope Green, "The Facebook Breakup," *New York Times,* 12 March 2016, http://www.nytimes.com/2016/03/13/fashion/facebook -breakup-compassion-team.html?_r=0.

129: *"we must accept the idea":* Carlo Rovelli, *Seven Brief Lessons on Physics,* trans. Simon Carnell and Erica Segre (New York: Riverhead, 2016), 20, 33.

130: *"There are always flowers":* "Henri Matisse," *BrainyQuote,* accessed 23 August 2016, http://www.brainyquote.com/quotes/quotes/n/nikoskazan176145.html.

131: *By becoming a divergent thinker:* Toni Bernhard, "What Type of Thinker Are You?" *Psychology Today* 28 February 2013, https://www.psychologytoday.com/blog/turning -straw-gold/201302/what-type-thinker-are-you. You can learn more about the differ- ent types of thinking by reading this article.

132: *"try harder to get another person's perspective":* Nicholas Epley, *Mindwise: Why We Mis- understand What Others Think, Believe, Feel, and Want* (New York: Knopf, 2014), 172.

133: *"How do you tell the difference":* "These Jokes Are for Intellectuals Only: The Fifth One Had Me Confused," *Higher Perspective,* accessed 30 July 2016, http://www.higher perspectives.com/jokes-for-intellectuals-1406161830.html.

133: *"Who earns a living by driving:* "Riddle Thirteen: Money for Nothing?" *Laugh and Learn English,* http://www.laughandlearnenglish.com/riddle13.html, accessed 24 August 2016.

133: *radio shows such as:* Ask Me Another, NPR, http://www.npr.org/programs/ask-me -another/, accessed 6 August 2016.

133: The Diving Bell: Jean-Dominique Bauby, *The Diving Bell and the Butterfly: A Memoir of Life in Death,* trans. Jeremy Leggatt (New York: Vintage, 1998).

133: Mindwalk: Bernt Amadeus Capra, Floyd Byars, Fritjof Capra, *Mindwalk,* directed by Bernt Amadeus Capra, 1990, http://www.imdb.com/title/tt0100151/fullcreits?ref_=tt _ov_wr#writers.

133: *board and electronic games, such as: Dungeons and Dragons,* http://dnd.wizards.com, accessed 7 August 2016.

137: *Temple Grandin's autobiography:* Temple Grandin, *Thinking in Pictures and Other Reports from My Life with Autism* (New York: Vintage, 1995).

137: *"The world needs different kinds of minds":* Temple Grandin, "Temple Grandin: The World Needs All Kinds of Minds," *TED2010,* February 2010, http://www.ted.com/talks /temple_grandin_the_world_needs_all_kinds_of_minds.

137: *"this effect is especially marked":* Keith Oatley, "Fiction: Simulation of Social Worlds," *Trends in Cognitive Sciences* 20/8 (August 2016): 618.

137: *"The secret to understanding each other":* Epley, *Mindwise,* 183.

138: *"hyper-anxious chronicler of the minute details":* Josh Jones, "David Foster Wallace's 2005 Commencement Speech 'This Is Water' Visualized in Short Film," *Open Culture,* accessed 3 August 2016, http://www.openculture.com/2013/05/david_foster_wallaces _2005_commencement_speech_this_is_water_visualized_in_new_short_film.html.

138: *The point of the fish story:* Jones, "David Foster Wallace's 2005 Commencement Speech."

138: *"The findings across dozens of studies":* Paul Piff, "Does Money Make You Mean?" *TED Talk,* December 2013, https://www.ted.com/talks/paul_piff_does_money_make_you _mean/transcript?language=en.

139: *Recent studies at the University of Zurich:* "Empathy Enhances Altruistic Behavior in Selfish People," *Neuroscience News,* 5 March 2016, http://neurosciencenews.com /altruism-empathy-brain-connectivity-3803/; Grit Hein et al., "The Brain's Functional Network Architecture Reveals Human Motives," *Science* 351/6277 (March 2016): 1074–78, http://science.sciencemag.org/content/351/6277/1074.full.pdf+html.

139: *Piff's work has also shown that:* Piff, "Does Money Make You Mean?"

139: *The "nudges" and "bumps" can occur:* Piff, "Does Money Make You Mean?"

140: *"can be written down and passed on":* E. F. Schumacher, *Small Is Beautiful: Economics as if People Mattered* (New York: Harper & Row, Perennial Library, 1975), 97.

140: *All issues in "human relations":* Schumacher, *Small Is Beautiful,* 97.

140: *"If this [convergence] were the case":* Schumacher, *Small Is Beautiful,* 97–98.

141: *Sometimes you don't see the possibilities: Brookfield Cares,* accessed 24 August 2016, http://brookfield-cares.org.

142: *"a molecule that would light up":* Adam Cole, "Our 'Golden Mole Winner' Used to Paint Wasps for a Living," *NPR,* 1 March 2016, http://www.npr.org/2016/03/01/468673964 /golden-mole-award-winner-to-be-announced.

142: *what fossilized viruses might look like:* Cole, "Our 'Golden Mole Winner.'"

142: *"Errors . . . are the portals of discovery":* James Joyce, *Ulysses: A Reproduction of the 1922 First Edition* (New York: Dover, 2002), 182.

142: *"If you keep making the same mistakes":* Robert I. Sutton, "Learning from Success and Failure," *Harvard Business Review,* 4 June 2007, https://hbr.org/2007/06 /learning-from-success-and-fail.

142: *Spencer Silver, a scientist:* Daven Hiskey, "Post-It Notes Were Invented by Accident," *Today I Found Out,* 9 November 2011, http://www.todayifoundout.com/index.php /2011/11/post-it-notes-were-invented-by-accident/.

143: *"Kids perform better":* Mikaela Conley, "Kids Fail Less When They Know Failure Is Part of Learning, Study Finds," *ABC News,* 14 March 2012, http://abcnews.go.com/blogs /health/2012/03/14/kids-fail-less-when-they-know-failure-is-part-of-learning-study -finds/; Frédérique Autin and Jean-Claude Croizet, "Brief Report: Improving Working Memory Efficiency by Reframing Metacognitive Interpretation of Task Difficulty," *Journal of Experimental Psychology* 141/4, (2012): 610–18, http://www.apa.org/pubs /journals/releases/xge-141-4-610.pdf.

143: *"When one door closes":* "Quotes of Alexander Graham Bell," 6 August 2016, http:// inventors.about.com/od/bstartinventors/a/Quotes-Of-Alexander-Graham-Bell.htm.

143: *when men were told:* Sharon Begley, "Pink Brains, Blue Brains," *Mindful,* 29 December 2015, http://www.mindful.org/pink-brains-blue-brains/.

144: *How we speak about the future:* Derek Thompson, "Can Your Language Influence Your Spending, Eating, and Smoking Habits?" *Atlantic,* 10 September 2013, http://www .theatlantic.com/business/archive/2013/09/can-your-language-influence-your -spending-eating-and-smoking-habits/279484/.

144: *"Multilingual exposure, it seems":* Katherine Kinzler, "The Superior Social Skills of Bilinguals," *New York Times,* 11 March 2016, http://www.nytimes.com/2016/03/13 /opinion/sunday/the-superior-social-skills-of-bilinguals.html?_r=0.

144: *"the key difference between bilinguals and monolinguals":* Yudhijit Bhattacharjee, "Why Bilinguals Are Smarter," *New York Times,* 17 March 2012, http://www.nytimes .com/2012/03/18/opinion/sunday/the-benefits-of-bilingualism.html.

145: *"The only difference between success and failure":* "Alexander Graham Bell," *AZQuotes,* accessed 23 August 2016, http://www.azquotes.com/quote/543446.

6. Act to Solve

147: *J.T. started a foundation: Newtown Helps Rwanda,* accessed 24 August 2016, http://www.newtownhelpsrwanda.org. Please take a moment to visit the foundation's website.

148: *"It wasn't that hard to do":* Jim Dwyer, "Making the Journey from Menace to Neighbor, All on One Brooklyn Block," *New York Times,* 3 March 2016, http://www.nytimes.com/2016/03/04/nyregion/making-the-journey-from-menace-to-neighbor-all-on-one-brooklyn-block.html?_r=0.

148: *It's one of the reasons:* Sean McElwee, "Most Americans Don't Vote in Elections. Here's Why," *Al Jazeera America,* 27 July 2015, http://america.aljazeera.com/opinions/2015/7/most-americans-dont-vote-in-elections-heres-why.html.

148: *only slightly more than half:* Drew Desilver, "U.S. Voter Turnout Trails Most Developed Countries," *Pew Research Center,* 2 August 2016, http://www.pewresearch.org/fact-tank/2016/08/02/u-s-voter-turnout-trails-most-developed-countries/.

148: *We are so routine oriented:* Marie C. Reed, "Why People Change Their Health Care Providers," Center for Studying Health System Change, May 2000, Data Bulletin No. 16, http://www.hschange.com/CONTENT/81/.

148: *"70 percent of Americans":* "5 Lessons to Learn from Patients' Complaints About Doctors," *Elements,* e-newsletter, 25 March 2015, https://www.pbahealth.com/5-lessons-to-learn-from-patients-complaints-about-doctors/.

148: *"linked physical inactivity to more than 5 million deaths":* Ryan Jaslow, "CDC: 80 Percent of American Adults Don't Get Recommended Exercise," *CBS News,* 3 May 2013, http://www.cbsnews.com/news/cdc-80-percent-of-american-adults-dont-get-recommended-exercise/.

148: *"The path of least resistance":* "Henry David Thoreau," *AZQuotes,* accessed 24 August 2016, http://www.azquotes.com/quote/347906.

149: *"transform[ed] into agents":* Daniel M. Wegner and Kurt Gray, *The Mind Club* (New York: Viking, 2016), 109.

149: *helping others when you are in a stressful situation:* Michael J. Poulin et al., "Giving to Others and the Association Between Stress and Mortality," *American Journal of Public Health* 103/9 (September 2013): 1649–55.

150: *"If you want to lift yourself up":* "Booker T. Washington," *BrainyQuote,* accessed 24 August 2016, http://www.brainyquote.com/quotes/quotes/b/bookertwa382202.html.

150: *"Fear has never been a good adviser":* Karl Vick, "Person of the Year: Chancellor of the Free World," *Time,* 21 December 2015, http://time.com/time-person-of-the-year-2015-angela-merkel/.

152: *"minimizes social anxiety":* Pamela Weintraub, "The Voice of Reason," *Psychology Today,* 4 May 2015, last reviewed 9 June 2016, https://www.psychologytoday.com/articles/201505/the-voice-reason; Ethan Kross, "Self-Talk as a Regulatory Mechanism: How You Do It Matters," *Journal of Personality and Social Psychology* 106/2 (2014): 304–24, http://selfcontrol.psych.lsa.umich.edu/wp-content/uploads/2014/01/KrossJ_Pers_Soc_Psychol2014Self-talk_as_a_regulatory_mechanism_How_you_do_it_matters.pdf.

152: *Kross explains that the positive results:* Weintraub, "Voice of Reason."

152: *my go-to guide is Rick Hanson: The Practical Neuroscience of Lasting Well-Being,* accessed 25 August 2016, http://www.rickhanson.net. You can learn more about Rick Hanson by accessing the link.

153: *Researchers, beginning with Albert Bandura:* Barry J. Zimmerman and Dale H. Schunk, "Albert Bandura: The Man and His Contributions to Educational Psychology," in

Educational Psychology: One-Hundred Years of Contributions (New York: Routledge, 2002), https://www.uky.edu/~eushe2/Pajares/ZimSchunkChpt5.pdf; Heidi Grant Halvorson, "Be an Optimist Without Being a Fool," *Harvard Business Review,* 2 May 2011, https://hbr.org/2011/05/be-an-optimist-without-being-a.

153: *"Realistic optimists" are those who:* Erika Andersen, "Want a Better Life? Be an Optimist—With a Twist," *Forbes,* 17 March 2014, http://www.forbes.com/sites/erika andersen/2014/03/17/want-a-better-life-be-an-optimist-with-a-twist/#2407faf35cf8.

153: *"Idealistic optimists" are:* Andersen, "Want a Better Life?"

153: *"Social relationships—both quantity and quality":* Debra Umberson and Jennifer Karas Montez, "Social Relationships and Health: Flashpoint for Health Policy," *Journal of Health and Social Behavior,* 4 August 2011, http://www.ncbi.nlm.nih.gov/pmc /articles/PMC3150158/.

154: *I regularly listen to songs:* Louis Armstrong, *Louis Armstrong's All Time Greatest Hits,* UMG Recordings, Inc., 1994, iTunes; The Script, *No Sound Without Silence,* Sony Music Entertainment, released 12 September 2014, iTunes.

154: *"Every time they face an issue":* Tia Ghose, "Realistic Optimists May Have More Success and Happiness, Study Suggests," *Huffington Post,* 26 August 2013, updated 26 October 2013, http://www.huffingtonpost.com/2013/08/26/realistic-optimists_n_3816827 .html.

155: *"talk about failures without apologizing":* Peter Economy, "17 Brene Brown Quotes to Inspire You to Success and Happiness," *Inc.,* 8 January 2016, http://www.inc.com /peter-economy/17-brene-brown-quotes-to-inspire-you-to-success and happiness.html.

155: *"to prove to the coach":* Scott Steinberg, "5 Spectacular Examples of Turning Failure into Success," *The Blog* (blog), *Huffington Post,* updated 17 March 2015, http://www .huffingtonpost.com/scott-steinberg/5-spectacular-examples of_b_6477532.html.

156: *Jimmy Stewart plays a small-town banker: It's a Wonderful Life,* IMDb, 1946, accessed 25 August 2016, http://www.imdb.com/title/tt0038650/.

158: *The organization was founded:* Rob Morris, interview by Lucy Nalpathanchil, *Where We Live,* NPR, 23 June 2016, http://wnpr.org/post/human-trafficking-around-world-and -connecticut#stream/0.

158: *"heard about child trafficking":* Morris, *Where We Live.*

158: *"We collaborate. We don't reinvent":* Morris, *Where We Live.*

158: *It is the only environmental treaty:* Justin Gillis, "The Montreal Protocol, A Little Treaty That Could," *New York Times,* 9 December 2013, http://www.nytimes.com/2013/12/10 /science/the-montreal-protocol-a-little-treaty-that-could.html?_r=0.

159: *The organization has grown from:* "Volunteer Pilots in Arizona Fly Blood Where It's Needed," *Here & Now,* National Public Radio, 6 January 2016, http://www.wbur.org /hereandnow/2016/01/06/flying-blood-where-its-needed.

159: *"assist other volunteer flight organizations":* Flights for Life, Inc., Mission Statement, accessed 9 August 2016, http://www.flightsforlife.org/mission_statement/flights_for _life_mission_statement.pdf.

159: *More Americans died of drug overdoses:* Jeanne Whalen, "Mothers of Addicts Turn to New Networks to Fight Stigma, Sorrow," *Wall Street Journal,* 30 March 2016, http://www.wsj.com/articles/mothers-of-opioid-addicts-form-support-networks -online-1459351509. A print version of this article was published in *the Wall Street Journal* on 1 April 2016.

159: *"events to combat stigma":* Whalen, "Mothers of Addicts."

159: *"Men Against Domestic":* Women's Center of Greater Danbury, "Men Against Domestic and Sexual Violence," community program, website of the Women's Center of Greater Danbury, accessed 26 August 2016, http://wcogd.org.

160: *Pagan Kennedy's book* Inventology: Pagan Kennedy, *Inventology: How We Dream Up Things That Change the World* (New York: Houghton Mifflin Harcourt, 2016), 13.

160: *"free space where sharing is the norm":* Kennedy, *Inventology,* 13.

162: *"But the line dividing good and evil":* "Aleksandr Solzhenitsyn," *BrainyQuote,* accessed 24 August 2016, http://www.brainyquote.com/quotes/quotes/a/aleksandrs405286.html.

163: *As one study examining the persistence of working:* Ken Ceulemans, Petra A. Karsdorp, and Johan W. S. Vlaeyen, "Effects of Responsibility and Mood on Painful Task Persistence," *Journal of Behaviour Therapy and Experimental Psychiatry* 44 (2013): 191.

163: *"students in these programs reported":* Vincent Tinto, "Learning Better Together: The Impact of Learning Communities on Student Success," *Promoting Student Success in College,* Syracuse University, https://www.sdbor.edu/administrative-offices/student -affairs/sac/Documents/LearningBetterTogether_Tinto.pdf.

163: *"The name Love146":* Morris, *Where We Live.*

163: *The Slovics have shown:* Scott Slovic and Paul Slovic, "Introduction," in *Numbers and Nerves: Information, Emotion, and Meaning in a World of Data,* eds. Scott Slovic and Paul Slovic (Corvallis: Oregon State Univ. Press, 2015), 7.

163: *"rescued over 20,000 abandoned infants":* "Abdul Sattar Edhi Laid to Rest in Karachi," *Radio Pakistan,* 9 July 2016, http://www.radio.gov.pk/08-Jul-2016/edhi-in-critical -condition-shifted-to-ventilator.

163: *"My religion is humanitarianism":* "10 Abdul Sattar Edhi Quotes That Will Leave You Inspired for Life," *Express Tribune,* 9 July 2016, http://tribune.com.pk/story/1138171 /10-abdul-sattar-edhi-quotes-will-leave-inspired-life/.

163: *I define the sacred as:* Webster's *New Universal Unabridged Dictionary,* 2nd ed., s.v. "sacred."

165: *"No man is an island":* John Donne, *Meditation XVII,* accessed 24 August 2016, http:// www.online-literature.com/donne/409/.

165: *"The story of our bodies":* Karel Schrijver and Iris Schrijver, *Living with the Stars: How the Human Body Is Connected to the Life Cycles of the Earth, the Planets, and the Stars* (Oxford: Oxford Univ. Press, 2015), 194–95.

165: *the less interconnected a society is:* Robert D. Putnam, *Bowling Alone: The Collapse and Revival of American Community* (New York: Simon & Schuster, 2000).

165: *how and why interconnections are so important:* Robert D. Putnam with Robert Leonardi and Raffaella Y. Nanetti, *Making Democracy Work: Civic Traditions in Modern Italy* (Princeton, NJ: Princeton Univ. Press, 1994).

165: *"social capital":* Putnam, Leonardi and Nanetti, *Making Democracy Work,* 167.

165: *"features of social organization such as networks":* Robert D. Putnam, "Bowling Alone: America's Declining Social Capital," *Journal of Democracy* 6/1 (January 1995): 65–78.

165: *Social capital has been found:* Shannon H. Rogers, Kevin H. Gardner, and Cynthia H. Carlson, "Walking Builds Community Cohesion," *Carsey Institute,* Regional Issue Brief #14 (Winter 2014): 2.

165: *"higher levels of social capital":* Rogers, Gardner, and Carlson, "Walking Builds Community Cohesion," 1.

166: *people without empathy have:* Liz Else, "The Man Who Would Banish Evil," *New*

Scientist 210/2807 (9 April 2011); Simon Baron-Cohen, *Zero Degrees of Empathy: A New Theory of Human Cruelty and Kindness* (London: Penguin, 2011).

167: *"Fault is backward looking":* John Coleman, "Take Ownership of Your Actions by Taking Responsibility," *Harvard Business Review,* 30 August 2012, https://hbr.org/2012/08/take-ownership-of-your-actions.

168: *Every hospital in Maryland:* Audie Cornish, "In Maryland, A Change in How Hospitals Are Paid Boosts Public Health," NPR, 23 October 2015, http://www.npr.org/sections/health-shots/2015/10/23/451212483/in maryland-a-change-in-how-hospitals-are-paid-boosts-public-health. The article and radio recording are both available at this link.

168: *"It's an ethical responsibility":* Ira Flatow, "Tricking Tumor Cells to Accept a Lethal Payload," interview with Mauro Ferrari, *Science Friday,* transcript and recording, 18 March 2016, http://www.sciencefriday.com/segments/tricking-tumor-cells-to-accept-a-lethal-payload/.

169: *"the process of adapting well":* American Psychological Association, "The Road to Resilience," accessed 25 August 2016, http://www.apa.org/helpcenter/road-resilience.aspx.

169: *"that the experience of overcoming":* Rachel Nuwer, "The Right Stuff: What Psychological and Physical Traits Separate the World's Athletes from the Rest of Us?" *Scientific American Mind,* July/August 2016, 38–44.

169: *"Your objective is to use":* Eric Greitens, *Resilience: Hard-Won Wisdom for Living a Better Life* (New York: Houghton Mifflin Harcourt, 2015), 23, 25.

169: *Scarlett is a model of how to:* American Psychological Association, "The Road to Resilience," accessed 25 August 2016, http://www.apa.org/helpcenter/road-resilience.aspx.

169: *Through her nonprofit organization: Jesse Lewis Choose Love Movement,* accessed 25 August 2016, http://www.jesselewischooselove.org. You can learn more about this foundation by visiting the website.

169: *"Hope is the belief that the future":* Elizabeth Bernstein, "An Emotion We All Need More Of," *Wall Street Journal,* 21 March 2016, http://www.wsj.com/articles/an-emotion-we-all-need-more-of-1458581680.

170: *There is "strategy" and "agency".* Bernstein, "An Emotion We All Need More Of."

170: *The next day Tabby took the pages:* Lucas Reilly, "How Stephen King's Wife Saved 'Carrie' and Launched His Career," *Mental Floss,* 17 October 2013, http://mentalfloss.com/article/53235/how-stephen-kings-wife-saved-carrie-and-launched-his-career.

171: *When you can laugh:* Steven J. Wolin and Sybil Wolin, "Reframing: How to Resist the Victim's Trap," in *The Resilient Self: How Survivors of Troubled Families Rise Above Adversity* (New York: Villard, 1993).

171: *when people choose to look at an overwhelming situation:* Al Siebert, *The Survivor Personality: Why Some People Are Stronger, Smarter, and More Skillful at Handling Life's Difficulties . . . and How You Can Be, Too,* ed. Kristin Pintarich and Molly Siebert (New York: Penguin, 2010).

171: *"Laughing reduces tension":* Siebert, *Survivor Personality,* 194–95.

171: *"rise above a situation":* Victor E. Frankl, *Man's Search for Meaning,* trans. Harold S. Kushner and Helen Pisano (Boston: Beacon, 2014), 41.

171: *showing how laughter changes the body:* American Physiological Society. "Laughter Remains Good Medicine," *ScienceDaily,* https://www.sciencedaily.com/releases/2009/04/090417084115.htm, last viewed on August 26, 2016; University of Maryland Medical Center, "School of Medicine Study Shows Laughter Helps Blood Vessels Function Better," University of Maryland, http://umm.edu/news-and-events/news-releases/2005/school-of-medicine-study-shows-laughter-helps-blood-vessels-function-better, last viewed on August 26, 2016.

171: *you are thirty times more likely*: Sophie Scott, "Why Is Laughter Contagious?" *TED Radio Hour*, NPR, 4 March 2016, http://www.npr.org/2016/03/04/468877928/why-is -laughter-contagious, last viewed on 26 August 2016.

172: *"dividing big assignments"*: Judy Willis, "The Science of Resilience: How to Teach Students to Persevere," *Guardian*, 12 January 2016, https://www.theguardian.com /teacher-network/2016/jan/12/science-resilience-how-to-teach-students-persevere.

172: *"Helping people focus"*: Amy Wrzesniewski and Barry Schwartz, "The Secret of Effective Motivation," *New York Times*, 4 July 2014, http://www.nytimes.com/2014/07/06 /opinion/sunday/the-secret-of-effective-motivation.html; A. Wrzesniewski et al., "Multiple Types of Motives Don't Multiply the Motivation of West Point Cadets," *Proceedings of the National Academy of Sciences of the USA* 111/30 (29 July 2014): 10990–95.

173: *"the most important psychosocial factor"*: Caroline Cassels, "Sense of Purpose Predicts Mental Health Outcomes Following Severe Trauma," *Medscape*, 25 November 2008, http://www.medscape.com/viewarticle/584181.

173: *"What evils have you cured"*: Pierre Hadot, *What Is Ancient Philosophy*, trans. Michael Chase (Cambridge, MA: Belknap, 2002), 200.

174: *"The way to do"*: "Laozi," *AZQuotes*, accessed 26 August 2016, http://www.azquotes.com /quote/545904.

174: *"When these girls sit"*: Leymah Gbowee, "Unlock the Intelligence, Passion, Greatness of Girls," *TED Talk*, transcript (March 2012), https://www.tcd.com/talks/leymah_gbowee _unlock_the_intelligence_passion_greatness_of_girls/transcript?language=en.

174: *"unlock all of the great things"*: Gbowee, "Unlock the Intelligence."

175: *"Luck is what happens"*: "Seneca the Younger," *AZQuotes*, accessed 26 August 2016, http://www.azquotes.com/quote/519812.

178: *"Don't be afraid, just play"*: "Charlie Parker," *AZQuotes*, accessed 26 August 2016, http://www.azquotes.com/quote/357837.

178: *"the act of unplanned"*: Keri Smith, *The Wander Society* (New York: Penguin, 2016), 7.

179: *"The stationary wanderer"*: Smith, *Wander Society*, 8.

179: *"the last brain region"*: Robert M. Sapolsky, "The Benefits of Mind-Wandering," *Wall Street Journal*, 19 June 2015, http://www.wsj.com/articles/the-benefits-of-mind -wandering-1434716243.

179: *"Idle though it may seem"*: Scott Barry Kaufman and Carolyn Gregoire, *Wired to Create: Unraveling the Mysteries of the Creative Mind* (New York: Perigee, 2015), 32.

179: *"The only people who ever get"*: "Henry David Thoreau," *AZQuotes*, accessed 26 August 2016, http://www.azquotes.com/quote/811634.

180: *"The Tao does nothing"*: Hu Shih, "The Scientific Spirit and Method in Chinese Philosophy," in *The Chinese Mind: Essentials of Chinese Philosophy and Culture*, ed. Charles Alexander Moore (Honolulu: Univ. of Hawaii, 1968), 110.

181: *"If each of us hires people"*: David Ogilvy, *Ogilvy on Advertising* (New York: Vintage, 1985), 47.

181: *Free yourself by embracing*: Gbowee, "Unlock the Intelligence, Passion, Greatness of Girls."

7. Conquest of the Common Virtue

185: *"Give light, and the darkness"*: "Desiderius Erasmus," *AZQuotes*, accessed 26 August 2016, http://www.azquotes.com/quote/90466.

185: *"If you have cooperative"*: Garett Jones, *Hive Mind: How Your Nation's IQ Matters So Much More Than Your Own"* (Stanford, CA: Stanford Univ. Press, 2016), 13.

187: *"Patriotism consists not in"*: James Bryce, "Allegiance to Humanity," *The Bankers' Magazine: Rhodes Journal of Banking and the Bankers' Magazine Consolidated*, vol. 79 (New York: Bankers Publishing, 1909), 81.

188: *"Everyone thinks of changing the world"*: Leo Tolstoy, "Three Methods of Reform," in *Some Social Remedies: Socialism, Anarchy, Land, Rationalism, Communism, etc.*, pamphlet published by the Free Age Press in 1900, digitized by the University of Michigan in *Pamphlets: Translated from the Russian* (Ann Arbor: Univ. of Michigan, 2008), 29, https://books.google.com/books?id=kVBYAAAAMAAJ&pg=RA1-PA46&dq=Pamphlets.+Translated+from+the+Russian+%281900%29+Leo+Tolstoy&cd=1#v=snippet&q=Everybody%20thinks%20of%20changing%20humanity%2C%20but%20nobody%20thinks%20of%20changing%20himself.&f=false.

188: *"psychophysically numb"* or *"fall prey to"*: Scott Slovic and Paul Slovic, "Introduction," in *Numbers and Nerves: Information, Emotion, and Meaning in a World of Data*, eds. Scott Slovic and Paul Slovic (Corvallis: Oregon State Univ. Press, 2015), 7.

188: *They borrow the poet Zbigniew Herbert's phrase:* Slovic and Slovic, "Introduction," 20.

189: *his mission was personal and worth the risk:* Lauren Frayer, "Risking Arrest, Thousands of Hungarians Offer Help to Refugees," *All Things Considered*, NPR, 29 September 2015, http://www.npr.org/sections/parallels/2015/09/29/444447532/risking-arrest-thousands-of-hungarians-offer-help-to-refugees.

189: *"Stories and images have the power"*: Slovic and Slovic, "Introduction," 21.

189: *"I alone cannot change the world"*: "Mother Teresa," *GoodReads*, http://www.goodreads.com/quotes/49502-i-alone-cannot-change-the-world-but-i-can-cast.

189: *"creating too much space"*: Sally McGrane, "German Forest Ranger Finds That Trees Have Social Networks, Too," *New York Times*, 29 January 2016, http://www.nytimes.com/2016/01/30/world/europe/german-forest-ranger-finds-that-trees-have-social-networks-too.html.

190: *"a great civilization"*: "A great civilization is not conquered from without until it has destroyed itself within." Will Durant's quote about Rome can be found here with a citation to the original source published in 1944: Bartleby.com, http://www.bartleby.com/73/1646.html.

Conclusion: The Modern Spartacus

191: *"To do more for the world"*: "Henry Ford," *GoodReads*, http://www.goodreads.com/quotes/470128-to-do-more-for-the-world-than-the-world-does.

192: *And if walls are constructed:* Robert Frost, *Mending Wall*, http://www.poetryfoundation.org/poems-and-poets/poems/detail/44266.

192: *the "alpha male stereotype"*: Carl Safina, "Tapping Your Inner Wolf," *New York Times*, 5 June 2015, A19.

192: *"The main characteristic of an alpha male wolf"*: Safina, "Tapping Your Inner Wolf."

194: *"We are not simply individuals"*: Greg Graffin, "'Survival of the Fittest' Is a Sham," *Time*, 21 September 2015, 15.

194: *The strongest argument for the work-jerk approach:* Rachel Sugar, "Being a Jerk May Have Its Perks—But Don't Underestimate the Power of Being Nice," *Business Insider*, 23 June 2015, http://www.businessinsider.com/why-being-a-jerk-is-bad-for-business-2015-6.

194: *"their success comes at a price":* Tomas Chamorro-Premuzic, "Why Bad Guys Win at Work," *Harvard Business Review,* 2 November 2015, https://hbr.org/2015/11/why-bad -guys-win-at-work?utm_campaign=HBR&utm_source=linkedin&utm_medium =social.

195: *Porath shows that incivility at work:* Christine Porath, "No Time to Be Nice at Work," *New York Times,* 21 June 2015, SR1; Alina Tugend, "Incivility Can Have Costs Beyond Hurt Feelings," *New York Times,* 20 November 2010, B6.

195: *"sooner or later, uncivil people sabotage":* Sugar, "Being a Jerk."

195: *"Nasty was not necessary":* Tony Schwartz, "The Bad Behavior of Visionary Leaders," *New York Times,* 26 June 2015, http://www.nytimes.com/2015/06/27/business/deal book/the-bad-behavior-of-visionary-leaders.html?_r=1.

195: *"Being a jerk":* Jerry Useem, "Why It Pays to Be a Jerk," *Atlantic,* June 2015, http:// www.theatlantic.com/magazine/archive/2015/06/why-it-pays-to-be-a-jerk/392066 /?utm_source=nl_weekly_link12_052215.000.

195: *"I never lose. I either win or learn":* Jim Schleckser, "Nelson Mandela's Secret to Win-ning," *Inc.,* 21 June 2016, http://www.inc.com/jim-schleckser/nelson-mandela-s-secret -to-winning.html.

196: *Couney learned about the incubator:* This section on Martin Couney relied heavily on the following sources: Elizabeth Yuko, "The 'Child Hatchery' of Coney Island," *Atlan-tic,* 29 October 2015), http://www.theatlantic.com/health/archive/2015/10/the-child -hatchery-of-coney-island/413080/; William Brangham, "How a Coney Island Sideshow Advanced Medicine for Premature Babies," *PBS NewsHour,* 21 July 2015, http://www .pbs.org/newshour/updates/coney-island-sideshow-advanced-medicine-premature -babies/; "Babies on Display: When a Hospital Couldn't Save Them, A Sideshow Did," *NPR Morning Edition,* 10 July 2015, http://www.npr.org/2015/07/10/421239869 /babies-on-display-when-a-hospital-couldnt-save-them-a-sideshow-did.

197: *John Riordan's entire family was threatened:* John P. Riordan with Monique Brinson Demery, *They Are All My Family: A Daring Rescue in the Chaos of Saigon's Fall* (New York: Public Affairs, 2015).

Index

Acting, 23, 24, 36–37, 147–81, 192
  Skill 1: overcoming fear, 150–61
  Skill 2: strengthening responsibility
    and resilience, 162–73
  Skill 3: power of nondoing, 174–81
  to solve, 147–81
Adams, Ansel, 43, 48, 49
adaptation, 67, 171–72
addiction, 19, 141, 159
adjectives, 116–17
Administrative Science Quarterly, 21
Aetna, 19, 20
Afghanistan, 13
agriculture, 142
Ahern, Laurie, 173
alcohol, 19, 141
alpha males, 192–93
altruism, 12, 13, 15, 139
ambigrams, 80
American Red Cross, 157
anagrams, 80
Anderson, Amy Rees, 118
anger, 83, 84, 88–89, 114, 128
Animal Behaviour, 29
ants, 13
anxiety, 60, 70, 86
Apple, 194
Apple Watch, 88, 89
Aquinas, Thomas, 82
arm crossing, 57
Armstrong, Karen, 3
artificial intelligence, 56, 87, 94, 97
astronomy, 175–76
Atlantic, 195
Autrey, Wesley, 25

Baard, Paul, 19, 20
BABA game, 101

Bandura, Albert, 153
Baron–Cohen, Simon, *Zero Degrees of Empathy*, 166
Barsade, Sigal, 18, 20
baseball, 67–68, 105
BBC, 97
Bell, Alexander Graham, 143, 145
Bible, 73–74
bilingualism, 144–45
bitterness, 84
blood pressure, 17, 22, 87
  high, 4
body language, 36, 57–58, 62, 84, 87, 90
Bond, James, 9
bonobos, 82
books, 133, 137
brain, 2, 14–15, 18, 31–32, 48–50, 59–61, 84, 139, 152
  chemistry, 14–15, 19, 49, 60, 92
  compassion and, 14–16, 92
  connections and, 95–96
  coupling, 48
  emotions and, 83–88, 94, 153
  evolution, 14
  music and, 53–54
  size, 105
  sleep and, 79
  wandering, 179
Breach (film), 57
Breuer, Hans, 189
British Secret Intelligence Service, 9
Brookfield Cares, 140–41, 186
Brown, Brené, 155
Bryce, James, 187
Buddhism, 60, 152
Budin, Pierre, 195
bullying, 4, 12, 19, 58, 72, 129, 141, 157, 176–77

burnout, 93
business, 11, 32, 61, 72, 96, 107–8, 186
    compassion in, 19–21
    jerks, 194–95
    See also workplace
butterfly effect, 127
bystander effect, 148

Camus, Albert, 67
    The Plague, 115
Canada, 102, 188
cancer, 168
capabilities, connecting to, 109–45
Carnegie, Dale, 121
Carnegie Mellon, 119
Carver, George Washington, 96
Center for Compassion, Creativity and
    Innovation (CCCI), 3–4, 121
Central Intelligence Agency (CIA), 197
Chabris, Christopher, 122
Chamorro–Premuzic, Tomas, 194–95
Charlie Rose, 125
Charter for Compassion International, 3,
    4, 185–86
children, 4, 5, 134, 147, 173, 180, 186
    premature, 196–97
    sex trafficking, 158, 163
China, 67, 180
Chou, Sophia, 153, 154
Christov-Moore, Leonardo, 14
Churchill, Winston, 118
civility, 4, 115–17, 150, 186
Claremont Graduate University, 19
clarity, 175–76
climate change, 158–59, 188
Coleman, John, 167
collaboration, 157–58
Columbia University, 18
community, 4, 5, 19, 62, 92–93, 107–8, 111,
    140–41, 150
    local interactions, 185–86
    working with others, 156–61
compassion, 1–5, 185–90
    definition of, 2, 91–92
    difference between empathy and, 91–94
    dwindling of, 21–22
    evolution and, 10–14
    hardwiring for, 14–16
    success and, 2–5, 9–22
compassionate achievers, 3, 185–90
    acting and, 23, 24, 147–81

    connecting and, 24, 109–45
    listening and, 23, 29–63
    understanding and, 23–24, 65–108
Compassionate Listening Project, 30
Compassion Group, 186
competition, 10, 11, 13, 19, 117–19, 166
    reducing, 166
computers, 87, 88, 96–97
concepts, turning facts into, 95–100
confusion, 101
Connecting, 23, 24, 109–45, 192
    to capabilities, 109–45
    Skill 1: hidden potential, 111–24
    Skill 2: web of connections, 125–29
    Skill 3: shifting your perspective, 130–45
connections, 11, 95–108
    between compassion and success, 2–5,
        9–22
    brain and, 95–96
    effective, 102–4
    embracing counterintuitive, 100–102
    identifying and developing, 96–100
    social networks, 104–8
    turning facts into concepts, 95–100
consequences, accepting, 167
Constitution, U.S., 74
contempt, 83, 84
context, 66–67
cooperation, 10, 11, 12, 13, 14, 117–20, 150,
    156–61
    collaboration, 157–58
    coordination, 158–60
    fostering, 117–20
    negative space and, 160–61
    working with others, 156–61
coordination, 158–60
Cornell University, 144
cortisol, 22, 60
Costa, Albert, 144
Couney, Martin, 196–97
counterintelligence agents, 2, 9–10, 57, 123
counterintuitive connections, embracing,
    100–102
courage, 1, 2, 3, 10, 86, 150–61
    building, 150–54
    cooperation and, 156–61
    handling failure and, 154–55
    overcoming fear and, 150–61
creative solutions, fostering, 106–8
crime, 19, 61, 79–80, 102, 159, 195
criticism, 177

crowdsourcing, 126
cyberbullying, 129
cyberstalking, 129

Dalai Lama, 3
Damasio, Antonio, 86–87
    Descartes' Error, 87
Danbury Hackerspace, 107
Darwin, Charles, 10–14, 117, 177, 192
    compassion argument, 10–13
    The Descent of Man, 10, 11, 177
    On the Origin of Species, 10
da Vinci, Leonardo, 58
Dawkins, Richard, 15
    The Selfish Gene, 10
Dearlove, Sir Richard, 9–10
debate, 137
decency, human, 115–17, 121, 122
Deci, Edward, 20
depression, 4, 17, 84
Descartes, René, 86
diabetes, 4
Diamond, Ronald, 30
Dias, Marley, 125
dignity, 164
Disability Rights International, 173
discussing, 137
disgust, 83, 84, 86
distractions, eliminating, 36
divergent thinking, 139–41
diversity, 107, 108
domestic violence, 159–60
Donne, John, 165
dopamine, 2, 15, 60, 92, 104
Dörner, Dietrich, The Logic of Failure, 78
Dostoyevsky, Fyodor, 1
doubters, of compassionate achievers, 193–95
Doyle, Sir Conan, 52
    The Adventure of Silver Blaze, 52–53
DRD4, 2
drowning, 132
drugs, 19, 141, 159
"duck or rabbit" drawing, 58–59, 66
Duke University, 112
Durant, Will, 190
Dweck, Carol, 70, 71
Dworkin, Ronald, 164

economics, 16, 17, 19, 62, 72, 102, 138–39,
    186, 187
    compassion and, 19–21

Edhi, Abdul Sattar, 163
Edhi Foundation, 163
editing, 38
Edmondson, Amy, 119
education, 2, 3, 4, 5, 32, 65, 70, 72, 77, 78,
    113, 116, 131, 136, 157, 186
    compassion in, 18–19, 21, 117–20
    cooperation in, 117–20
    self–, 152–53
    standardized tests, 103
Education Digest, 32
effective connection, 102–4
efficiency, 102–4
Egger, Helen, 112
Egger, Sasha, 112
Einstein, Albert, 103
Eisenberg, Nancy, 16
either–or situations, 48
Ekman, Paul, 11, 83
elderly, 141
Elite SEM, 18
Ellen DeGeneres Show, The, 125
Elliott, Jane, 116
e–mail, 36
Emerson, Ralph Waldo, 108
Emmons, Robert, 120
emotional intelligence, 82–94
    feelings and, 83–88, 89
    how to develop, 88–91
    importance of, 83–88
emotions, 59–60, 81, 82–94, 153
    brain and, 83–88, 94, 153
    –feeling gap, 83–88, 89
    managing, 89
    nondoing and, 177–78
    of others, 89–91
    recognition of, 88–89, 90
    understanding, 82–94
    universal, 83
    See also specific emotions
empathy, 2, 13, 14, 89, 91–94, 139, 166
    definition of, 2, 91
    difference between compassion and,
        91–94
    fatigue, 92–93
endorphins, 18, 171
enhanced interrogation techniques, 9–10, 43
Enron, 195
entrainment, 31
Epley, Nicholas, 104, 105, 137
    Mindwise, 132

Erasmus, Desiderius, 185
Estonia, 98, 123–24, 132–33, 156–57
eusociality, 13
"everyday" compassion–success
  connection, 16–19
evil, 82
evolution, 10–14, 23, 177, 192
excuses, looking beneath, 112–14
exercise, 35, 148
expanding your reach, 125–29
expectations, avoiding, 122–24
extrinsic values, 16–17
eyes, 57, 59–60, 81, 86
    closing, 36–37
    emotions and, 59–60
    looking through someone else's eyes,
        137–39
    pupil dilation, 57
    reading, 58

Facebook, 105, 127, 129
facial expressions, 55–57, 58, 61, 62, 83, 84,
  87, 90
facts, 98–99
    turning into concepts, 95–100
failure, 77, 89, 100, 101, 141–43, 154
    handling, 154–55
    as opportunity, 141–43
falling forward, 155
fear, 70, 81, 83, 84, 85–86, 89, 150–61, 162
    overcoming, 150–61
feelings and emotions, interaction
  between, 83–88, 89
Ferrari, Mauro, 168
Ferrari Lab, 168
fight response, 16, 70, 73
first name, self–talk using, 151–52
fixed mindset, 71
flight response, 16, 70
Flights for Life, 159
Florida State University, 17
focused attention, 34–40
    acting and, 36–37
    reviewing and, 37–39
    thinking and, 35
food, 14, 15
    stealing, 79–80
Forbes, 118
Ford, Henry, 32, 191
Fordham University, 19
forgetting, 101, 103

forward looking, 167
Fossey, Dian, 13
Frankl, Viktor, 171
Franklin, Benjamin, 79
freeze response, 70, 75, 76
friends, 151, 156
Frost, Robert, "Mending Wall," 189–90, 192
Fry, Art, 142
functional magnetic resonance imagery
  (fMRI), 31
future, 144

games, 133
Gandhi, Mahatma, 24
Gates, Bill, 96, 97
Gbowee, Leymah, 174, 175
General Mills, 19–20
generosity, 12
genetics, 10
genocide orphans,147
Genovese, Kitty, 148
George Mason University, 18
Georgetown University, 195
Gladwell, Malcolm, The Tipping Point,
  109–10
Global Alliance for Genomic Health, 168
global interactions, 187–89
Goebel, Rainer, 92
Golden Mole award, 141–42
Goleman, Daniel, 88–91
    Working with Emotional Intelligence, 83,
        88–91
Golem effect, 123
Goodall, Jane, 13
Godman, Paul, Speaking and Language, 54
Google, 19
Google News Alert, 127
government, 4, 19, 61
Graffin, Greg, Population Wars, 194
Grandin, Temple, Thinking in Pictures, 137
gratitude, expressing, 120–22
Gray, Kurt, The Mind Club, 148
Great Escape Room, 109
Gregoire, Carolyn, Wires to Create, 179
Greitens, Eric, Resilience, 169
Grondona, Mariano, 17
group selection, 11–12
growth mindset, 70

Hakanen, Mila, 31
Hambrick, Donald, 194

Hanson, Rick, 152
Hanssen, Robert, 57
happiness, 15, 84, 85
Harvard University, 12
    Business School, 20
    Graduate School of Education, 5
Hasson, Uri, 31, 48
Hawking, Stephen, 96, 97
Haydn, Joseph, "The Joke," 53
health, 4, 17, 20, 112–14, 142, 143, 148, 154,
    159, 180, 195, 196–97
    insurance, 113–14
    sharing responsibility and, 167–68
hearing, 29–30, 34, 60, 81
    listening vs., 32–33
heart, 15
    rate, 16
    vagal tones and, 15–16
heart disease, 4
Herbert, Zbigniew, 188
Heskett, James, 20
    The Culture Cycle, 20
hidden potential, 111–24
    acting with human decency, 115–17
    avoiding expectations, 122–24
    expressing gratitude, 120–22
    fostering cooperation, 117–20
    looking beneath excuses, 112–14
Hirsch, Joy, 31–32
Hitler, Adolf, 157
hobbies, 105
holding back, 180–81
holistic understanding, 106
Holmes, Oliver Wendell, 32, 95
Holocaust, 82
homelessness, 101–2, 106, 147–48
homosexuality, 73–74, 187
hope, 169–70
hopelessness, 77
hormones, 14–15, 92
Horowitz, Alexandra, On Looking, 106
hospitals, 4, 102, 159, 167–68, 196, 197
Housing First, 101–2
Hsing, Courtney, 21
Humane Society, 157
human rights abuses, 158
humor, 133, 171
Hypatia, 69

IBM, 97
identity, 134–35

combining, 135–37
    failure vs., 155
    limitations, 134–35
    multiple identities, 130–31, 133–37
    new, 135
    recognizing, 134
IDEO, 18
imagination, 93
immigration, 188–89
Immordino-Yang, Mary Helen, Emotions,
    Learning, and the Brain, 94
incivility, 4, 115–17
incubators, 196–97
inefficiency, 102–4
InnoCentive, 126
insanity, 81
insects, 13
instinct, 85
intelligence, emotional, 82–94
Internet, 125–29
interruption, 36
intracranial EEG (iEEG), 31
intrinsic values, 16, 17, 20, 172–73
introspection, 174–81
"invisible gorilla" experiment, 122–23
Irish Republican Army, 10
Isaacson, Walter, 195
Italy, 106
It's a Wonderful Life (film), 156

Jaws theme, 54
jazz, 178
jerks, 194–95
Jesse Lewis Choose Love Movement, 169
Jobs, Steve, 194, 195
Johansson, Frans, The Medici Effect, 106–8
Johns Hopkins University, 17
jokes, 133
Jones, Garrett, Hive Mind, 185
Jordan, Michael, 155
Journal of Behavior Therapy and
    Experimental Psychiatry, 163
Journal of Experimental Psychology, 143
Journal of Health and Social Behavior, 154
Journal of Memory and Language, 60
joy, 83, 84
Joyce, James, Ulysses, 142
judgments, 60–61

Kaltschnee, Mike, 108
Kaufman, Scott Barry, Wired to Create, 179

Kazantzakis, Nikos, 111
Keillor, Garrison, *A Prairie Home
 Companion,* 32–33
Kelley, David, 142
Keltner, Dacher, 16, 22
Kennedy, Pagan, *Inventology,* 160
Kenyon College, 138
kindness, 7–26
  survival of the kindest, 10–14, 177
King, Stephen, *Carrie,* 170
Kinzler, Katherine, 144
kneers, 75–78, 79–81
knowledge, and understanding, 65–108
knownauts, 70–71, 78–81
knoxers, 71–75, 78–81
Konrath, Sara, 21
Kross, Ethan, 152
Kurdi, Alan, 188, 189

labels, dropping, 116–17
language, 143–45
  learning, 98, 144–45
Lao-Tzu, 21, 174
laughter, 171
law, 187
Lawler, Kathleen, 17
leadership, 124, 186
Leadership, Compassion and Creativity
 Certificate (LCCC) program, 186
"learning for teaching," 119
Lee, Harper, *To Kill a Mockingbird,* 116
Le Guin, Ursula K., 31
Lewis, J. T., 147
Lewis, Scarlett, 169
LGBT community, 187
Liberia, 174
Lieberman, Matthew, 96, 119
lifeguards, 132
Lincoln, Abraham, 103, 155
LiquidSpace, 108
Listening, 23, 29–63, 93, 104, 119, 177, 192
  attentive, 30–31, 34–40
  hearing vs., 32–33
  Skill 1: focusing your attention, 34–40
  Skill 2: questions, 41–51
  Skill 3: silence, 52–63
local interactions, 185–86
logic, 86–88
Lorenz, Edward, 127
love, 2, 92
Love146, 157–58, 163

LUCA, 23–26, 27–181, 192–93, 198
  Acting, 147–81
  Connecting, 109–45
  followers, 192–93, 195
  Listening, 29–63
  Understanding, 65–108
lungs, 15
lying, 57

Madoff, Bernie, 195
Mandela, Nelson, 71, 195
manipulation, emotional, 90–91
Mann, Horace, 23
mantra, power, 151
Maran, Meredith, 18
marriage, 89, 90, 120, 134
Massachusetts Institute of Technology, 119
mathematics, 99, 101, 193
Matisse, Henri, 130
Max Planck Institute for Chemistry, 81
Max Planck Institute for Human Cognitive
 and Brain Sciences, 2
Mayes, Bernard, 30
Mayo, Elton, 37
McGill University, 53
McIntyre, Rick, 192
Medici Effect, 106–8
MediConnect Global, Inc., 118
Medina, John, 49
meditation, 22, 36, 152
memory, 79, 84
Menon, Vinod, 53
mental illness, 4, 112
Merkel, Angela, 150
metal, 162
mettle, testing your, 162–73
Michigan State University, 12
microexpressions, reading, 55–57
Mikati, Mohamad, 112
military, 2, 3, 9–10, 60, 77–78, 152, 164,
 197–98
Miller, Roger, 111
Mindful Leadership, 19–20
mindful listening, 61–62
mindfulness, 19–20, 22, 61
mind over matter, 117
mindset, 69–81
  kneers, 75–78, 79–81
  knownauts, 70–71, 78, 79–81
  knoxers, 71–75, 78, 79–81
  recognizing, 69–81

Mine Ban Treaty, 188
mirrors, 174–75
MI6, 9
money, 17, 79, 138–39
monkeys, 82
Montreal Protocol, 158–59
moods, 59–60
Moore's law, 96, 97
morality, 13
Morris, Rob, 158, 163
motivation, 89
movies, 9, 133, 191
Mozart effect, 53
multiple identities, 130–31, 133–37
muscles, 15
    cramps, 100
music, 34, 53–54, 93, 135, 154, 177–78
Musk, Elon, 56, 96, 97

Nar–Anon, 159
National Center for Education Statistics, 4
national interactions, 187
National Public Radio, 141
natural disasters, 126–27, 156
Nazism, 189
negative space, fostering cooperation
    through, 160–61
neighborhood watches, 159
nervous system, 100
networks, 13, 104–8
    social, 104–8
neuroscience, 14–16, 31–32, 53–54, 59–61,
    73, 86–87, 92, 95–96, 101, 153, 179
news media, 115, 156
Newtown Helps Rwanda, 147
New York City, 106
New York Mets, 105
New York Times, 129
Nhat Hanh, Thich, Silence: The Power of
    Quiet in a World Full of Noise, 53
nondoing, 174–81
    practicing, 175–79
non–zero–sum people, 119–20
Northeastern University, 22
nucleus accumbens, 15

Oatley, Keith, 137
O'Brien, Edward, 21
Ogilvy, David, 181
O'Neill, Olivia, 18, 20
opportunity, failure as, 141–43

optimism, 15, 160, 169, 170
    realistic, 153–54
organ donation, 126
Orion Holdings, 18
owls, 29
oxytocin, 14–15, 16, 19, 22, 49, 92

pain, 15, 92
Pakistan, 163
Paleolithic Era, 11
paradox, 71, 132
    Parrondo's, 100–102
paramedics, 102
paraphrasing, 37–38
Parker, Charlie "Yardbird," 178
Parrondo, Juan, 100
Parrondo's paradox, 100–102
Pathfinders, 25
path of least resistance, 148
patience, 179
Perry, Michael, 164
perspective, 66–67, 129, 130–45
    divergent thinking, 139–41
    language matters, 143–45
    looking through someone else's eyes,
        137–39
    multiple identities, 130–31, 133–37
    power of, 131–33
    seeing only opportunity, 141–43
    shifting your, 130–45
    triangulation of, 152
    understanding and, 66–67
pets, 144
phosphors, 50
photography, 41, 42, 43, 48, 49
Piferi, Rachel, 17
Piff, Paul, 138, 139
Pinker, Susan, 121
Plato, 86
pleasure, 14–15
police, 3, 4
politics, 19, 105, 148, 158, 186, 187
    global, 187–89
Porath, Christine, 195
Porges, Stephen, 15–16
positivity, 153–54
Post–It notes, 142
power mantra, 151
predictive coding, 59, 60
primates, 13, 14, 82
Princeton University, 48

problems, 30, 66, 100, 109, 142
  compassionate solutions for, 24–26
  seeing only opportunity, 141–43
  solving, 66, 78, 79, 80, 81, 100, 109,
    131–32
Prochnik, George, *In Pursuit of Silence*, 54
Program for International Student
  Assessment (PISA), 103
psychological safe zone, 119
psychology, 13, 14, 16, 59, 83, 101, 140
  positive, 153–54
Putnam, Robert, 150
  Bowling Alone, 165
  Making Democracy Work, 165
puzzles, 66, 109, 162
Pygmalion effect, 123

quantum physics, 128, 194
questions, 37, 39, 41–51, 54, 71, 107, 137–38,
  153, 160
  closed, 42–51
  open, 42–51
  understanding through, 42–51

racism, 116
radio, 35, 133, 141
reading, 93, 133, 137
real estate, 72
realistic optimism, 153–54
recreation, 105–6
reflection, 174–81
refugee/immigrant issue, 188–89
relationships, managing, 89–91
religion, 73–74, 163–64
Renaissance, 106
Rende, Richard, 119
resilience, 17–18, 93, 169–73
  developing, 170–73
respect, 30, 114, 186
responsibility, 162–68
  developing, 166–67
  sharing, 167–68
reviewing, 37–39
Ricard, Matthieu, 92
Rieux's Routine, 115–16
Riordan, John, 197–98
robotics, 56, 87
Rolling Stones, 41
Ross, Jerilyn, 17–18
Rousseau, Jean-Jacques, 14
Rovelli, Carlo, 129

Rowling, J. K., 170
Rumi, 9
Russell, Joyce E. A., 117
Russia, 123–24
ruthlessness, 9, 10, 12
Ryan, Richard, 20

sacredness, 163–64
sadness, 83, 84, 85, 86
safe zone, 119
Safina, Carl, 192
San Francisco, 30
Sapolsky, Robert, 179
schools, 3, 4, 5, 32, 70, 72, 113, 116, 131,
  136, 141, 157, 180, 186
  bullying, 4, 19, 129, 176–77
  compassion in, 18–19, 21, 117–20
  SEL programs, 18–19, 169
  See also education
Schrijver, Karel and Iris, *Living with the
  Stars*, 165
Scott, Sophie, 171
Schumacher, E. F., 140
self-confidence, 150, 151–52
selfishness, 10–13, 14, 139
self-talk, using first name, 151–52
SEL programs, 18–19, 169
Seneca, 173, 175
senses, 81
serotonin, 15, 92
Seuss, Dr., 70
  Oh, the Places You'll Go!, 70
sex, 14, 116
  child trafficking, 158, 163
  violence, 159–60
shame, 86
shared space, 107–8
Shatterproof, 159
Siebert, Al, *The Survivor of Personality*, 171
silence, 52–63
  embracing, 52–55
  interpreting, 55–58
  removing static, 58–62
Silver, Spencer, 142
Simons, Daniel, 122
Singer, Peter, 25
Singer, Tania, 2, 92
sixth sense, 104
slavery, 74, 96, 157, 187, 191
sleep, 79
  lack of, 79

Slovic, Scott and Paul, 163
    Numbers and Nerves, 188, 189
smartphones, 36, 127
smell, sense of, 81
Smith, Anna Deavere, 62
Smith, Keri, *The Wander Society*, 178–79
social capital, 165–66
social media, 105, 125–29, 156
social networks, 13, 104–8
    power of, 104–6
    strengthen understanding and foster
      creative solutions, 106–8
Social Neuroscience, 14
socioeconomic class, 138–39
Socrates, 54–55, 193
solar system, 99
Solzhenitsyn, Aleksandr, 162
Soudunsaari, Aki, 31
Soul Sisters, 159
South Korea, 67
Spacious, 108
Spartacus, 191–92, 195, 198
Spencer, Herbert, 10
Sporns, Olaf, *The Future of the Brain*,
    95–96
sports, 9, 11, 12, 105, 106, 151, 155, 169
standardized tests, 103
Stanford University, 17, 43, 53, 142
Star Trek, 86, 87, 88
static, removing, 58–62
stealing, 79–80
stepping up, 166
stereotypes, 117, 143
stress, 4, 17, 20, 70, 149
    hormones, 22, 60
Strevens, Michael, 97
Strier, Karen, 13
success, 3–5, 32, 67, 77, 92, 100, 105,
    125, 153
    compassion and, 2–5, 9–22
    counterintuitive connections and,
      100–102
    definition of, 3
    evolutionary, 10–14
    inclusive, 19–21
    jerks, 194–95
suicide, 30, 129, 141, 156
sunlight, 130–31
support, mobilizing, 171
surprise, 83, 84
survival of the fittest, 10–11, 12, 13, 117

survival of the kindest, 10–14, 177
sympathy, 10–11
Syrian refugee crisis, 188, 189

Taking on the World, 38
Taoism, 180
Target, 19
taste, sense of, 81
teamwork, 11–12, 25
television, 9, 35, 115, 130
Teresa, Mother, 189
terrorism, 9–10
thinking, focused, 35
Thoreau, Henry David, 52, 148, 179
3M, 142
Three Wise Monkeys maxim, 82
tolerance, 13, 116–17
Tolstoy, Leo, 188
touch, sense of, 81
traffic accidents, 67
trauma, 58
trees, 93, 95–96, 189–90
    rings, 190
triangulation, 152
trust, 31, 78, 107, 150, 160
Twain, Mark, 54
Twitter, 125, 126–27
"Two Truths and a Lie," 57

ultraviolet light, 50
Underground Railroad, 157
Understanding, 23, 65–108, 192
    to know, 65–108
    questions and, 42–51
    Skill 1: mindset, 69–81
    Skill 2: emotional intelligence, 82–94
    Skill 3: connections, 95–108
United Nations Declaration of Human
    Rights, 188
University of Kansas, 165
University of Maryland, 60, 117, 171
University of Michigan, 152
University of Minnesota, 16, 17
University of New Hampshire, 165
University of Oregon, 15
University of Pennsylvania, 18
University of Tennessee, 17
University of Wisconsin–Madison, 22, 30
University of Zurich, 139
Useem, Jerry, 195
Utah, Housing First program in, 101–2

vagus nerve, 15–16
veterans, 30, 77–78
Vietnam War, 197–98
violence, 4, 19, 72
    domestic, 159–60
virtual world, compassion in, 128–29
viruses, 142
vital signs, monitoring, 89
vocalization, 15, 90, 94
Vohs, Kathleen, 16
Voltaire, 41
voting, 148

Walker, Gordon, 102
walking, 93, 165–66, 179
Wallace, David Foster, 138
Wall Street Journal, 20
wandering, 178–79
war on terror, 9–10
Washington, Booker T., 150
water, 114, 132, 138
web of connections, 125–29
websites, 127–28
Wegner, Daniel, The Mind Club, 148
Western Connecticut State University,
    3, 186
West Point, 17, 172
Wharton, Edith, 125
Wiesel, Elie, 82
    "Night," 82

Willis, Judy, 172
Wilson, David Sloan, 11–12
Wilson, Edward O., 10, 11–14
    The Meaning of Human Existence, 12
    The Social Conquest of Earth, 11
Wilson, James Q., 12–13, 14
    The Moral Sense, 12
WithumSmith+Brown, 18
Wohlleben, Peter, The Hidden Life of
    Trees, 189
Wolin, Steven and Sybil, The Resilient
    Self, 171
Women's Center, Fairfield County,
    Connecticut, 159–60
workplace, 4, 18, 83, 90, 181
    civility, 4, 116
    compassion in, 18, 19–21, 117–20
    cooperation, 117–20
    emotional intelligence in, 83, 90
    gratitude gap, 120–22
    jerks, 194–95
    shared space, 107–8
    turnover, 4, 195
worry, 84

Yale University, 31

Zak, Paul, 19, 22, 150
    The Moral Molecule, 15, 16
zero–sum thinking, 119–20, 166

About the Author

Dr. Kukk is Professor of Political Science and Social Science at Western Connecticut State University, a Fulbright Scholar, founding Director of the Center for Compassion, Creativity and Innovation, a faculty adviser at WCSU and City of Compassion initiatives (Danbury and Milford, Connecticut), Director of the Kathwari Honors Program, founder of the university's debate team, and a member of Phi Beta Kappa. He is also cofounder and CEO of InnovOwl LLC, a research and consulting firm that solves micro and macro problems through innovative education.

He received his Ph.D. in political science from Boston College and his B.A. in political science from Boston University. He was an international security fellow at Harvard University's Belfer Center for Science and International Affairs. His research and publications focus on education issues, the political economy of natural resources, and the creation and sustainability of civil society. Dr. Kukk was a counterintelligence agent for the U.S. army and a research associate for Cambridge Energy Research Associates.

He has provided the Associated Press, National Public Radio, The Economist magazine, NBC-TV, CableVision, and local radio stations with analysis on a wide range of topics and issues. He has spoken at the United Nations on issues ranging from freshwater scarcity to nuclear disarmament and has won several national and international grants as well as teaching awards.

Dr. Kukk is a compelling and in-demand speaker whose message about compassion resonates with business leaders, educators, parents, the medical community, governments, and nongovernmental organizations.